Alexander Wilson Author and Spy Website:
https://alexanderwilsonauthorandspy.com

THE SECRET LIVES OF A SECRET AGENT

The Mysterious Life
and Times of
Alexander Wilson

SECOND EDITION

TIM CROOK

The Secret Lives of a Secret Agent: The Mysterious Life and Times of Alexander Wilson, Second Edition

By Tim Crook

Epigrams

"So much depends on the Secret Service man. He must learn absolutely that his own honour, his life, count for nothing. He must be prepared to face desperate odds, danger, death, with the realization that there is no reward except the abstract one which goes with success in the service of the country he loves. Failure and exposure invariably mean complete obliteration; he can expect no help from the authorities; no help can be accorded him. Governments cannot recognize secret agents. A little carelessness, a lack of forethought, an impulsive word or action, may cause disaster."
Page 12 *Wallace Intervenes (1939) by Alexander Wilson*

"I simply could not live without female companionship."
Page 197, *The Sentimental Crook (1934) by Alexander Wilson*

"…the magnetic field of one's mind gets dispersed, with the particles flying here, there and everywhere. Instead of straining after an integral self, one becomes first two, then maybe several selves, functioning independently. Which of them happens to be uppermost at a particular moment depends on circumstances; on the chance of mood, whimsical or otherwise, pushing on in this, that or the other direction. It is rather like living, instead of writing, a novel; being each character in turn, experiencing their adventures, their hopes and disappointments and moments of exaltation, as, for instance, Dickens did when his novels – sometimes two or three at a time – were being serialised while he was writing them."
Page 280 *The Infernal Grove (1975) by Malcolm Muggeridge*

Dedication

This book is dedicated to the extended family of Alexander Wilson whose generosity of spirit has made this book possible and in respectful memory and acknowledgement of Gladys, Dorothy, Alison, Elizabeth Wilson, Adrian Wilson, and Mike Shannon.

Preface

The Secret Lives of a Secret Agent, and the television drama series *Mrs Wilson* arising from it, have been surprising outcomes out of a deeply personal and confidential enquiry I offered to take on for the actor and poet Mike Shannon in 2005.

The introduction and catalyst had been his son Richard, an award-winning director and playwright whom I had been friends with since childhood. Richard's instinct and good judgement in this situation deserves profound respect and consideration.

As a researcher and academic at Goldsmiths, University of London I had been committed to the college's ethos of doing whatever can be done for people less fortunate than ourselves. Mike wanted some help in unravelling the mysteries of his family history, the father who had apparently been killed in action during the Second World War when he was only a small child, and the lives of his parents who had seemingly met, fallen in love and married in British India. The development and dignity of the human personality is rooted in knowledge and understanding of identity. This is a fundamental and inalienable human right.

Such investigations are done for private purposes and not for public and commercial exploitation. Over five years I was able to introduce Mike to a wider family that he never knew he had, and a story that defies belief, but brought him happiness, many answers and some understanding of his past. Most importantly all of the families of his father, Alexander Wilson, came together offering him love, friendship, warmth and comfort; particularly during the months of illness that would end his life in 2010.

His father was an extraordinary man: a scallywag, a rogue, and larger than life character blessed with immense talent and the many flaws that created the many parts and lives he performed in different parts of the world. Mike was insistent that I wrote a book that told the research story, analysed the mysteries of his father's life as was possible at that time, and assessed his achievements and importance as a writer.

Mike's then newly discovered niece, Ruth Wilson, has through her unique and award-winning talents as an actor and producer created a three-part television dramatization of Alexander Wilson's life primarily through the point of view of her grandmother and Wilson's third wife, Alison. This story is now reaching a wider and global audience.

With the cooperation and permission of this remarkable family I have written a second edition of the biography to offer a factual benchmark to the narrative.

3

This is the culmination of 13 years of research and investigation. There are still many more questions that need answering. But I hope in the spirit of the enquiring though caring leopard represented in the Goldsmiths' coat of arms, it tells this story accurately, honestly and with full respect and consideration for everyone involved.

Professor Tim Crook
Goldsmiths, University of London, New Cross. 30th October 2018

Contents

Chapter Three - Dorothy and son - Page 43

Dorothy was the beautiful, and self-resourceful touring actress standing in for Dame Sybil Thorndike in British India. She was one of the first actors and directors in Indian radio drama. She first met Alexander Wilson on the ocean-going liner taking them both out to British India in 1925. They would live together as man and wife in Lahore- the Paris of the Punjab and North West Frontier during the febrile period of insurrection, bloody terrorism and the struggle for independence. Alexander Wilson saved her from the Tribesman's bullet and the fatal sting of the world's deadliest snake. He wrote the plays, Dorothy directed and performed them for productions raising money for charity; something Dorothy would do all her life. Dorothy could well have been the muse who inspired him to start writing best-selling novels. She would be his literary secretary during the 1930s when they lived in Little Venice bringing up their son Michael. Alexander's love for Michael was so intense he took on Michael Chesney's name as a writing pseudonym for another military intelligence fiction series. But this happy, romantic and exciting life crashed with the onset of the Second World War, the blitz and recruitment into MI6. What led to the violent row, followed by Dorothy taking Michael to the Yorkshire Dales and never to return? Why did she hate him so much she forced him to agree to a plot to make Michael falsely grieve when only 9 for the father he would never see again?

Chapter Four - Alison and sons - Page 67

Their love blossomed dodging the bombs that fell on London during the Blitz of 1940 and '41. Despite the twenty odd years between them an intense mutual attraction developed in the MI6 bomb shelters during air-raids. He was the respected British Indian Army Colonel whose fluency in Arabic, Persian, and Urdu made him a leading intelligence analyst eaves-dropping on embassy and diplomatic legation communications in war-torn London. She was the MI6 secretary typing up and filing his 'special material' reports stamped 'Top Secret' for the eyes only of Prime Minister Winston Churchill, the war cabinet and intelligence chiefs. Her family were suspicious and her boss tried to warn her against the mysterious though charismatic charm of a man who self-effacingly showed reluctance in wearing his decorations and who claimed a family connection with the Marlborough dynasty. In 1942 after marriage and childbirth their world came crashing down around them. Disgrace and dismissal at the Foreign Office, hand to mouth existence, arrest and imprisonment, humiliating poverty. Why did they become destitute? Why did their first son have to be sent to a children's home and their second considered for adoption? How did they survive and stay together for 22 years? Why was Alison's love so blind? How and why did she learn to forgive when Dorothy had learned to hate?

Chapter Five - Elizabeth and son - Page 91

It was the affair and marriage that many members of Alexander Wilson's family have found it hardest to understand or explain. It was the breaking point for Oscar Wilde's famous homily by Lady Bracknell on misfortune. One bigamy might have been an accident. A second perhaps a misfortune. But a third? Wilson embarked on the adventure of a fourth marriage and family close to the hospital where he worked, but far away enough to avoid the risk of being seen by Alison and her two boys. How and why? They met while working in the early years of the National Health Service. She was the nurse. He worked in A&E bringing in and taking out the dead and living. Was it madness on his part? To Elizabeth this was a charming and exciting love that she cherished and protected to the very end. She took their young son Douglas to Scotland where she waited for the promised return to India. Where the Urdu language teaching books remained on the book-shelf. Douglas remembers receiving his father's presents at Christmas and the sad moment his mother told him of his passing away.

Chapter Six – The Buddha of St James's - Page 103

Analysing Alexander Wilson's career in intelligence. The faint traces of espionage during the 1920s and 30s. Why did he begin writing spy novels characterising people with an uncanny resemblance to real life spooks? Why did he take his young son Michael to meet the notorious Nazi London ambassador and foreign minister Joachim von Ribbentrop? His exhortations to do something for his country during the growing World crisis led to an interview most probably with the second 'C' of MI6 Admiral Hugh Sinclair. By September 1939 he was using his many languages to spy on telephone lines of friendly and neutral embassies and diplomatic legations in London. After three years in the service his reputation was so high he may have been known to War-time leader Winston Churchill and his colleagues affectionately called him 'Buddha' owing to experience in India and penchant for wearing the uniform of a British Indian Army major.

Chapter Seven – 'A Great Public Danger?' - Page 119

Alexander Wilson had given three years of his life during the Second World War to the Secret Intelligence Service from 1939 to 1942. He had been responsible for collecting intelligence on people whose perfidy and unreliability could have undermined what turned out to be the British Army's first ever land victory against Axis forces- the full defeat and retreat of Irwin Rommel's Africa Corps at El Alamein. He had fallen in love and married a beautiful 19-year-old secretary working in his top secret unit. Life and duty to King, country and Empire were good. But this exciting and fulfilling life would crumble ignominiously. The Secret Service would dismiss him when the police decided a burglary at his London flat was something he had faked- perhaps to provide cover for his selling of precious jewellery so he could pay for expensive drugs that saved his young wife's life. And then an MI5 investigation would claim the Buddha of SIS also faked his reports on the telephone calls of the Egyptian Ambassador and his Embassy in London. The consequences of being condemned as 'a great public danger' would be very harsh indeed.

Chapter Eight - 'One of the best' – Compton Mackenzie - Page 137

The super-star writer of the 1930s Compton Mackenzie announced in Britain's biggest selling newspaper the *Daily Mail* that Alexander Wilson had written the best novel of the season in *The Magnificent Hobo*. There was a Hollywood film option. Wilson's 24 published novels received critical acclaim throughout the world in tiptop reviews from New York to Singapore. He was a leading seller for Longmans and P.G. Wodehouse's publisher Herbert Jenkins. He was a versatile story-teller commanding the genre of spy novelist, romantic fiction, crime thriller, and comedy. He could tackle abortion, child abuse, and rape and fashion pioneering depictions of betrayal and treason at the heart of espionage. Wilson made a huge contribution in propagandising the myth of global intelligence power for the British Secret Service through the nine *Wallace of The Secret Service* spy novels published between 1928 and 1940. He was particularly brilliant at addressing journalistic and current affairs issues in his fictional plots. He showed insight and understanding of the terrorist's mind and the dangers of fundamentalism in *The Crimson Dacoit* and throughout his books there is a pioneering tendency to advance the characterisation of women as intelligent action heroines.

Chapter Nine - Killing The Author - Page 151

Why did this brilliant and successful author never have anything published after the Second World War? Another four unpublished novels never saw the light of day. Just how good are they? Wilson is now acknowledged as the missing link in spy writing between Buchan and Fleming- some say without Wilson there would never have been Bond or Bourne. What did this country lose when Wilson's brilliant writing career was unaccountably shut down? Three of his unpublished books show that he never lost his touch in developing the spy genre or advancing the crime thriller. In one he has a homicidal judge challenging the authority and reach of justice during the age of capital punishment. In another he has a special league of retired service chiefs deciding to organise their own private and covert national intelligence service to tackle the growth of organised crime. Is it possible Wilson's style simply declined in popularity in the midst and wake of a World War, or was there a greater misfortune and injustice at play? There was every sign that his second intelligence series, Colonel Callaghan of military intelligence, was poised to continue after three novels. Is it possible he was unable to resurrect his writing career in a new name after an agreement with his second wife that he should die a hero at the Battle of El Alamein in 1942 and abandon his son from his second marriage?

Chapter Ten - Scoundrel or Sentimental Crook? - Page 167

A concentrated and objective analysis of Alexander Wilson's career in crime. Strip away the chaff and decoy of possible intelligence fantasy, the nonsense about the undercover operation which for reasons of national security he could never explain. Wilson was a crook. He even confessed to being one with the title of his 1934 novel *The Sentimental Crook*. He may have been a villain with emotions, but also recognised perhaps that he was a dyed in the wool cad and scoundrel. *The Sentimental Crook* had been sold to another publisher with the title *Confessions of a Scoundrel* - only the first and last chapters were changed. Everything else was largely word for word. A New Zealand critic spotted the con. He contacted the publishers. Had Alexander Wilson ripped off Geoffrey Spencer or Geoffrey Spencer ripped off Alexander Wilson? He never twigged they were one and the same man. Wilson was busted, perhaps for card sharping returning Great War veterans of their hard-earned savings having risked life and limb in the trenches of the Western Front, and did six months hard labour in one of North America's toughest penitentiaries. But he got away with employment as an English professor in British India with a fake CV, a degree and masters from Oxford he never earned. He even went round Lahore as Sir Alexander Wilson.

He inveigled himself into MI6 with another fabricated CV- Repton School, Cambridge University, cousin to Winston Churchill? All lies. He faked a burglary at his home in war-time London. That got him chucked out of MI6. MI5 were convinced he even made up the bugged calls he was listening to. He was arrested for wearing a Colonel's uniform and medals he was never entitled to and did time in Brixton Prison in 1944. He left his hand in the till when cinema manager in Hampstead and did three months in 1948. For the rest of his life he got away with fraud and pecuniary advantages by deception. He forged his third wife's signature to get educational grants their sons were not entitled to. She had to pay everything back after he 'dropped dead' in their kitchen. He had promised that the truth of his heroic life as a great spy would be revealed to her after his death if she cared to examine his wallet. When she did so in front of the priest administering the last rites, it was empty.

Chapter Eleven- Discovery, forgiveness and reparation - Page 185

Alexander Wilson's life and times is a truth-defying narrative of mystery, paradox, charm and alarm and enduring humanity and in the end heroic forgiveness, love and understanding. All his children remember him as a wonderful father who gave them love and confidence and hopes and dreams. He was a quintessential story-teller dancing and spinning on the edge of fantasy and reality, fact and fiction. Perhaps we should remember Spike Milligan's recollection of being woken up at 3 o'clock in the morning by his father Leo to confess: 'The tiger…I never shot him. I'm sorry. But honestly. What would you have preferred? The entertaining lie, or the boring truth?'. All of Alexander Wilson's children decided that the dramatic truth of their father's chaos, adventure, and indeed patriotism was the thing to take from the extraordinary heritage he left for them. His third wife Alison investigated, interrogated, tried and condemned the man who gave her so much love, grief, sorrow and fun. She articulated the forgiveness that his surviving children would agree on when they consecrated a gravestone in 2008 at Milton cemetery Portsmouth bearing the words from Shakespeare's *Othello* 'He loved not wisely, but too well.'

In the end there is a balancing of scales, where the good in a complex, perplexing and enigmatic man could be recognised over the troubling chaos of a charm and patriotism that became for him unavoidably misanthropic. And the real triumph rests with the women he loved and who loved him, and children who went on to have successful and fulfilling lives.

Appendices – Timeline and literary output. - Page 201

A detailed chronological timeline of Alexander Wilson's life from his birth in 1893 to his death in 1963 and followed by the fortunes of his family and how they eventually began to unravel some of the mysteries of his double, triple and quadruple existences with four different families.

A table setting out the detail of all his published novels and non-fiction work, along with four unpublished manuscripts that have survived.

The Secret Lives of a Secret Agent: The Mysterious Life and Times of Alexander Wilson, Second Edition

Chapter One

A very unusual funeral

Milton cemetery, Portsmouth, Wednesday April 10th 1963. There has never been a funeral like it. Four widows, two attending and not a divorce in sight. Two requiems, two priests, and one coffin. One daughter too upset to attend and successfully encouraged to stay away. Four sons attending. Two knowing their half-brothers were present. The other two having no idea they were in the company of half-brothers, having been deceived into thinking they were cousins. This is the story of four Mrs Wilsons, their children and the man at the centre of it all, encased in the coffin about to be consigned into the ground.

He had two identities: Alexander Joseph Patrick Wilson and Alexander Douglas Gordon Chesney Wilson. He had two birthdays; one around seven years earlier than the other. Another son was not attending because he had been led to believe his father had died an heroic death at the Battle of El Alamein in October 1942. Another son was not attending because the fourth Mrs Wilson had moved to Scotland. There is the possibility that at least one more son was completely unaware of his true father's identity and existence. In the end the deceit, the confusion and consternation meant that Alexander Wilson lay in an unmarked grave for 46 years. The third Mrs Wilson visited a few years later and observed: 'So he who in life lied his true identity out of existence, is equally nameless in death; he lies in an unnamed grave, an unresolved enigma.'

It was a telephone call by Alison, the third widow, to somebody she had been led to believe was an aunt or cousin that like a butterfly flapping its wing set off a hurricane through the lives of so many people and fifty five years later much of the enigma is still unresolved.

Gladys, Dorothy, Alison and Elizabeth were the four wives of Alexander Wilson. He married each of them in four different decades of the twentieth century. With Gladys whom he married in 1916, there were two sons, Adrian and Dennis and a daughter Daphne. With Dorothy whom he married around 1928 there was a son called Michael. With Alison whom he married in 1941 there were two sons, Gordon and Nigel, and with Elizabeth whom he married in 1955 there was a son called Douglas. There is evidence that he may have had another son as the result of an extra-marital affair during the 1930s.

The second son of his first marriage, Dennis Wilson, had survived life-changing injuries in the Second World war, was married with two children and developing a successful career as a sales manager for *Encyclopaedia Britannica* in Southampton when in 1963 his mother Gladys took a telephone call from a woman she thought was his father's landlady: 'She was told he had passed away and all my mother could say was "Alec's dead," she dropped the phone and she was overcome with distress. I took over the telephone call and said I would be coming up to London to deal with the arrangements.' This Dennis did with his very laid back older brother Adrian who was a school teacher: ' We were shown into a house in Ealing and the woman who I thought was his landlady presented herself as my father's widow. I explained that my father's widow was my mother living in Southampton. The woman said she had guessed that this was the case and asked if we would be discreet. I have to say I liked her. Her first name was Alison and I wanted to stay in touch, but after the funeral we lost contact. She gave me four manuscripts of my father's unpublished novels. Three of them were typed, and the fourth in his wonderful handwriting.'

Rather like the frontline infantry officer he was during the Battle of Normandy, Dennis took command of the situation: 'We agreed that to her two sons, Gordon and Nigel, we would be known as father's cousins and my mother would be an aunt. They seemed the most impressive young men. Gordon was in naval uniform. There were also the feelings and sensitivities of my sister Daphne who adored our father. She was too upset to attend the funeral and burial and that was a blessing in disguise. It would have broken her heart to have discovered this side of father's life. All three of us, that's my mother, Adrian and I believed it was in her interests to keep this from her.'

Dennis explained that it was really left to him to organise these things: 'I thought we had agreed we would avoid the issue of any status for chief mourners. This would have required some discretion in terms of clothing, but unfortunately, when Alison arrived she was dressed from head to toe in mourning black. And this was in striking contrast to my mother. My mother was also very much affected by the appearance of one of Alison's sons in smart royal naval uniform. He looked the spitting image of how my father must have seemed to her when she first met him.

Alexander Wilson had been in the Royal Navy before joining the army and this was how they must have met in early 1915: 'Yes, it was a trying day. Afterwards I remember saying to my wife and brother-in-law something along the lines "No doubt you are very curious, but I would prefer it if you did not ask any questions that I would rather not answer. I can't stop you drawing your own conclusions, but I hope you will have the good sense to keep them to yourselves."'

While Alexander Wilson was being buried in an unmarked grave in Portsmouth, his second wife Dorothy was living a retired life in the East Yorkshire seaside resort of Bridlington. She had left him in 1941 and made it very clear to their son Michael that she hated him. In 1963 somebody informed her of his death. She did not send any flowers or sympathy cards. She had been part of a plot to deceive their son Michael that his father had died in General Montgomery's battle with Rommel at El Alamein. Michael was only a young boy of nine at the time. In 1963 he was a young father with two young children and making his way in the world as a professional actor.

Alexander Wilson's fourth wife, Elizabeth was in Edinburgh and had also been informed by somebody that Alec had died. There is no evidence she sent any flowers or cards, but she did sympathetically tell their very young son Douglas that his father had passed away.

Galsworthy, Dickens, and Tolstoy would have struggled to write anything so poignant and ironic. And so it was widow number one, Gladys and widow number three, Alison who faced each other among the tombstones of Milton cemetery to say goodbye to the same husband in such bizarre and fraught circumstances.

Alison Wilson had been the first person to come across Alexander after he passed away in the kitchen of their Ealing home, less than two years after he had completed the writing of his last novel:

'On the evening of my second day back, 4th April, Alec dropped dead. He had obviously been very ill when I went into hospital and the anxiety of having to leave him to cope alone with the children had exacerbated my condition. However, he had recovered sufficiently to return to work and had been to work the day he died. After my part-time day, I had gone to an instruction in the early evening. [Alison was preparing to convert to Roman Catholicism] On returning home, as I opened the front door I had a sensation which I can only describe as the Angel of Death going out as I came in. I knew instantaneously before I set foot in the house, that something was very wrong.'

Alison remembered being overcome with the feeling of the house being wrapped in silence and an atmosphere of thick and deathly hush. She looked in the sitting-room. It was empty. She moved quickly to the kitchen, and there she found her husband on the floor. She surmised that he must have died instantaneously, fell backwards and hit his head with great force on the stone floor. He had not been dead long. She sent for a priest to come and anoint him in the Catholic tradition.

Alison had known that sudden death could have happened at any time. His health was poor and he was now elderly. But she was stunned, stupefied and desolate at losing him all the same. He had told her that there was a secret compartment in his wallet containing papers verifying his identity, which she would find after he died. Alison recalled: 'I suggested to the priest that perhaps we ought to remove his wallet before the undertakers came. I have often wondered what he thought; no doubt he was shocked, thinking I could not wait to get my hands on the money. But how wrong we can be in our judgments. I did not want the money; I wanted the verification for which I so yearned. There was no special compartment, and no verification.'

Alison had managed to capture the pathos of her husband's death as well as the black comedy in the searching of Alexander Wilson's wallet which would be bereft of the fortune of true identity and any hidden riches. It may be the case that there had been a misunderstanding between the couple in that Alexander indicated that she would find papers explaining his past when he died though talk of a secret wallet compartment would be typical of a practiced author of spy fiction.

Two remarkable written recollections of Wilson's funeral have been left to history. Alison's memoir provides the perspective of a grief-stricken and disillusioned young widow. Dennis Wilson has written about the day from the perspective of a grief-stricken and bewildered adult son who had taken on the responsibilities of managing funeral arrangements that would have defied the imagination of the famous Russian playwright Anton Chekhov and the master of French farce Georges Feydeau.

Alison had been suspecting that in the previous decade her husband had been concocting a fantasy of returning to work at the Foreign Office. She had observed that he 'had gone out every day, but to somewhere and to a life which' she knew nothing. It is entirely conceivable that by this time there was a part of Alexander Wilson that had been consumed by so much false-consciousness he himself was none the wiser.

Alison wrote: 'Because I wanted to prevent the boys from finding out any of the facts about Alec, I had to keep all the arrangements strictly under my control and not seek their help as I would otherwise have done. Now that his statement about his work, at any rate since he had claimed to have returned to the F.O.

[Foreign Office], had been shown to be pure fabrication, it was probable all the rest was equally unfounded and I was fearful of what was going to be uncovered.'

She had no recollection of how she informed Gladys and could not remember the telephone exchange. But she did remember when her two sons came up to London to see her. She remembered that they 'were quite pleasant, but insisted that he be buried under his proper Christian names and the correct date of birth, which meant that he was in his seventieth year, and that he be buried not in Ealing as I had arranged, but in Portsmouth, where there was a grave reserved with a place for their mother.'

Alison walked up and down outside the undertakers' premises panic stricken. She was worried that 'The names I had given and which were already on the coffin and the death certificate were those he had claimed from the Marlborough connection and the date of birth was seven years later. I thought that by requesting the alterations I would be unleashing a hive of police enquiries. Would they not ask why I did not know who I was burying? And surely it must be illegal to bury someone with a different identity from that on the death certificate?'

As these desperate questions kept churning around in her head she could not bring herself to go into the Undertakers and phoned the priest who was instructing her instead. She next found herself being advised by a solicitor he'd recommended and 'Strangely, it did not seem to matter. I could have the nameplate changed without any problem. So I went back to the office of the undertaker, who received my instructions for the new plate and burial at Portsmouth without any disturbance to his habitual suavity. To me it seemed an enormity; to him it was all in the day's work. No doubt it is quite common for people to do the strangest things under the stress of grief.'

Alison recalled her sense of shock and disillusionment when Dennis and his older brother Adrian had assured her that there had never been any divorce nor any annulment. She asked her parish priest not to preach any homily at the Requiem in West London: 'I was afraid he would extol Alec's apparent virtues which, in the circumstances, would have been unendurable, adding sacrilege to sacrilege, in which I could bear to have no part and which I would have wanted to denounce. Consequently, when asked if I wished Alec's body to rest overnight in front of the Blessed Sacrament, I said "No".'

'The church was surprisingly full for Alec's requiem and I was touched to see several of the boys from Nigel's school. The Mass, with no homily, was soon over. To add to the macabre situation, the body had to be whisked hurriedly away for a post-mortem before being taken down to Portsmouth the following day for burial.

That journey to Portsmouth, following the coffin, was a torment; grief and anxiety overwhelmed me. I had no idea what was going to happen or what course events would take. At the graveside we would meet Alec's wife, his daughter and the two sons. I had had to adopt Alec's deception and tell Gordon and Nigel that they were his sister-in-law, nephews and niece. I did not know whether they would say anything which would expose the truth. I did not know what the procedure was at a Catholic funeral, let alone this one. I wondered what the undertakers thought was going on, and how much, if anything, they knew. What would 'she' be like? Who would take precedence at the graveside? All the way I was petrified with anxiety to protect Gordon and Nigel from the awful truth. I could not bear, least of all, at this moment to shatter their love and respect for their father.

We met at the graveside; an elderly, sad, non-descript looking woman. We all huddled round the grave. It was a very simple ceremony and no problems arose. I suppose the two groups spoke to each other, but nothing significant was said and we separated. Gordon and Nigel still unaware of anything untoward. That, at least, was a relief, and the journey back was that much better.'

Dennis remembered the drive to London to meet his brother Adrian, who was teaching at a private boarding school in one of the outlying districts, and together they went to the address in Ealing. Alison introduced herself to Dennis and Adrian at the front door and invited them into a front room. They noticed two young men at the end of the hall, but had the feeling she did not want to introduce them. She said that she had married Alec. They replied that his marriage to their mother had never been ended. She had suspected this to be the case. They discussed the urgent matter of his funeral which was a financial problem for all of them, apart from its other difficulties.

Because Dennis had arranged his aunt's funeral some years earlier and he still had the deeds to her grave in Portsmouth he suggested it would be less expensive for Alec to be buried there. There was room for one more coffin and it would be good for him to be with his mother and sister. Alison made it clear that she did not want her sons Gordon and Nigel to know the truth of their father's bigamy and its significance for both of them. Adrian and Dennis were equally eager, along with their mother later, that their sister Daphne should never know the truth. She idolized her father. Could they altogether hide the truth and persuade the funeral director to be part of the cover-up?

Dennis recalled that although Adrian was four and a half years older than him and 'head of the family' for some reason he always left anything awkward for him to deal with. After a brief settling of the funeral details Alison and Adrian left him alone with the funeral director. He said: 'I can't stop you from jumping to conclusions, but I hope I can rely on your discretion. There will be two ladies at the funeral. It is Mrs Wilson's wish and approval (i.e. Alison) that you must on no account give precedence to either of them.'

Dennis was sure that the funeral director had fully sized up the situation. He assured Dennis that he would fully comply with these arrangements.

And so he returned to Southampton to relate the sad truth to his mother; something he had not been relishing. But Gladys was only surprised that her husband had agreed to marry Alison when she had known him as such a committed and strong Roman Catholic. She knew him too well to think that he would have been all that time in London without living with another woman. She told Dennis: 'I may as well tell you now that he had an affair with an actress years ago, and they had a son.' Dennis was more worldly in his youth than his mother realised. 'Oh, I knew that' he replied. When she asked how this was possible when she had cut out the embarrassing report from the newspaper in the house, Dennis explained he had simply gone out and bought another copy to satisfy his curiosity to which she replied: 'Oh! I never thought of that!'

Dennis has always admired his mother's equanimity and compassion in being prepared to go along with the charade of being introduced as her late husband's sister, their 'Aunt Gladys' and for her sons to be introduced as cousins. This is what Alexander Wilson had always led his third apparently bigamous wife and two technically illegitimate sons to believe. Gladys put the feelings and considerations of the two young men, Gordon and Nigel, before her own. Her distraught daughter Daphne did not know how she was going to be able to endure the funeral. The problem was solved when they urged 'Then don't go!'

Dennis had always been an excellent infantry officer. The historian of his battalion, the 1st Tyneside Scottish Black Watch obtained an eye witness account of the battle in Normandy in 1944 when a young officer was felled by two blasts of Wehrmacht shrapnel and while lying wounded 'was trying to get up and rally his men.' This account related to the exact location where Lieutenant Dennis B. Wilson had received his appalling wounds on 1st July 1944. Kevin Baverstock later wrote to Dennis Wilson: '…it is astonishing to think that you survived such a dreadful ordeal.'

Dennis was leading his family in a wholly different kind of battle when his father Alexander Wilson had to be buried and mourned one troubling April day in 1963. The shrapnel was wholly emotional. He deliberately arranged the journey of his family from Southampton to Portsmouth so that there would be no contact between the families beforehand outside the church. He had arranged a Requiem Mass there. Unfortunately, there was an unforeseen delay on the road so they actually arrived after the service had started. Dennis remembered: 'That was just as well because the Parish Priest at St Swithin's Church in Southsea was Canon Lindsay, who knew father and mother because they attended Mass there when we were all staying with my Auntie May. He would have known Alison was not the real widow. He also knew me well because he had been Parish Priest at my local church in Portswood, Southampton.'

Luckily for Dennis, Adrian and Gladys, Canon Lindsay only officiated at the Mass. His Curate was left to deal with the actual committal service. And the funeral director had been true to his word. But Dennis caught his breath and his heart lost more than a few beats when Alison appeared all in black mourning dress from head to foot. His mother Gladys had no money of her own, had received nothing from her impecunious husband for a great many years and could not afford any kind of black outfit appropriate for her husband's funeral. To any observer there was only one widow present.

Dennis's operation 'funeral containment' continued after the simple interment service by the graveside. There would be no reception or wake afterwards. Alison and her boys had to be driven straight back to London. There would be no time for extended small talk. A few quick and polite introductions as Aunt, nephews and cousins, the briefest of conversations, and the ritual would be over with interested, deceived and curious parties scattered hither and thither from whence they came.

The knowing widows spoke to each other. What they said was not overheard and they never said what passed between them. Gladys later said to Dennis that she did not attach any blame to Alison. She had great sympathy for her and her sons. Over the years Dennis has reflected on why Alison decided to act upon this stage in heavy mourning. Was it thoughtlessness? Was it a deliberate action to grab the most prominent position at the funeral? If it were the latter case Dennis thinks such behaviour was 'unkind and extremely ungrateful' to his mother.

He has never forgotten how his mother nearly collapsed on first seeing Gordon in his naval uniform. He was like a ghost from her past. He was the living image of her husband Alec when she first saw him wearing a naval uniform early in 1915 in the New Forest village of Lyndhurst.

Dennis realised that after Alison and her boys had gone it was time to avoid answering questions thereby doing everything he could to quell the bursting curiosity of his wife who was incapable of keeping any secret, even if implored to do so. Dennis knew that she would never actually give it away explicitly, but would deliberately let something slip, and then say 'Oh dear! Have I said something I shouldn't?'

The absent gravestone was more due to a disagreement over the form it should take and the set of Christian names to go on it, rather than any divine revenge for having led a mendacious and duplicitous life. Because of the potential expense of a large enough tombstone Dennis had suggested the money would be better spent on living families.

Secret lives and many lies were buried in Milton Cemetery that fine spring day in April 1963. In his lifetime Alexander Wilson had more than an air of mystery about him. His son in Royal Naval uniform was very curious to find out more. There had been a connection with the Foreign Office, but there was nothing in his papers to support or confirm this.

And so Gordon as a very young naval officer who had completed his training at the Britannia Royal Naval College in Dartmouth decided to ask some questions. He was serving on his first seagoing ship, a recently completed frigate working up an operational level in Home Waters, before deploying to the Middle East. He telephoned the Foreign Office, and was not optimistic. But he hoped he might find out something about his father. Gordon recalled: 'Interestingly, I was not immediately dismissed, but passed around several departments before reaching an extension which invited me to wait while a check was carried out to see if his name could be located. Whether the individual put the phone down beside himself for several minutes or actually went away to carry out a check I shall never know, but the answer when it came was a blank. There was, he said, no record of my father.'

Gordon later reflected how incredibly naïve he had been. When in his later distinguished and long career he found himself in his own appointments at the Ministry of Defence and got to know the ways of Whitehall, he said he quickly realised 'how ridiculous' his approach had been.

Gordon had in fact reproached himself rather too severely. Had he been given access to his father's War Office file containing papers of his service during the two World Wars of the twentieth century, he would have seen very clearly that his father was indeed employed by his majesty's Foreign Office where his gift for languages was needed and appreciated. A lieutenant-general in the army had assessed him at territorial barracks in Westminster in March 1940. In the emergency officer reserve he could have been deployed as a transport officer for ships from Avonmouth near Bristol anywhere in the world having done this during the First World War before being invalided out because of a disabling injury to his knee and catastrophic wounds that left unexplained scars across his arm and torso. The War Office believed it was in the Foreign Office that he could be most useful. Gordon may also have noticed the Second World War annotation 'S.S.' scribbled in red pencil by the assessment panel.

This was a Whitehall acronym for the Secret Service during the 1940s.

In fact, if Gordon had ever been told by his mother, she too could have revealed what his father was doing in MI6. The work was so sensitive that the actual section number for the unit was not made public until 2010. Because that is where Alison Wilson née McKelvie was working when she met his father in the spring of 1940.

Everyone involved in the dark *commedia dell'arte* funeral at Milton cemetery returned to their daily lives having buried into their psyche the sharp shards of conscience, shame, regret, anger, confusion and despair about Alexander Wilson. But like the shrapnel left in Dennis Wilson's flesh by the Wehrmacht in 1944, their future direction could not be certain. Alexander Wilson's mysterious and mischievous life and times were like the Luftwaffe ordnance Dennis had been fighting against when serving in home artillery batteries during the Battle of Britain. Incendiaries and bombs with long term time-delay devices had been buried in special Pandora's boxes deep into the clay and sand of their family heritage.

Would Alison one day decide to offload her agony and grief? Would Dorothy's white heat rage against the man who had lied and humiliated her let rip the ultimate revenge she could visit upon him- to deny and utterly disillusion the respect and pride her only son Michael had for him? Would the sagacious patience and compassionate understanding of Gladys crumble amidst the shabby poverty of her circumstances? As the young naval officer Gordon Wilson advanced in rank and joined the dimensions of the clandestine world of military intelligence, would he be able to unlock the chambers of official secrecy and learn the truth about the father he loved and gained so much inspiration from? Would Douglas in Scotland unleash the brilliant research skills he gained in higher education with qualifications at Masters' and PhD level and answer the question they were all asking- Who was Alexander Wilson?   What was the meaning of his second middle name 'Chesney', his connection with the Marlborough family, and would they ever regain the family seat called 'Ringwood' set amidst the outstanding beauty of the New Forest and requisitioned by the military during the Second World War?

Chapter Two

Gladys and children

The marriage and lives of Alec and Gladys Wilson were rooted in romance and adventure. It is believed they first met socially in the village of Lyndhurst in the New Forest area of Hampshire. When Gladys Kellaway first saw 23-year-old Alexander Wilson, he was in naval uniform. It was early 1915. He had been in the Royal Navy prior to the Great War serving in the cruiser HMS Andromeda which patrolled home waters between Plymouth and Southampton. He was undergoing training to join the Royal Army Service Corps as a second lieutenant.

A clue as to why he moved from the navy to the army may lie in notes taken down by a Lieutenant-General in Westminster in March 1940 during an assessment interview for emergency war commission service. He said he had crashed his plane. This means he may well have started in the Royal Naval Air Service. The plane smash, in what would have been a flimsy and wooden structure, might account for whitish near vertical scars on his abdomen. Dennis remembered that as a child his father would jokingly invite him to feel his knee in order to discover 'the wires implanted to repair the injury.'   There is perhaps an element of truth in the plane crash story as it hardly represents something heroic or fantastic.

Wilson had a noble and dramatic military pedigree. His grandfather Hugh had been one of the founding members of the Army Hospital Corps and gained a medal during the British China war of 1861. He died from fever at the age of 31 in 1870 and was buried in the grounds of Netley Hospital overlooking the Solent.

Alexander Wilson's father- Colonel Wilson

His father, also called Alexander, joined the army at Aldershot at the age of 15 and had a distinguished career in what became the Royal Army Medical Corps serving during the Boer War and during the First World War reaching the rank of Lieutenant Colonel. In the bloodiest fighting of late 1918 he was responsible for all the medical provisions to soldiers on the front line in France and received a mention in despatches for his work.   There was a powerfully romantic back-story to Colonel Wilson's marriage to Annie O'Toole. They met in

Ireland and fell in love. Both sides frowned upon the liaison. The British Army was hated in Ireland. The army disapproved of the idea of one of their NCOs romancing a young woman from a Fenian family. Her family forbade her to marry him. And to make it quite clear that the Army did not want him to have anything to do with her, the Army posted him to Hong Kong. That ought to have been the end of the affair. But she was made of sterner stuff. As Dennis recalled: 'It doesn't surprise me because when she was older she was a pretty formidable figure.'

When she reached the age of 21 she left her family and travelled out to Hong Kong, a considerable adventure for a young Irish woman in the 1880s covering thousands of miles across the world to be with the man she loved. They married in Hong Kong, the Colonel of the Regiment gave her away, and exchanged vows in the Church of the Immaculate Conception.

He was 55 years old when he came home on leave from Boulogne in the middle of the Spanish influenza epidemic in 1919 that was killing more soldiers than the fighting had done in the trenches. He must have been exhausted and asked to take to his bed on his first night at the Wilson seaside home in Minster. Sadly he never woke up. He died from a heart attack in his sleep. Such was the importance of his contribution to the Great War struggle, three hundred soldiers from the Cheshire Regiment stationed at local barracks took part in a moving and spectacular military funeral. But his son Alexander missed it. He was in the Oakalla Prison Farm in British Columbia serving six months with hard labour.

Alexander Wilson had an older sister, Isabella Marie Wilson, who was known as 'Auntie May'. She had served in Malta during the Great War in Queen Alexandra's Imperial Military Nursing Service. A fiancé who died on active service left her enough money to start a hospital and nursing home called 'Bruerne' in Southsea. Alexander had two younger brothers. Harold who died in 1922 at the age of 23 after being brain-damaged in a childhood accident, and Leonard who went to Sandhurst and had a regular army career until after the Second World War with service in France, Northern Ireland, Sierra Leone and Germany.

Alexander's son Dennis remembered how 'My Auntie May adored her father. She was so proud of him, she kept a framed copy of the photograph of him hanging in a prominent position at her nursing home in Southsea, and also the house she rented in Devon during the war.' The family also held onto the special plaque and tribute to Colonel Wilson sent to them by King George V. Dennis said: 'My mother was at the funeral and always said that the 'Dead March' from Saul sent shivers up and down her spine. And Auntie May could not bear the final drawn-out note of the Last Post.'

Childhood and education

Alexander Wilson appears in a family photograph album as a teenage schoolboy, as a Royal Naval Midshipman most probably standing on the deck of the cruiser HMS Andromeda, and as a young man lounging on a chaise longue bristling with charm and good looks and stroking a mischievous looking mongrel puppy on his lap.

He had an excellent education, attending St Joseph's school in Hong Kong and St Boniface in Plymouth where he was taught by De La Salle brothers with bilingual classes in English and French. It is possible that he served in the merchant navy between the ages of 18 and 21 before he enlisted in the Royal Navy in 1914. Many of his novels show detailed knowledge of Australia, New Zealand and South America. He would later join the merchant navy again as purser in 1919 in a requisitioned German liner, the SS Prinzessin, which was returning North American servicemen from the Western Front.

Great War and marriage

War Office records reveal he served as a transport officer with the Royal Army Service Corps during 1915 escorting convoys of military supplies between Avonmouth and French ports supplying the British Army fighting on the Western Front. He sustained a disabling injury to his knee and this combined with indications that he was suffering from the psychological consequences of that event resulted in his medical discharge 25th May 1916 with the rank of lieutenant. He was awarded the Silver War Badge, a special decoration available to soldiers during the First World War invalided by battlefield wounds or injuries while on active service.

A striking sepia portrait of Alexander and Gladys on their wedding day in 1916 shows the groom looking handsome and noble wearing the uniform of an officer in the Royal Army Service Corps. The bridegroom is indeed beautiful in her white wedding dress. She had a kind and intelligent face. Proud families pose behind the couple on a wedding day in Lyndhurst. It was March and there was snow on the ground.

It is clear that they struggled to make ends meet particularly after Alec had to leave the army. He was sending a series of letters to the War Office desperately seeking information about a pension: 'Owing to the many bills I have had to pay to specialists, and to masseurs, and the costs of going away for the benefit of change of air, my financial position is at present very poor.'

By February 1917, Gladys had just given birth to their first son Adrian, and Alec was begging to do any work he could manage: 'I am in an exceedingly embarrassing financial condition, more especially as I am married. I understand that invalided officers are being offered appointments, and as they, in most cases, consist of very light duties, I feel certain that I could accomplish whatever is required of me, if you will be good enough to give me one of them.' Later on that year he even turned up at a recruiting office in 1917 unsuccessfully hoping to get his commission back.

The old and crumbling documents from Alexander's WWI War Office file suggest that any *Boy's Own* dreams of heroic service to King, Country and Empire had been met with the banal and prosaic reality that his Royal Naval service was terminated, probably as the result of crashing a plane, and his 15 month career in the British Army fizzled out in an accident, crude knee operations, ineffective physiotherapy, disability, depression, medical boards, begging letters and financial penury.

Gladys Kellaway was Alexander Wilson's Great War bride who stayed loyal to him with a compassionate understanding and humanitarian sacrifice that garners admiration and astonishment. They had a happy life together. Their children adored them, and were particularly excited when as a glamorous and famous author he returned from exotic trips and work abroad driving them through the New Forest in top of the range hired Rovers. But it was a marriage where they spent many more years apart than together.

Jail and travelling players

In 1919, he signed up for the merchant marine at Tilbury serving as purser on the SS Prinzessin bound for Vancouver, Canada. There is a photograph of him in the Merchant Marine archives looking hard, staring menacingly at the camera with none of the proud charm exhibited in his wedding pictures. There is a visible scar above his left eye.

It is not known if Gladys was ever aware of the six month jail sentence he received for stealing £151 from the SS Prinzessin. This is the equivalent of nearly £8,163 at 2018 financial values. He did not have to tell his family. He could have just shown up much later than they had expected and explained away his longer absence to getting more work on the liners. He would have had to work his passage back to Britain and this was probably under a false name.

From 1919 to early 1925 Alec and Gladys ran a touring drama company and travelled the countryside putting on revues and plays. That was why Dennis was born in Thame, Oxfordshire in 1921. His parents had been living in the scenic village of Cuddington and his father had played cricket for the local team. It was also why his sister Daphne was born a year later in Norwich.

Dennis explained: 'My parents were so busy putting on shows and taking their company around the country, they forgot to register my sister's birth. Years later she needed a passport and I can't tell you the fuss we had to go through to sort that out. My brother Adrian was old enough to remember Daphne being born and swore an affidavit and so did my mother, and that's why poor Daphne's birth did not appear on the National birth register until 1980!'

Absent father and British India

Dennis's earliest recollection of his father was when he went to India in 1925: 'We were living then in a bungalow at the end of Whartons Lane on the edge of the New Forest, Colbury. It was actually owned by my maternal grandparents. They lived there with my mother and three children. My brother Adrian went to the local school. I remember when my father was leaving for India; the bags were packed and the taxi was waiting. I can remember that very clearly. My sister Daphne always remembers that he bent down and put his foot on the running board of the taxi and tied his shoelace. I have that little mental picture of the family parting.'

From then onwards throughout the time he was in India Gladys and their three children only saw him when he came home on leave. There was no question of his family going with him to India. Daphne was quite tiny, four or five, and Dennis was a year older. In those days families did not follow their fathers on far away postings in the British Empire. Dennis said: 'He had a regular correspondence with my mother so she was able to tell us what happened. I suppose he would have put in little messages for us children although I can't actually remember.'

Dennis's memory of his father was that it was marvellous when he was there: 'Since he only saw us when he came home on leave he could indulge himself on us because he didn't have any other distractions. He would concentrate on his children and we would have an absolutely marvellous time.'

Dennis accepts that he did not take on the full responsibilities of a father but in every other respect he was what a child wanted a father to be: 'He was fun to be with and he was a very funny man. He always kept us laughing. He had a very quick wit. I remember one occasion when I was staying in Auntie May's nursing home in Southsea. It was a bit like playing truant with a medical certificate. My father was also staying and Auntie May informed him that a Mrs Gunner had arrived from London and he should go and introduce himself, and father quipped "Oh Well, I'd better go and say *Howitzer!*"

Dennis was emphatic: 'We loved him very dearly. When he did come home he would hire an expensive car, a bit on the sporty side too, he was always very keen on Rovers, and then he would drive us all over the place and pick us up from school. And we basked in his glory because by then he was a pretty well-known author, and a glamorous figure coming home from the Indian continent. And then he would disappear and we would go back to our humdrum existence again.'

Dennis remembered that his regular return to India which happened over a period of eight years would produce 'very much of a sad-heart day.' The rest of his Southampton family would revert to their normal rather banal and unexciting lives. Dennis said it was frustrating that they certainly never lived together as an individual family: 'We were always living with relatives. All the time he was away my mother was living with her parents. The house in Southampton was divided into flats. It was actually owned by my grandmother Kellaway's sister, Great Aunt Ruth, and she occupied the top half and we lived in the bottom half. My mother's brother Stanley was also living there. It was a big house with a very big garden too. And we had a very happy childhood.'

When Alexander Wilson returned from India it was like the arrival of Father Christmas: 'He would buy us presents to make up for the birthdays and Christmases he had missed. He was a great storyteller, he always had masses of tales of things he had done and he was also a very amusing man.'

Dennis believes his father enjoyed all the benefits of being a largely absent father: 'Although most of the time he was a distant figure, we loved him dearly because we never had the opposite side. He never had to discipline us, or anything like that. While he was on holiday we were all enjoying ourselves. The everyday matter of "Do this" and "Go to school" never went on. He didn't have any responsibilities like that.'

All the hard work had to be done by Gladys who brought up her children as Catholics. She was quite strict Church of England, and her mother was very strict too. At that time it was traditional for a non-Catholic marrying a Catholic to agree that their children should be brought up in the Church of Rome. Gladys was absolutely rigid and a disciplinarian. She never allowed her children to miss going to mass on Sunday. These were the days when Roman Catholic obligations were quite serious. She insisted that they observed all of the religious rituals. Dennis recalled: 'We fasted, we did penance and we went to confession and always had fish on Fridays. My mother, very commendably, ensured that we kept the faith. My brother and sister both went to Catholic schools. She always respected the Catholic faith and doctrine, but she could never quite bring herself to adopt it.'

Gladys was hugely respected by her children for providing what was in the end a one parent and very excellent upbringing: 'My mother was entirely responsible for it. She was a wonderful woman and did a jolly good job with all of us.'

Dennis could not recall any of the insecurity that children pick up from rowing parents emotionally estranged from each other: 'It was only after he came back from India that the financial side got a bit dodgy. I was never aware of there being any shortages before then.'

Dennis said his parents' relationship was always very loving: 'My mother always spoke of him with love. He was always loving to her. I can't remember my parents ever having a row. He was away so much that a lot of things people tend to row about in married life didn't arise really. My mother was able to keep from us the extent to which she must have been missing him. We always had a dream that he would come home and we would have a house of our own. I was conscious of that all my boyhood.' Dennis remembered walking to a nearby road and imagining that they would all move into a house and how lovely that would be.

Dennis was adamant that he did not believe there was a cruel intention or exploitative motivation behind his father's commitment of marriage to several women: 'My father had a very deep respect for women. He was a charming man. He respected women in the sense of always paying them attention and compliments; not for any selfish reason but because he genuinely romanticised about women. He had a romantic side to his nature and women were on a pedestal for him really. He was like the knights of old. I would agree with you if you said that that would attract a very positive reaction from women. I was even conscious of that when I was as young as ten. I would realise that he was getting on with women quite well because of his immense charm.'

When Dennis Wilson was a child, his father was a hero figure: 'When I got to school and people asked what does your father do and I said "he writes books", I, of course, made the most of that. I was immensely proud of him. His books were popular prizes on sports' days. He was this romantic figure in India. I started reading his books at an earlier age than children would normally have expected to. I remember reading his first novel *The Mystery of Tunnel 51*. I remember how excited I was reading that. The stealing of the plans when the train enters the tunnel and the lights are blacked out with the courier being stabbed to death. That's the thing about my father's books. They were so exciting. You didn't put them down. You couldn't wait to find out what was going to happen next.'

Return from India and 1930s

After his father's return from India he came to live with Gladys and his children in Westridge Road, Southampton for longer periods. They had no idea about his other life with Dorothy in Lahore which had evolved into an apparent marriage in 1928 when she and Alexander were appearing in public there as man and wife. This was after 1933, the year Alexander and Dorothy had their son born Michael Chesney. When he was at home in Southampton, he was consistently writing books. There were more than one published each year.

Dennis said: 'I do remember him writing *Mr. Justice* for the reason that I saw the first page he was typing and I read it. It starts off with a group of people discussing the inadequacies of the justice system and criminals getting away with their crimes. I went downstairs and I was young and an idiot and I said "Congratulations! You've been writing exactly what I think," and something impertinent like that and he was absolutely furious. It was the only time I can remember my father being cross with me. He said: "You've no right to read it. It's like reading somebody's personal letter." And that is a very, very vivid memory. It was so rare and chastening. I never did it again or if I did, I never told him!'

Dennis was able to recall the events that precipitated his father effectively leaving his family in Southampton for good. By this time they all thought they would be living together as a whole family forever: 'My Great Aunt Ruth owned the house and lived in the top half. I think I'd been cheeky or something. She'd made a remark to me and I'd responded rudely. She was ignoring me pointedly every time she saw me. My father could hardly fail to notice this. He wanted to know what it was. Of course, I wouldn't tell him. But eventually he did wheedle out of me that she had said that my uncle was the only one bringing money into the house. That was Stanley who'd trained as a chiropodist and had remained a private throughout the World War and was exceedingly jealous of Alexander.'

In Ruth Kellaway's eyes earning money was about going out to work to do a job, handing over the money of a weekly wage to the wife for house-keeping and so on. Alexander Wilson was probably contributing more to the budget than his brother-in-law, but it was in lump sums, and then when he got royalties. Dennis said: 'Anyhow I had to tell him in the end and he went to see her and there was an awful row and she apologised and she begged him to stay but he insisted on leaving and saying things like "I'll come back and collect you and we'll all live in our own house" to my mother. He stormed out.'

This was a breach and schism that was never fully healed: 'It was a terribly tearful scene and off he went. Except for brief periods when he and my Great Aunt were reconciled, and he used to stay for a few days at a time, we were never actually together as a family again.' Dennis looked forlornly into the distance when he said: 'We were all still living in this dream where my father was going to make a fortune and come and collect us, buy us a nice home, and we would all live happily ever after together as a family.' But this was never to be.

Alexander Wilson's dramatic departure must have taken place in April or May 1935. He had been with his first family for about sixteen months. He had been going up to London from time to time ostensibly so he could meet his publishers for what seemed like rather long stays. It was hardly a day return to Waterloo station. Dennis realised: 'It makes sense he would have been seeing Dorothy and Mike as a young baby.' He would always spend Christmases in those days with his sister Auntie May at her nursing home 'Bruerne' in Southsea.

Dennis was able to fix the time of the blow-up to one of those warm father and son experiences that define nostalgic memory for family life. They had been listening to the cup final between West Bromwich Albion and Sheffield Wednesday: 'The score was 2-2 and father had gone to the back door to pay the milkman when a goal was scored, and I rushed out to tell him that West Brom were leading, but when I returned I discovered it had been Sheffield who had scored a break-away goal that had defeated the second commentator, whose job it was to keep naming the square in the diagram of the pitch in which the action was taking place. The final score was 4-2 for Sheffield.' The precision of Dennis's recall was most impressive, but also poignant. He was remembering the joy and delight of the last time he was able to join his father listening to FA Cup Final commentary on the radio, who as a father for all intents and purposes, would leave him for good. Dennis also mentally cross-referenced his father's letters to his older brother Adrian: 'Father's letters to Adrian from London began in July 1935.' That was also the year that Adrian took the King's shilling and joined up with the Hampshire Regiment.

A permanent separation

In the early days of his move to London, Gladys, Dennis, Adrian and Daphne became accustomed to what is now known commonly as a one-parent family. At the beginning they saw more of him than when he had been in India, because quite frequently he would return to Southampton and book a room in an hotel, where Gladys would join him, and he would take everyone out for a meal and to the cinema.

He would only return to the house if Great Aunt Ruth and Uncle Stanley were out, in order to visit grandmother Kellaway, with whom he had a loving relationship. In those early days he sent Gladys money on a regular basis, but this support became further apart and inadequate. Gladys began to find it extremely difficult to pay all the bills and they soon became the 'genteel poor.'

Daphne and Dennis would have cardboard insoles cut for their shoes because Gladys could not afford to have them repaired. It was embarrassing when on rainy days their shoes left wet marks on the floor. Dennis had to wear a second-hand blazer that was too big for him. It wore out before he had a chance to 'grow into it.' Dennis also remembered feeling humiliated when he had to wear a cheap mackintosh when all his friends had gaberdine. The headmaster at this private school applied public humiliation whenever Dennis was not paying attention by calling out: 'I am sure YOUR father cannot afford to have his money wasted,' when fully aware that the school fees were always in arrears and sending Dennis home with a note addressed to Uncle Stanley complaining that he had not been paid for a long time. The deep embarrassment was felt by Dennis who opened the note to read on his way home, and also his mother Gladys who had to depend on her brother and aunt to pay for her children's education.

Well into his late teens Dennis always continued to cherish the dream of his father bringing them all together: 'In 1938 and 1939 he was negotiating with a studio in Hollywood because they wanted to film *The Magnificent Hobo*. He was going to write the script and on the basis of this tremendous success, he was going to be employed as a scriptwriter in Hollywood and we would all be over there and we would live a rich life in Hollywood. It got quite far I believe. I am sure I am right in thinking that they actually paid my father some sort of retainer. They may even have bought the copyright. They were certainly going to do it, but unfortunately the war started in 1939 and that ruled it out altogether. My father wanted to go into some kind of war service and in any case films for the European market had no future.'

Dennis remembered that after the family row and his father went off to London with all his baggage packed and so on, he had a picture of him arriving at Waterloo Station surrounded by suitcases and thought to himself 'What would I do? How do you find lodgings for the night?' At the time Dennis knew his father would not have had a lot of money.

Many, many years later the penny dropped: 'I now know he simply went off to his other home. To the best of my knowledge my mother had no idea at all. He continued to come and stay with us occasionally, and my parents were on good terms. I am quite sure I would have known if she had any suspicions.'

In that time long before the age of the Internet, and online digital street maps and databases it was not all that difficult living in two entirely different cities and not being discovered. Gladys never went to London alone. In Southampton they did their best to carry on as a family. Apart from the times he came to stay with them occasionally, they used to go up to London on trips to see him. They used to have trips to theatres; something he was very keen on. On anniversaries and birthdays they would go up to London and have a family party.

Dennis remembered that on 2nd April 1949: 'We all went to White Hart Lane and saw the Saints beat their promotion rivals one nil and we thought promotion was in the bag. Unfortunately, our leading goal-scorer was injured in that match and we scarcely won another match and missed promotion by one point. After the match we all went to see *Annie Get Your Gun*.' They were completely oblivious to the fact that Dorothy and Michael had long disappeared from Alexander Wilson's life in London to be replaced by Alison whom he married in 1941 and their sons Gordon and Nigel, born in 1942 and 1944.

Alexander the sporting hero

Dennis treasured his memory of his father as a dedicated sportsman. As a young man he and his parents Alexander and Annie lived in Plymouth, and there was a legend, entirely unconfirmed by any existing records, that he played as an amateur for Plymouth Argyle and he talked about playing two amateur Internationals for England.

Another family legend surrounded Dennis's birth. When his mother was actually in labour with him, his father had an important club cricket match. His mother insisted that he played the match and did not let the team down. It was a time when fathers were not expected to attend the births of their children. Dennis loved telling the story: 'He didn't do his pacing of the corridor outside. He'd gone out to bat and a message came to the pavilion that I had been born and they took a message out to him to the crease and everybody cheered, the opposing players cheered as well and congratulated him and then he went on to score fifty and win the match which is quite fantastic really.'

Alexander Wilson was a tremendous player and follower of cricket. It was more important to him than football. Dennis remembered that when he was working on a cruise liner just before the Second World War and they used to dock at Tilbury every fortnight through the cricket season he would join his father in London to watch matches at Lords and the Oval.

On one occasion, which Dennis has never forgotten, he actually introduced his son to Dennis Compton, who at that time was a colt on the Middlesex staff: 'The match had ended and we were sitting talking, and he was coming round and collecting the cushions and my father said "That's Dennis Compton. He's going to be a great player for England one day. Would you like to meet him?" We went over and he introduced me and we had a conversation, and Dennis Compton addressed my father as "Sir". That was way before Compton became the well-known and famous figure he became later.'

Cad or romantic?

Dennis said he found it difficult to recall any aspect of the scoundrel or old-fashioned bounder about his father: 'My father was a very popular character. He got on with men and women. Of course, I am romanticising I suppose, but I can never remember anyone saying a bad word about him. Except my Uncle Stanley on the Kellaway side. My mother's brother. He had also been in the army during the Great War, but he had stayed a private. He was a chiropodist actually. He was very jealous of my father's career. I do know that in later years he used to say when my father had come back from India "How's the gallant Major?" always laden with a sense of sarcasm.'

Dennis is adamant that his father's multiple relationships with women was not the behaviour of a sexual predator. He emphasised that as an author Alexander Wilson never wrote anything of an explicitly sexual nature. He did not travel beyond the bedroom door: 'All his heroes had his own attitude to women; that they were to be respected and cherished and I think my father could simply not write the modern sex novel.'

It is Dennis's theory that his writing career ended in the 1940s probably because the old fashioned conventions he expressed in his novels became unpopular and passé: 'I think also his precise writing style was getting out of date and I don't think he could have written anything else but precise English. Some of his later manuscripts, even allowing for the fact they were written in the late 1940s, were beginning to get dated for their time.' It is his view that if his father's unpublished manuscripts were to be published today, somebody would have to go through them and put them into the more everyday language which he would never have used.

Encouraging son Adrian

Alexander Wilson mentored his laid-back and sports mad, but thoroughly unambitious son Adrian with love and exasperation. He was sent to the best local schools, but his love of sports always won over the application required to pass exams.

In January 1935 he persuaded Adrian to follow the family tradition and join the British Army as a regular soldier and enlist with the local Hampshire regiment. He played every kind of sport for the Hampshire regiment, including cricket, rugby, athletics and even boxing, and he would have been in the British Olympic team were it not for the Second World War, which he served in Ciphers. But he would never respond to his father's pleas to take up a commission. Alexander would always be writing to him: "When are you going to get your 1st Class Certificate? When are you going to get your first stripe?' He was continually persuading very senior officers, and even at least one General to commend Adrian to his commanding officer. But Adrian would not be motivated. This is because as a sportsman he had such a wonderful life. He was in seventh heaven. In the peacetime army any sportsman with prowess led a privileged status, free from all duties, eating the best food in the Sergeant's Mess, and being able to train continually. Socially he was always in contact with the officer class who dominated the sports teams and were more in keeping with his intellect and background.

Adrian never had to do any square-bashing and going to Sandhurst was far too much like hard work. His father never stopped trying to persuade Adrian to show ambition. There was the example of Alexander's brother Leonard, who did get his school certificate when in the ranks of the Green Howards, and went on a scholarship commission to Sandhurst in the early thirties. He played cricket for his army corps and went on to gain promotion and service all over the world: Hong Kong; with the BEF in France in 1940; West Africa; and Germany and Austria in the army of occupation after the last war.

Alexander's Letters to Adrian

It is in the surviving letters from Alexander Wilson to his eldest son Adrian that there is the strongest documentary evidence that in his familial relationships, albeit multiple and simultaneous, he would consistently demonstrate respect, love and affection for his children and their mothers. In September 1935 after Adrian had embarked for his first service overseas, he expressed the profound bond he had with Gladys, even though by this time his parallel life and family with Dorothy was probably into its tenth year: 'Mummy was delighted that she was able to see you for a few minutes on the pier at Southampton. What a great soul she is, isn't she? So loyal and loving and devoted! She is almost bursting with pride for you: I'm rather that way myself. She is so grateful for the week-ends you have been able to spend with her, when you have proved yourself such a devoted son to her. During these bad times, when fate is taking such a malignant delight in upsetting everything I do, or attempt to do, it is a source of infinite consolation to me to know that you have stepped into the breach, and been able, by your thoughtfulness and love, to make her life a little less hard and put a little pleasure into her life.'

Another letter to Adrian in January 1937, when the young soldier was en route with the Hampshire Regiment for military operations in India, offers some insight into the complexity and humanity of Alexander Wilson's character: 'Please, for your own sake, concentrate chiefly on getting nominated for Sandhurst. Push yourself forward, make yourself and your ambition known to your officers; study hard to get your certificate and that very necessary stripe; and by doing everything eagerly and being always the first to do things, keep yourself in the limelight. Make a big effort to kill, or at least reduce, that reserve, diffidence and shyness which at present is so deeply rooted in you. An inferiority complex will get you nowhere, and though you may be in the ranks now, always remember that your birth is every bit as good as that of any officer you may meet or serve under, and that you have an honourable military tradition that few can equal. Please keep all that in mind mostly for your own sake and the sake of your future, but also for Mummy's and my sake, old chap, we want you back so badly. I know I feel the separation more than I could ever tell you to your face. I need you, and am longing for your return, not only because I am so keen for you to enter Sandhurst, but because I am never so happy as when you are with me or within easy reach of me.'

In this heart-felt correspondence Alexander Wilson revealed some of his inner-most hopes, fears and emotions: 'I am a very lonely man, Adrian, and often a very unhappy one. Life has played me some scurvy tricks and you mean far more to me than I can ever describe. When you were a little boy you always used to say you were "Daddy's number one boy." You still are and always will be. I hope you will not think these remarks are the sentimental outpourings of a middle-aged emotionalist. I'm neither emotional nor sentimental: merely your very devoted father, who regrets nothing so much as the fact that he has been able to accomplish so little for you. I shall not feel any happiness now until you are back with me again, but my joy and pride will be indescribable when you return, I hope before the year is out, you will be able to enter Sandhurst. There is another little wish I have. It is that you cease being quite so introspective. Let your feelings show themselves more, particularly with me. I want to be always your confidant: to feel that you confide all your perplexities, your troubles, your problems, to me. I yearn for you to have no secrets from me and never to fear to tell me anything, no matter what it may be. You will always find me understanding. I have been through the fires; made mistakes; suffered; been up against things. Let my experiences be of use to you; so avail yourself of it by letting the mantle of reserve that cloaks you fall entirely from you where I am concerned. I am very much reserved myself, which is all the more reason why you and I should be pals in every sense of the word. There are beastly, desperate pitfalls in life which you only avoid by experience: use me for all you're worth to avail yourself of my knowledge in order to keep out of them. Will you do this? Write to Dennis and Daphne as much as you can. Dennis was rather hurt by your remark about why he came to see you off. He, like Daphne is very fond of you and I honestly think that he was as upset as anybody at your going, though wild horses wouldn't have got him to admit as much but, between you and me, there were great tears in his eyes as the ship moved out. Dennis doesn't easily cry. [...] Attend Mass and Holy Communion as often as possible, won't you? And, with all my love, I ask you to pray for your ever loving and devoted Dad.'

Never an officer but eventually a teacher too

Adrian utterly refused all of his father's exhortations to apply for a commission, even though his father had been pulling strings for him at the War Office in London. The regiment was posted to India and Palestine. He adamantly refused to have anything to do with applying for a commission and in complete exasperation Alexander would affectionately refer to him as "That mysterious and lone figure in the Middle East!" When war broke out, the Regular Army realised Adrian was clearly officer material and then the pressure for him to apply for a commission would not only have come from his father. But he still would not budge. In the end there was a happy compromise. As Adrian was brilliant at doing crosswords and puzzles and was very intelligent, they lured him into the Royal Signals to work on ciphers and codes and he ended the war a sergeant- the highest rank he wanted to rise, above which he would have had to take on responsibilities beyond his inclinations.

Adrian become a general teacher. He took advantage of the emergency teacher training that came out of the war. He went to the famous Loughborough teacher training college, where he met his future wife Grace. They were very much in love and shared a total passion for sport. She played cricket and qualified as a Cricket Umpire. Dennis recalled that her good humour made her the perfect match: 'She was able to laugh him out of his surly moods that he had always been prone to. Sadly, however, she contracted cancer and died while still young, and quite literally the life went out of his life.'

Adrian had gone into general teaching at junior school level. He himself had a tremendous interest in literature and was extraordinarily well read. When he died in 1998, he had more than 900 bottles of wine in temperature-controlled cabinets, more than 4,000 hardback novels, over 3,000 paperbacks and more than 1,000 long-playing records. He'd been keen on science fiction right from his teens and he had a tremendous collection of *Wonder* and *Astounding* stories. He had magazines from the pre-war period that were unique. His collection sold for £1,200.

Encouraging son Dennis

Dennis had to leave school when he was fifteen in June 1937. There was not the money to fulfil his university potential. He began working with Ocean Pictures, a firm supplying photographers for ocean liners and was taught to develop and print. Every fortnight he went aboard the "Queen Mary" after she docked to process all the photographs taken during the voyage. He loved roaming the ship to his heart's content. He was fascinated to learn much later in life that his father took Michael on a visit to the ship at around the same time and wondered what they would have said if they had bumped into each other.

Alexander Wilson had great ambitions for Dennis and went out of his way to find him a job in the British Film industry and this included an actual approach to J. Arthur Rank. Wilson was not a hero with the cheque-book. He was, however, a hero with joie de vivre, the dreams that give sense, fun and purpose to living, and the indelible charm of the time-honoured storyteller. In 1938 Dennis spent six months on the Canadian Pacific liner SS Montcalm doing fortnightly cruises out of Tilbury Docks that took him to virtually every city in Europe with a port, and exotic and faraway places such as Helsinki, Algiers, Casablanca, Madeira, Tenerife and Naples. He once got lost in the Arab quarter of Algiers, but realising it was built on a hill, kept turning downhill until he reached the sea-front. He remembered seeing an American film in Copenhagen and laughing before the audience because it was sub-titled in Danish.

At the end of each cruise on a Saturday, when his father was living with Dorothy and Michael in their flat in Little Venice, Dennis would go up to London to meet him for cricket either at the Lords or Oval and in the evening they would go to the Gaumont State Cinema in Kilburn. Alexander would book lodgings for him. Dennis later worked as a commercial artist for an illuminated signs company and then for his Auntie May when she moved her nursing home for retired ladies from Southsea to Topsham in South Devon. It was there he was called up for service in the Second World War.

The Second World War

Dennis joined the Royal Artillery in a light Ack Ack and search-light unit for the early part of the Battle of Britain. When the British Army was 'desperately short of infantry officers' he was commissioned into the Middlesex Regiment, serving in the first Battalion Kensingtons, and then the Black Watch Tyneside-Scots.

He looked forward to visiting his father for lunch at the Authors' Club in Whitehall Court where everyone would salute him as he was wearing the uniform of a Lieutenant-Colonel at the time: 'He told me very little. In the same circumstances I think I would have told my son, but he was very particular. Of course, we were all very much aware of the motto "Careless talk costs lives". I didn't probe him about it. One time he did tell me that if anything happened to him the person to get in touch with was Lord Cadogan at the Foreign Office who would be able to put me in the picture.'

During the early part of the Second World War Alexander Wilson began giving Gladys some regular payments and she was able to rent a small house in Chandler's Ford. The Southampton family had been effectively blasted out of their house during the Blitz when a bomb totally demolished a modern house opposite. Daughter Daphne was working in London for the Ordnance Survey, making maps for the invasion of Europe. Alexander Wilson would visit Gladys in Chandler's Ford during the war and a number of times after it, sharing a bedroom with her and meeting local friends.

Dennis had a violent and distressing campaign as an infantry officer during the Battle of Normandy. Many close friends were killed in action. On the 1st July 1944 while leading his platoon in battle he was riddled with shrapnel from two German artillery shells and evacuated with disabling injuries. He had an affinity for army life and wanted to continue serving after the war as a regular officer, but his medical status was such that he had to leave in 1949 with the rank of Captain. All the while Dennis was writing poetry and it was his long poem 'Elegy of a Common Soldier', scribbled while in the slit trenches of the Normandy campaign, that would later gain him recognition as a significant poet of the Second World War. Five volumes of his poetry would be published when he was in his late 80s and such would be their success, he would be awarded a prestigious honorary fellowship from the University of Southampton, be a guest of honour for the Queen and Duke of Edinburgh at the Royal reception for contemporary poetry at Buckingham Palace in 2013, and be interviewed on the BBC Radio 4 *Today* programme where he was invited by John Humphrys to read some of his poetry aloud.

Dennis defied all the disappointment of his father's Micawber-style financial incompetence, that had consigned him to a declining private school in the 1930s, and inadequately prepared him for the school leaving certificate examination. From 1949, he worked for 49 years for Encyclopaedia Britannica and became their longest serving sales representative in the entire world. He held the financial tiller for his family with responsibility for bringing up two children, paying for every minute of their education, who went on to have successful professional careers. He was determined to give his family a good standard of living in a big family house with a large garden; something his father failed to do for all four of his families.

Bogus Colonel Wore Wings

In October 1944, while still receiving treatment for his war wounds, Dennis was devastated to read in the London newspapers that his father had been prosecuted for wearing a false uniform and decorations. He and his brother Adrian agreed not to mention it to him and he never mentioned it to them. He was brought up before the magistrate in Marylebone for posing as a Colonel in the Indian Army, and wearing decorations to which he was not entitled. They included Royal Air Force wings, and the Croix de Guerre. Dennis wore an apologetic smile as though the memory of this event still hurt him deeply when he said: 'I can vaguely remember the headline in the newspaper now. Yes, it was "Bogus Colonel Wore Wings." I did keep the newspaper cutting but then deliberately threw it away because I did not want the family to find it after I died.'

The shame of this experience was such to bring tears to his eyes when recalling it over sixty years later. Dennis, Adrian and the rest of his Southampton family were also completely unaware that he had been declared bankrupt in January 1944. He wrote to Gladys asking if she could lend him some money. This provoked Dennis into sending his father the only angry communication he had with him: 'I did write a letter back to him that would I suppose have upset him, although it was to the point. I remember saying to him that I didn't think he realised what the situation was: "Adrian, Daphne and I are supporting mother and that's the only income she has. We give her a regular amount, which none of us can really afford and yet you come and out of the blue write asking to borrow from her. You haven't contributed anything to her for years. Where on earth do you think she was going to get the money from?" I was, in fact, pretty cross. I don't think he replied to the letter. It was the only time it could be said that I had words with him really.'

Encouraging daughter Daphne

Daphne is the only girl among Alexander's known family of eight children. She was born in Norwich in June 1922, about a year after Dennis, when her parents' travelling theatrical company were touring East Anglia. Daphne was devoted to the art of dance and it was her ambition to perform and teach professionally. Such was her talent that the Elfin School of Dancing took her on as a student-teacher. Her father arranged for her to audition with Zelia Gray, a leading impresario and stage producer in the late 1930s, and she passed the audition. When the Second World War broke out she worked for Ordnance Survey and also gained a series of qualifications from the Royal Academy of Dancing, and Imperial Society of Teachers of Dancing which led to her teaching and performing through the late 1940s including pantomimes at the Theatre Royal Exeter.

Daphne fell in love and married Robert McGill- one of her enthusiastic and skilful ballroom class students. They set up and ran a successful School of Dancing in Eastleigh and then a theatrical stage costumes and dancing shoes suppliers shop. They said that they had never had an argument, but Dennis affectionately recalls: 'From my own observation this was untrue, because they would argue if each of them wanted to go to a different place on a day's outing. However, on such occasions they would be arguing in favour of what the other wanted.'

After the Second World War

In the post war period as Dennis, Adrian and Daphne pursued their adult lives of marriage and setting up their own families it would be inevitable that they saw less and less of their father who remained in London. They were oblivious to the struggles he had bringing up two young boys with his third wife Alison and his fourth marriage to Elizabeth in 1955.

There was, however, a memorable occasion in 1951 when Alexander Wilson attended the marriages of Dennis and Adrian on the same day. In those days there were tax advantages if you got married before April the fifth and it was a case of both brothers realising 'Oh you're getting married and so am I.' So Adrian was married in Enfield in the morning, and Dennis tied the knot in Southampton in the afternoon about two o'clock. Wilson attended one wedding in Enfield with a quick toast to the bride and groom and then got the train to Waterloo and came down to Southampton for Dennis's marriage where he was able to stay for the reception. It took a bit of planning but as became so very evident much later he was rather good at devising complicated plans and adventures in his private life.

Dennis recalled that his father was initially reluctant to attend the marriage of his daughter Daphne to Robert McGill. This was an occasion when Gladys, usually so tolerant and good-natured about her husband's unusual character, changed his mind with a telephone call. It is possible that she threatened Alec with the revelation of aspects of his past he would rather his daughter never knew. She never shared with anyone what that information had been.

Dennis suspects it might have been the information mother and son shared about newspaper coverage during the 1930s that Alexander Wilson had been named as a respondent in a divorce case and was alleged to have had a son as a result of the affair. Dennis discovered the report when at breakfast there had been a hole in their morning newspaper. He had gone out to buy an uncensored one and read its sensational contents. This is one of the more mysterious and unfathomable aspects of Alexander Wilson's complicated narrative. Despite extensive searches of national newspaper archives and court records, it has not been possible to verify the newspaper report or Family Division case file. Wilson is not cited as a co-respondent in any of the 80 per cent of divorce case files that have survived from this period.

Chapter Three

Dorothy and son

Dorothy was the beautiful, and self-resourceful touring actress standing in for Dame Sybil Thorndike in British India. She was one of the first actors and directors in Indian radio drama. On the 25th October 1925 at the age of 31 she embarked on the ocean-going passenger and general cargo ship, City of Nagpur, at Liverpool bound for Karachi in British India. She was described in the passenger list as a 'theatrical' and she was joined by other members of her touring group: the actresses Miss D N Wren, and Miss D Vellenoweth, the actor B. Bray, another 'theatrical' Mr A G E MacLean, and a Miss D E Pack who preferred to describe herself as 'an artiste.'

There was also a Professor of English Literature on board with the address, The Bungalow, Colbury, Southampton. His name was Alexander Wilson. He had just turned 32. The single-funnelled City of Nagpur with its red and black livery had a passenger list of 34 men and 55 women who in the quaint language of the time were 'not accompanied by husband or wife.'

It was going to be a long and very romantic voyage. The Ellerman City Steamship vessel would normally take three weeks to sail to British India stopping at Gibraltar, Marseilles, Port Said, and Aden on the way. The Glasgow registered ship was sparkling new and modern for its time, having only been built and launched three years before and at 10,146 tons was one of the larger ships plying the Karachi route.

She would be torpedoed, shelled, strafed with machine-gun fire and sunk by the German submarine U.75 while 900 miles west of Fastnet near Ireland in the early hours of the morning on 29th April 1941 with the loss of 16 lives though 452 survivors were picked up by a destroyer and made it back to Greenock two days later. One crew member died from his wounds in Hospital. The sinking of the City of Nagpur took place at around the same time that Alexander Wilson bade farewell to Dorothy and their 7-year-old son Michael on a railway station platform in Yorkshire. It was the spring of 1941 and they would never see or talk to each other again. There is some poignant symbolism in the passenger steamship that originally kindled their love sinking to the bottom of the sea at the same time as broken and resentful hearts parted on a railway platform, leaving a

43

little boy fatherless and forlorn for the rest of his life.

Was it not inevitable that Alexander Wilson and Dorothy Wick struck up an interest in each other on that long voyage through the Irish Sea, Bay of Biscay, Mediterranean Sea, Suez Canal, and Arabian Sea in 1925? They were the same age and background. They were both steeped in the theatrical world of touring, performance and story-telling. And they both had time on their hands. It was an exciting and luxurious adventure across the world they were sharing. They were in a social whirl of breakfast at 8:30, coffee at 10, lunch at 12:30, followed by teatime with little cakes and pastries at 4, dinner served at 7 and a 10 o'clock night buffet of little sandwiches and sweets. When they were not partaking of this constant restaurant silver service, they could spend their time sitting on deck, talking, reading, card playing, and going on excursions, perhaps to see the Pyramids when the ship stopped over in Port Said before sailing through the Suez Canal.

We do not have a detailed account of how their relationship developed. He would travel directly to Lahore to take up his teaching post at Islamia College, in Lahore. It is presumed that following the end of the theatrical group's tour of British India she decided to join him in the capital of the Punjab often described as the Paris of North West India. These were intense and dramatic years in the history of the Great Game of intelligence between the British and Russian Empires. The Russian Revolution had violently catalysed the Soviet Union and the International Comintern that continued to fuel Anglo-Russian rivalry and intrigue in Afghanistan and across the North West Frontier. It was a febrile period of insurrection, bloody terrorism and the struggle for independence.

The first references to an Alexander and Dorothy Wilson on the social scene of Lahore would begin from around 1928. They would both be resident as man and wife at number 11 Masson Road, Lahore. Alexander Wilson would save Dorothy from the Tribesman's bullet and the fatal sting of the world's deadliest snake. He wrote plays staged in the city and Dorothy directed and performed them for productions that raised money for charity; something Dorothy would do all her life.

Dorothy could well have been the muse who inspired him to start writing best-selling novels. She would be his literary secretary during the 1930s when they lived in Little Venice bringing up their son Michael. Alexander's love for Michael was so intense he took on Michael Chesney's name as a writing pseudonym for another military intelligence fiction series. But this happy, romantic and exciting life crashed with the onset of the Second World War, the blitz and recruitment into MI6. What led to the violent row, followed by Dorothy taking Michael to the Yorkshire Dales and never to return? Why did she hate him so much she forced him to agree to a plot to make Michael falsely grieve when only 9 for the father he would never see again?

Michael Chesney Wilson decided to change his name to Mike Shannon when he was a young man. He did not like the surname he was born with in a Kensington nursing home in 1933. And he needed a new professional working name for acting.

The last memory he ever had of his father belongs in some imagined film sequence that could be iconic of the Second World War in Britain. It was March or April 1941. He was living with his mother in the Yorkshire village of Wensley and was seeing his father off at Leyburn railway station. His father was all dressed up in Khaki, carrying his tin hat and in Lieutenant Colonel's uniform: 'He looked absolutely splendid. I remember that when war came I had always known him in civvies, or as a part-time policeman. Then suddenly there was this magnificent figure in Khaki with a brown Sam Browne belt, the ribbons and the hat, and something that was always of great pride to me; when we went out for our walks service personnel who used to approach used to salute to him.'

The only photograph Mike had of his father in army uniform presented the handsome features of a senior officer with Royal Flying Corps insignia and ribbons which in black and white colours are difficult to make out. One of them appeared to have a star; somewhat reminiscent of the RAF distinguished flying cross usually known as the D.F.C.

Mike was seven going on eight when he last saw him. The bright sunshine and blue sky and rolling green Wensleydale countryside, the smell of the burning coal, the huffing and puffing of the steam engine, the chatter of people saying goodbye. The deep and everlasting emotions of grief, longing, and loss would be expressed in Mike's poem 'Goodbye 1941.'

'Be a good boy and take care of mum.'
A familiar figure, strange in khaki uniform
Leans out of the carriage window.
I'm lifted up to kiss the large smiling face.
'Don't cry, there's a brave chap,
Won't be away long you know.'

I can't say it's the train's escaping steam
That brings a smarting tear -
It wouldn't be true.
I can't say anything at all
Only cling on tight

Until a whistle shrieks
Announcing departure.

We wave until there's only a toy train
Dissolving in the dusk.

Do I TRULY remember -
Or over the years have I imagined
My own scene copied from War Movies?
Did I IMAGINE my hand enclosed in his:
His laughter, crinkling bright blue eyes?
Our Sunday walks from Little Venice
By the Regent's Canal,
Past the horse-drawn barges bright with colour,
To a large, red painted pub
Where we sat outside on benches?
He with his ale and pipe, me with my ginger beer,
Listening to the tales he invented
Just for that day, just for ME,
Am I INVENTING NOW?
I never got to know this man called 'DAD'
Only as a child I felt his love and the joy of his company
IF I dreamed my memories and they are all I have of him -
Then in dreams we shall meet and be glad.

The bright light and emotion of that day on a railway station platform in 1941 was something that creatively resonated and he could write down. He felt it captured something of the feeling and world of his existence as the young boy he was on that day and also his 'sense of loss,' after all these years. It was obvious that for however long Alexander Wilson lived beyond 1944, he had denied himself the privilege of knowing a son whose talent and qualities would have given him immense pride.

Alexander Wilson and Islamia College, Lahore

Alexander Wilson responded to an advert in *The Times* on Thursday 3rd September 1925 in which Islamia College, Lahore said it required a Professor of English literature with the ability to organise and run cricket and sports (described as essential). The salary was 500 Rupees a month with annual increments of 50 Rupees rising to a maximum of 1,000 Rupees on a three-year contract, with passage money of £75. The college specified: 'state qualifications and experience.' Wilson's second published novel *The Devil's Cocktail* (1928) reveals how closely he set his fiction in the reality of his life. The novel is hugely autobiographical and he compliments and mocks fictional characters who are barely disguised representations of people he actually worked with in Lahore. *The Times* advert for the post is printed virtually word for word in his novel:

'A Professor of English Literature is required for Sheranwala College, University of Northern India, Lahore, at a salary of Rupees 500-50-1000, for a period of three years. Applicants must be graduates of an English University and preference will be given to one who is a sportsman. Apply with copies of testimonials, references etc, to Mahommed Abdullah, C.I.E., Savoy Hotel, Strand, London.'

In 2018 the value of the £75 passage money would be £4,342. The equivalent in today's money of the starting salary on offer of 500 British Indian rupees a month from 1925 would have produced an annual salary of just over £23,000. These were modest earnings, but the adventure on offer and chance to be a Professor of English literature must have been alluring.

Mr. Abdullah Yusuf Ali C.B.E., was Islamia College's Principal and travelled to London to actively run the recruitment. His full qualifications were listed in the *Punjab University Enquiry Committee, 1932-33 Report* of which he was an active member and author: 'A. Yusuf Ali, Esquire, C.B.E., M.A., LL.M. (Cantab.), I.C.S. (retired), formerly Principal, Islamia College, Lahore.' He received written applications at 12 Grange Park, Ealing, W.5. We do not know if he interviewed short-listed candidates at the Savoy Hotel. Ali was a well-established figure in the Indian government hierarchy, both as a civil servant and academic. He was Principal of the college until 21st November 1927 when Alexander Wilson took over. Wilson's salary would have been tripled to the equivalent of over £60,000 in 2018 money.

Abdullah Yusuf Ali was also the world's leading English speaking scholar on Islam. His English translation and commentary on the Koran ranks as one of the most celebrated and highly respected achievements in the field of Islamic scholarship. The translation, first published in 1934, 1938 and then revised in 1940, remains one of the most widely used to this very day.

We can only speculate that Yusuf Ali was recruiting a European who could combine the role of improving the college through higher educational leadership with the monitoring of the boys at the College who were drawn from the region's Islamic elite, North West frontier farmers and the agitating tribal chiefs of Waziristan.

Islamia College was the only all Muslim college of the University in Lahore and Indian Political Intelligence and the Indian Intelligence Bureau may have realised the College could play a significant role in combating the Muslim perception of discrimination by Hindus in British Imperial India. They could have realised that it was through higher education that they could influence the minds of the sons of Muslim community leaders in the Punjab state.

Yusuf Ali had all the hallmarks of being connected with Indian Intelligence Bureau interests. He worked as a propagandist during the Great War in support of Great Britain in recruiting Urdu speaking soldiers, and consistently represented the interests of the British Empire in higher education and at international conferences. He had been twice married to English women, but the unions did not last and he became estranged from his children. He died in some conditions of deprivation in London in 1953. His contribution and allegiance to Britain was marked by a detailed obituary in *The Times* on December 15th 1953. If Alexander Wilson had been employed and placed in Islamia College for intelligence purposes, Abdullah Yusuf Ali could have been a key figure in recruiting and 'running him'.

In fact, Wilson clearly portrayed the real Abdullah Yusuf Ali in his sympathetically drawn character 'Mahommed Abdullah', in *The Devil's Cocktail* and many of Wilson's descriptions of the fictional Sheranwala College exactly match the characteristics of Islamia College set out in the *Punjab University Enquiry Committee, 1932-33 Report*. Wilson derived the fictional college's name from 'Sheranwala Gate' the location in Lahore of Islamia High School.

Wilson's fictional Abdullah is the mirror of the real Yusuf Ali: '...the new Principal of Sheranwala College was a man of very deep learning. He had taken his Master of Arts degree at Cambridge, was a barrister, a retired financial commissioner, and an eminent economist. At the end of the interview Shannon had acquired a deep respect for the quiet-mannered little man, who had proved himself so adept in questioning him.'

The fictional Abdullah informs Captain Hugh Shannon of the British Secret Service: 'Sheranwala College, which is a Muslim institution affiliated to the University of Northern India, has not been upholding Mahommedan traditions. The governing body has, therefore invited me to return to India, and take over the Principalship in the hope that I may be able to raise the College to the position it once held. For some time I hesitated, as I had fully made up my mind to settle down in this country for good. However I was eventually persuaded to accept. I have been empowered to engage a first-class Englishman as Professor of English, and thus my advertisement. I may tell you that I desire the man I select to act as vice-principal and in fact to be my right hand man and general aide-de-camp. The salary is not large, of course, and I fear that most Englishmen would find it difficult to live on five hundred rupees a month.'

Wilson's novel depicts the central character Captain Hugh Shannon as applying for the job as part of a British Secret Service operation. Is it possible that Wilson set out the plot in order to deflect and ridicule any suspicion that his role had anything to do with intelligence objectives? He even managed to incite *The New York Times* in its review of the novel to question the very idea of a British agent travelling to Lahore with his batman to take on the job of English Literature Professor in an undercover operation.

As soon as Alexander Wilson appears in Islamia College records in addition to being called Professor, he is also called Major- presumably on account of the fact he is responsible for commanding half a company of University student cadets for the British Indian Army Reserve. He also appears to have been conferred a knighthood. He is consistently represented as Prof. Major Sir Alexander Wilson, Bart. B.A. (Oxon), D.S.O., M.C., Legion of Honours.' He was certainly not the holder of a baronetcy, a hereditary title awarded by the British Crown. He had not been knighted. He did not have a degree from Oxford. He had never been awarded the Distinguished Service Order, Military Cross, or the French Legion of Honour. A researcher into the history of Islamia College in 2009 decided that Wilson was the closest match to an Alfred Alexander Ball Wilson who gained a pass degree at Oxford University in 1898. This was certainly not Alexander Wilson as he would have been only 6 years old on his graduation.

If the rather far-fetched idea of intelligence cover being the reason for the multiple adornment of qualifications and titles is not true, there is the other possibility that Wilson forged his Oxford University BA and MA, and other gongs. And Abdullah Yusuf Ali was so enraptured by the charm and confidence of his protégé that he never thought to seek official corroboration of his Oxford qualification and other adornments.

If *The Devil's Cocktail* is the voice of the author, Alexander Wilson laboured against academic corruption, intimidation and bribery from students, over-work and very poor standards of teaching and inadequate facilities. There was so much lecturing in any working day, Wilson's voice was literally worn out. However, he committed over five years of his working life to Islamia College, most of them in the top position as Principal. And he successfully raised standards in all areas.

By 1929 Wilson reported a fine year of sporting success with the College being first in the University in cricket and second in soccer out of a federation of 53 colleges. An Islamia College athlete held the half-mile Punjab run record, and another broke the all India record for the longest javelin throw. Five of the College's cricketers were in the Punjab University team. Wilson's commitment to education extended to sponsoring his own student prize: 'The Alexander Wilson-Gulam Husain Medal in Economics.'

While at the College Wilson edited and contributed to at least three educational textbooks: *Selected English Prose Stories For Indian Students* (1926), *Four Periods of Essays* (1928), and *Selected English Essays: From Steele to Benson* (1930). All three texts contain writing, analysis and annotation of a talented academic who you would have expected to have obtained a substantial degree qualification from an English University. *Selected English Prose Students For Indian Students* was co-edited and jointly written with Mohammad Din, the Head Master of Islamia High School, Lahore and the published stories selected were described as depicting: 'the lives of young people, and give examples of perseverance, endurance and courage, and point out a courage which is good for all.' These successful books were a source of great inspiration and Alexander Wilson was highly respected throughout the Punjab.

His resignation in April 1931 was due to world-wide economic recession and the fact that many of the colleges in Lahore could no longer afford the relatively high salaries they had to pay European academics. Wilson kept some papers, in which the University of the Punjab placed on record 'its great appreciation of the services rendered by Major Alexander Wilson in the cause of Higher Education in this Province. The name of Major Wilson will remain always as a memorial of efficiency and high and successful endeavour.'

In October 1931 the University awarded him an Honorary Fellowship for life. He kept a reference in which the University's Vice-Chancellor wrote that he was: 'A brilliant scholar, he did a tremendous amount of good in raising the standard of the university, particularly with regard to the classics.' It was a very great pity, said Vice-Chancellor Woolnar, that 'the financial collapse of Islamia College has caused him to sever his connection with the University.' Woolnar said Wilson's, 'seven years' splendid work in the Punjab in general and Lahore in particular will always be remembered with real gratitude.' There was a reference to Islamia College being 'probably the most backward and badly administered institution of the University' before Wilson took over. Had Wilson forged this reference? Was he writing his own script again? The document is not signed by Woolnar. The criticism and condemnation of Wilson's predecessor, the greatly revered Yusuf Ali does not ring true, and by October 1931 Wilson had been in the Punjab for just less than six years, not seven.

Mrs Dorothy or Lady Wilson

By 1929 the actress Dorothy Wick appears in the official Islamia College photograph of the university's staff as Mrs Wilson, or perhaps she was addressed as 'Lady Wilson' on account of her husband's apparent knighthood. *Selected English Essays* (1930) credits the editor as 'Sir Alexander Wilson, M.A. (Oxon).' Dorothy begins to appear in English-speaking newspapers published in Lahore as Mrs Wilson from 1928. She is reported as organising revues for charities and supporting her husband's reading of his plays.

They lived at 11 Masson Road, and a photograph album left by Dorothy to Mike Shannon after her death in 1965 presents images of their apparently happy and exciting life in North West India. They are seen in and around motor vehicles, socialising with Europeans on a bungalow veranda, and in at least two photographs, appear garlanded; perhaps for a wedding ceremony.

But no official record or certificate of their marriage exists. Wilson's great grandson Christopher McGill, visited Lahore in 2015 seeking to unravel some of the mysteries surrounding the spy writer's time there between 1925 and 1933. He tried to find out if he could trace any official document proving that Alexander Wilson had ever married Dorothy Wick.

Christopher was greatly assisted in his research by the Bishop of Lahore. The Bishop sent out a team of researchers in search of any information that could be found. Looking firstly in the Anglican Church they were unable to find anything. They were adamant that if a Catholic such as Alexander Wilson were to marry it would most definitely have taken place in the Catholic Church, as no records of Catholics marrying have ever been found in the Anglican Church.

Catholic researchers went through all the records held in Lahore, and unfortunately once again were unable to find anything. This led the Bishop to believe that the marriage must have purely been a staged event. They had the records of every other British national who had married whilst in Lahore and had checked every one.

Christopher discovered that nine years previously the bungalow at 11 Masson Road where Alexander and Dorothy lived had been pulled down. Three impressive modern houses had been built on the site. He discovered that: 'this was an area where many Britons (or 'Britishers' as the locals say) used to live. It is still a desirable area, with many of the residents owning cars.'

He also visited Islamia College which he found to be 'in an ultra-conservative and rather deprived area of the city.' The campus was quite some distance away from where Alexander and Dorothy lived. Although back then the population was smaller, Wilson's daily commute would most likely have been up to an hour. Christopher was delighted to see the name of his great grandfather written on the board of Principals. Portraits of present and past principals hang on the walls of the College's main lecture room.

He was taken to the English department whose location had not changed since Alexander's time. The whole university, despite the extreme heat outside, was very cool and Christopher observed that it 'must have been a lovely working environment due to the building's traditional architecture.' Looking out from one of the windows he could see the university's playing field and 'could imagine Alexander judging Islamia College sports day.' The field has also been used for many political rallies over the years and the College is associated closely with the political development of Pakistan as an independent state.

Alexander and Dorothy

Alexander Wilson clearly adored Lahore and was deeply committed to the Muslim community of scholars and students he served. Muslims were a minority in a cosmopolitan and volatile mixture of religions and races in the city that was often referred to as the Paris of Northern India. It was the centre of a thriving newspaper and publishing industry and the University of Punjab played a key educational role in a province bordering the North West Frontier and Afghanistan. It was the city of Rudyard Kipling's 'Kim'– where the famous writer had cut his teeth and honed his pen working as a journalist on the *Civil and Military Gazette*.

This was the North West Frontier region of the Great Game of intelligence between Russia, its 20th century post-revolutionary incarnation as the Soviet Union, and the British Empire. Life had to have been intense, dramatic, and exciting on so many levels. While Gandhi's Congress movement was agitating for Home Rule, more radical 'extremists' were using terrorism to achieve independence. The Deputy Police Commissioner of Lahore John Saunders was gunned down when dismounting from his red motorcycle in 1927 only a stone's throw from Alexander Wilson's College. Alexander and Dorothy may have been present during a bloody assassination attempt on the Governor of the Punjab during a university degree presentation ceremony in 1930. Terrorist conspiracy trials took place in Lahore and executions of political activists in 1931 generated unrest and a security crisis throughout the Punjab.

The British India photograph album shows two attractive young adults in love and having the time of their lives. Dorothy told her son Mike Shannon that on one occasion they were up in the hills touring in a car in the North West Frontier. She was warned that although it was a beautiful and stunning view, and so high up you could see for miles around great care and caution was required. If you got out of the car and strayed off the road into the fields, it was a matter of life and death.

Fierce tribal gunmen not only resented strangers, but bitterly resented white Europeans. Mike related: 'They drove on and on and up and up and eventually she wanted to get out and get a breath of fresh air, look round at the mountains and the wonderful scenery and without thinking she did stray into the fields and the next thing, there was a loud ping next to her ear.' This was the ricochet of a bullet, and out of nowhere appeared a very tall, bearded man, cartridge cases slung over his shoulders, holding a rifle that looked like a blunderbuss because it seemed to be a very ancient looking gun. Alexander calmly coaxed her back to the car shielding her with his body. The tribesman had given his warning. One more time off the road and they would have been shot dead.

Dorothy also used to credit her husband Alexander for saving her life one late night when a deadly krait snake had entered their bedroom. With the electric fan on to try and cool the hot air, beds draped in mosquito nets, this sinister and very lethal snake disguised itself as the fringe of an Indian carpet. Just before she put the light out she thought 'that's funny.' She had another look. She just saw the fringe move. Very frightened she turned to Alexander and whispered 'I think there's a krait at the foot of our bed.' He said: 'Stay there. Don't move,' and he got out on his side.

Using one of those large cabin trunks that people always used to have for long sea journeys, he managed to manoeuvre the trunk so that it was between the snake, the rug and the wall, and he made a mad rush and squashed it flat against the wall. Mike proudly recalled his mother's story: 'But those things apparently move very quickly, like lightning and you had to be quick to get it. If she hadn't seen it and she had put her foot out, she could have been killed. It was a story of admiration for my father because he had saved her life. And I think they must have been very much in love and happy in India.'

Always the Raj

Many of Alexander Wilson's novels were set in Imperial India and Mike was able to recall the legends and resonance of his parents having been part of the British Raj. He remembered his mother speaking Urdu on a rather embarrassing occasion after the war. They had come back to London and she insisted they went to a rather magnificent Indian restaurant near Regent's Street, a very splendid and palatial place with all the gentlemen waiters serving in the full regalia of long white coats.

This is likely to have been the famous restaurant Veeraswamy that had been founded in 1926. Mike was about twelve or thirteen at the time. His mother summoned one of the waiters in what he presumed to be Urdu, but she spoke in a very commanding tone as though she were a memsahib all over again. Mike said: 'I just wanted to die, wanted to vanish through the floor. I could feel myself getting absolutely scarlet. You know whispering, "be quiet mother, be quiet!" But they were sweethearts. They bowed and they salaamed, they called her "memsahib" and she got away with it. I am sure it made her very happy. I even remember her clapping her hands for service.'

The photograph album shows Alexander and Dorothy having a lovely time in the hills in the North West region of British India, at Murree, Peshawar and Simla. They seemed to be having a lot of fun. They also led a very privileged life. They had servants. Dorothy was in show business. She was what was called a soubrette in those days. She did concert parties and pantomime. Mike recalled her telling him horror stories when she knew that he had wanted to go into the drama business. She used to say: 'You don't want that. There's no security. You can be out of work all the time.' So he said to her one time 'How long were you in the business mum?' She replied 'Eleven years.' He also asked her how often she had been out of work and she replied 'Two weeks.'

Mike admired her record of only a fortnight out of work in eleven years. She had done variety for most of her career before going to India. She was a very good singer and could play the piano for concert parties. Her booking in British India had initially been with a concert party tour but she was asked to fill in for Sybil Thorndike who at the last minute had pulled out of a tour of *grand guignol* theatre. She would have been performing in a blood and thunder, kind of Sweeney Todd and slaughter old-fashioned melodrama.

A marriage with hidden fears and tensions

Mike was always aware as a child that all was not well with their relationship as he grew up with them in London during the 1930s. He said: 'I think as a child one is very perceptive and perhaps more emotionally sensitive, I suspected they had an uneasy truce for my sake. *Pas devant les enfants*.' There was one occasion when all these tensions erupted in an explosion of violence that he was never able to forget. The volcano that had been simmering blew up before his very eyes.

He said: 'It was a pretty nasty thing for a young lad to see. I can't have been very old then; about five I suppose. It was very violent.' To his eternal shame he seemed to remember he took his father's side and the guilt stayed with him for the rest of his life: 'The only son hooked on the father figure. He struck my mother and hurt her very badly. These things you never forget. He broke a couple of teeth. Blood pouring out of her mouth, poor old love.'

Mike remembered that physically his father was a strong man. He was about five foot eight, but very solidly built: 'I think he forgot how strong he was on that occasion. She was physically only a little woman, but she was very tough mentally.' His father told him afterwards that he bitterly regretted what had happened and chastised him for taking sides. This account of Alexander Wilson being responsible for such a dreadful and inexcusable manifestation of domestic violence is something none of his children by his other marriages can understand or relate to. Those who knew him and lived with him had no recollection at all of any incident where he had raised his hand to anyone.

Life in Little Venice

Mike recalled living in London's Little Venice area in the 1930s. In those days barges were horse-drawn in different motifs and beautiful colours: 'When we set off, we walked along the canal bank, along the Regent's canal, and then we must have turned off at Warwick Avenue and then found ourselves near Lords cricket ground. There used to be this wonderful large pub painted red as I said in my poem. I sat outside on a bench and he brought me some ginger beer. He sat there with a pint in a pewter tankard and his pipe. These were the most magical days.'

Mike's father had plotted and based the 1938 novel *Wallace At Bay* in the area of his childhood. While they lived at 53 Blomfield Road, Alexander Wilson conjured and plotted a vicious thriller of international terrorism and assassination. His characters hopped on and off the Number 6 double decker red bus and travelled on the brown coded Bakerloo underground line between Waterloo and Warwick Avenue. Mike's childhood home was literally around the corner from the terrorists' safe house in Shirland Road staked out by his father's fictional secret service agents commanded by 'C' Sir Leonard Wallace. The real 'C' of SIS in these years was Admiral Sir Hugh 'Quex' Sinclair and his service was based at Broadway Buildings opposite St James's underground station. The Security Service, MI5, with its first Director-General, Sir Vernon Kell, still in charge, operated out of a building opposite the Victoria & Albert Museum in the Cromwell Road.

Mike Shannon had no idea at the time that his father was an author: 'He used to start a story at the beginning of the walk and complete it when we got to the pub. It had a real beginning, middle and end. He was a complete and spontaneous storyteller, off the top of his head. Sometimes he asked me to give him a theme. But usually he would just look at something and say "oh did I ever tell you the story about..."'

Mike was an enchanted little boy. His father had taken him into a magical world. His imagination was enriched with the most beautiful fairy stories. Mike reflected: 'He could have been the most wonderful writer of fairy tales. With his gift he could have written some wonderful radio scripts and given the most wonderful radio talks because he had a great voice. I do remember that.'

The richness of Mike's memory recreated his father's presence in sound and colour. He came from an age when electronic media was recording sound, filming publicly and privately in black and white, and in colour. He remembered his father's voice as being a light-baritone: 'A little touch of Scots or Irish. I couldn't decide which it was. There was certainly a suggestion of an accent there, but hardly any. He spoke beautifully as you were expected to do in those days. Very clear, well-educated English.'

Mike could recall his father's 'twinkly' sense of humour: 'He'd test you. He would look at you for quite a long time and he would say something and you were not sure if he meant it. Was he in earnest, was he having a go? He taught me quite a lot about reading the human face. He had a very nice sense of humour. Soft irony. Not cruel; not at all cruel.'

But there was also humanity, an intrinsic quality that Mike could remember with warmth and affection: 'I can never remember him being angry with me. He was very, very generous with toys. I always remember my first real Easter gift was this huge bunny holding a very large basket of Easter eggs. Another great favourite was a Mickey Mouse that used to stand up.'

Alexander Wilson bought his son Michael a beautiful model yacht and they went sailing with it on the Round Pond on Sundays in Kensington Gardens. He loved that area of London: Kensington Gardens; Hyde Park, and the Serpentine. They would pay homage to the statue of Peter Pan. Wilson also bought his young son a lovely Hornby railway set, all the stations and railway track, including signal boxes. Mike remembered how wonderfully generous he was: 'He was very kind and very sweet. As we say in Yorkshire "Now't but the best for my son."'

When living together as a family in London during the 1930s they did not have an affluent lifestyle. It was not Upstairs of the Downstairs and it was not exactly Downstairs; not what you would call a hand to mouth existence. Dorothy and Alexander were able to afford to hire a nanny for their son, although they may have been on the cut-price line of quality and care. Mike used to call one of them to her face 'Potty Nanny.' That's because as a little boy that was what he thought she was. He recalled: 'I think we were somewhere down the river and there was a bit of a slope. I was strapped in my pram and she just let go. I thought it was great fun whizzing down this hill with no adults. And we ended up on the Embankment. Apparently, it was a *rendezvous* with her boyfriend. And they started to canoodle and when my mother turned up, I was hanging upside down by the pram held in by the reins. My mother was not best pleased. I remember a terrible din above my head.'

They rented the top floor of a three-story house in Blomfield Road at the top of a dangerous steep staircase. One morning when it was early closing day at the shops and his mother was in a bit of a hurry and he was slow keeping up, he missed his footing on the top step and went rolling head over heels all the way down three flights to the bottom, bang, bang, bang, bang until he got to the bottom. Mike remembered his mother and friend screaming all the way behind him: 'There was a lump the size of an egg on my head. "Are you alright love?" mother kept asking. Fuss, fuss, fuss. I remember I was simply rather angry.'

Alexander Wilson, with several million other Londoners, was determined to do what he could to defend London after the German invasion of Poland in September 1939. Mike remembered in the early part of the war his father coming home in a policeman's uniform with a conical hat. He had signed up as an emergency constable, and he would fill his hat with shrapnel for his son's growing collection of 'war debris.' Mike remembered that he used to wear white over-gloves when he did traffic duty. He was out one night in a blackout when there was very thick fog and a bus nearly ran him down. His father had explained it was not the driver's fault. He just could not see a thing and they had to keep their lights so dim: 'So you had the combination of a black-out with virtually covered headlamps and pea-souper fog, which was very, very dangerous.'

Mike remembers that the decision taken to move to Yorkshire was largely to keep him safe from the London blitz of late 1940 and early 1941. There had been plans for him to be shipped out to his cousins in St Catherine's, Ontario whose name was Shannon. They had emigrated some years before. He had been booked on a liner, but the ship that went before his was the *City of Benares*, which was torpedoed. Transatlantic trips with British children stopped immediately. Hendon was hardly a suburban refuge from the blitz as they were living quite near Hendon aerodrome. The bombing was often day and night. His mother would go out shopping between raids. They lived in a crescent and every morning they would come out into the smoke, the dust and the smell of bombed houses. The crescent shrunk bit by bit with fewer houses standing. Mike remembered that people with no house to speak of would still be there brushing their steps and the milkman wearing his tin helmet would continue delivering the milk saying 'Morning Missus. Bit of a rough night wasn't it?'

The false legend of El Alamein

Mike recalled how the legend sprang up, he thought from his mother, that his father had died in the desert around the time of El Alamein: 'Funnily enough I think the battle broke out on the day of my birthday, October 23rd 1942. That's what I was led to believe, that's what I did believe, and that's what I wanted to believe. My father was a war hero.' It was the adults around Mike in those years that had told him his father had died a gallant death in battle: 'It came from my uncle Reg who got on rather well with my father. Being rather an old fashioned family the ladies didn't feel that it was up to them, but the man of the family, as Reg had then become. After my grandfather it was left to him. On one of my visits to Hull to see the grandparents, Reg took me to one side and said: 'Well, I don't know how you are going to take this Michael, but your father died.' He told me where and everything and of course at that age you are sad, but at the same time you are very proud, very proud indeed. My father was a hero. I didn't question it. Not until many, many years later.'

He pointed out the jaunty portrait of his Uncle Reg from the surviving photograph album, a happy go lucky man with a cheeky grin and captured riding a donkey in plus fours on a holiday beach. He and Mike's father had the look of kindred spirits and it was not difficult to imagine them slipping out of a stiff and suffocating family gathering to play truant with a pint of beer and pipe tobacco in the local hostelry.

Dorothy came from a close-knit family based in what is now the university district of Hull. When the national register was taken in September 1939, Mike was staying in the home of his grandparents Matthew and Edith at 40 Warwick Avenue, in the district of Sculcoates. Grandfather Wick, a retired senior clerk, was 76 years old, and his grandmother 67. Dorothy's brother Reginald had emigrated to Canada at the age of 17 in 1914, and had been working as a fruit farmer in Newfoundland when he joined up to serve in the Canadian Expeditionary Force in France during the Great War. He had been a private in the Canadian Light Horse which had been in action in most of the great battles from the Somme in 1916 to the defeat of the German armies in 1918.

Dorothy's youngest sister Gwendoline had served in the RAF between 1918 and 1920. She along with Dorothy's other sister Marjorie were both married, and it is possible to see how the Wick family pulled together to protect Dorothy and her young son from the ignominy and fall-out of Alexander's great betrayal. They had to have worked together to create a great deception to conceal what they all no doubt thought was the greater deception that Alexander had perpetrated on Mike's mother. He had been oblivious to the plot and it would not unravel and become known to him until he was in his 73rd year in 2006, by which time the protagonists and authors of this sophisticated web of deceit were long dead and beyond reproach.

Mike recalled the moment when he realised that his father had not died the hero's death he had been led to believe: 'I received the cutting. I spotted the address in NW11. I was pretty shaken, if not stirred.' The small extract from the front page of *Times* for 1st January 1944 read: 'From the London Gazette, Friday Dec. 31. The Bankruptcy Acts 1914 and 1926. Receiving Orders. Wilson, Alexander, 54 Denman Drive, London, N.W.11., an officer in his Majesty's Army.'

He was astonished. The address in Denman Drive NW11 is where they were living before he and his mother left for Wensleydale. It is difficult to imagine the shock that the information on that small slip of paper must have been for Mike Shannon. All through his life he had believed his father died serving his country heroically at El Alamein in the fall of 1942. The implications were tragic. Mike as a 9-year-old boy had been totally deceived into grieving for the loss of his father. He realised that the deception had to have involved his mother and uncle and perhaps other relatives. What would make these adults force a child to falsely grieve in this way? Why all the lies?

In Dorothy's will that she had signed and dated 5th March 1951 she declared: 'I have made no provision in this my Will for my Husband Alexander Jocelyn Wilson for reasons set out in a Declaration of even date herewith.' This declaration did not survive the shredding of solicitors' and legal archives. But the short sentence in the will disclosed a combination of new mystery about his father's name, and the confirmation that it was likely that when she had it drawn up and witnessed in 1951 she knew that her husband was still alive and had not died in 1942.

Mike Shannon could not make sense of the introduction of the middle name 'Jocelyn' to his father's identity. Was this an attempt to throw her son's future enquiry off the trail? His mother's Will was further documentary proof that she had been part of the conspiracy. What had been so serious and catastrophic to motivate a group of adults to lie and deceive a 9-year-old child with the fake revelation that his father had died? The Will raised further issues. As she was described as a widow by the time of her death in 1965, how had she found out about his death in 1963? Who had informed her? These implications were devastating for Mike. It must have hurt him deeply to realise that his father could have been alive as he developed his successful acting career, married and had children himself.

Why had he not tried to contact Mike after he had turned 18, or 21? It was a matter of enormous regret to Mike that he had been deprived of the choice and right to contact his father while he was still alive. Perhaps courage should not be measured merely as the red mist of gallantry when charging the barricades, but also as the bravery of an individual coming to terms with truth on their own at 3 a.m. in the morning or 3 p.m. on a Sunday afternoon. Mike's priority was to find answers so he could explain these deepening mysteries to his adult children of whom he was most proud and always praising.

Mike reflected: 'Really that was my first inkling that the stories I had formerly been told were not necessarily true. Clearly he led several different lives on different levels at any one time.' He was happy to appreciate the positive outcomes of his investigation into his family history. It had been a sense of amazement for him to find that the one novel he had found would lead to a writing portfolio of more than twenty books.

He remembered that when his mother died in 1965 and he had to travel up to Bridlington to clear things up he was hoping and hoping that he would come across something in her papers that would reveal more about his father. A letter, photographs; anything at all. But here was nothing apart from the novel *Wallace Intervenes.* That was the first time he knew his father had actually been a real writer. Not just an enthralling teller of fairy tales to a little boy.

Mike had been astonished to discover that his father had at least 24 books published under different names. He had no idea that he had such an output. He was also overwhelmed by the knowledge that all these novels had been published during the 12 years he and his mother were together, even though he now discovered that there had been a secret parallel first family he had been returning to while in India and visiting in Southampton when they moved to London.

Mike remembered the clattering of a typewriter at home, but he was not aware that he was writing several novels a year, which was his output in the thirties: 'I seem to remember him showing me once and saying "That's a typewriter". "Can I try it?" I asked. "No", was the reply.'

Mike appreciated he was a popular novelist and clearly enjoyed quite a vogue in the twenties, thirties and early forties: 'Now I have been able to read some of them, even though I say this about my own dad, well done! They were what we used to call "ripping yarns". Boy's own stuff, but beautifully written and you do get involved in the characters. You care about them. He develops some wonderful characters in the Secret Service. It's also very obvious that he travelled very, very widely indeed. He has immense knowledge of so many different countries; probably different languages as well.'

His mother's apparent hatred for Alexander Wilson

Mike did not find it very easy bringing up the subject of his father with his mother: 'There was one rather horrible occasion. I was quite rightly very persistent in wanting to know more about him. And she suddenly lost it. She said "Don't you ever, ever mention that man's name in my hearing again." I was about thirteen or fourteen. I didn't persist all of the time. But I was worried. I wanted to know more. How did he die? Who were his friends? He was an unknown. He was a stranger to me. My memories of him by then were very fragmented.'

Mike had a clear memory of a number of exciting outings with his father. He was once taken to the Queen Mary in Southampton to have tea with the Captain. He also remembered going with his parents on H.M.S Rodney to watch

60

the parade of the Fleet at Spithead when all of the Royal Navy's battleships, cruisers, destroyers and aircraft carriers would switch on all their lights- an occasion made famous in 1937 after a freelance BBC announcer, Commander Tommy Woodroffe, had imbibed himself with an excess of alcoholic refreshment and stumbled and slurred his way through a broadcast punctuated with the shouts 'The Fleet is all lit up! Like thousands of fairy lights. And now it's gone!'

Mike treasured other memories. They went to Regent's Park Zoo: 'I remember I had a big bag of buns, we were sitting on this bench, there were some elephants coming past and the next thing I knew there was this large trunk that took most of my buns in one go. I was livid. That was a treat.'

He was taken to the coronation of King George VI and saw that on his father's shoulders. He was able to see the procession and the new King and his Queen in 1937. He remembered going with him to one of his father's rather exclusive clubs: 'I seem to remember a rather smoky atmosphere of pipe tobacco and cigar tobacco and a lot of elderly burbling going on. You'd hear an old boy saying "And when we were in the trenches in the Somme..." that kind of background murmur going on. I must have been a bit young to be in a club like that. I am amazed they admitted him with me. I seem to remember it was called the Authors' Club.'

His father was a devotee of cricket and an enthusiastic member of the MCC which meant he spent a lot of time watching cricket matches at Lords: 'I felt his love and enjoyed his company. Unfortunately for my mother, she didn't give the same wonderful feeling of belonging; of being somebody who mattered. A man.'

Mike felt that his father never treated him as a child whereas his mother Dorothy did for most of her life; even after he got married and had children of his own: 'She was still treating me like her kid. One mother and one only son and no siblings; no father; can often go horribly wrong that. She had expectations of me, which were wildly off kilter and nothing to do with what I wanted. She wanted me in a nice, safe, secure, routine, deadly dull job for the rest of my life. She was shocked when she realised that there was something else I wanted.'

On the other hand, Mike had the greatest admiration for his mother's tenacious and hardworking spirit. Throughout her life she made her own living and had considerable talent and professional discipline to be employed for more than eleven years in showbusiness: 'My mother did do some broadcasting in India. She was involved in the opening of a radio station in Calcutta. During the First World War she was working in the Hull telephone exchange where she met her lifelong friend Dorothy Jubb who ended up living with my mother in Bridlington. She was the lady I went to after my mother died and said: "Dolly can you tell me anything more about my father?" He was a mystery to her as well.'

Mike realised that his mother had done a very good job indeed of liquidating his father's existence from her life and, indeed his. There were no letters from him at all in her flat after her death; only this one novel. And he often wondered whether she had overlooked that. Perhaps she had intended to put that with the rubbish just before being taken seriously ill and moved into the Cottage hospital. Mike had had only two weeks to sort out all his mother's affairs after her death in Bridlington. In the process of organising the funeral arrangements, closing up her rented flat, he could find no traces or clues about his mother's marriage, relationship and life with his father.

The search for truth

Mike had a highly respected career in professional acting with long periods of performing the greatest classical plays with the Royal Shakespeare Company, going on world tours and long periods of repertory performance in a wide canon of popular and modern plays. He played the role of Samuel Pepys in an award-winning radio dramatization broadcast on UK independent radio and produced in spoken word for an exclusive cassette series 'The Drama Collection' promoted by WH Smiths. His radio acting was heard throughout the USA on NPR radio stations in classical dramatizations of Sherlock Holmes, The Spanish Armada, Mary Queen of Scots, and Jane Austen's *Pride and Prejudice*.

He had two children both of whom have had award-winning and successful careers in professional drama as directors, and producers. It was in 2005 when he was 72 years old and was still working professionally as an actor and performance poet that he wanted to find out more about this father. He enlisted the help of a former colleague in radio drama who was now working as a research academic at the University of London. First he discovered the extent of his father's writing success and career. Then he discovered the bankruptcy notice and appalling deception over his father's death.

It gave him a great feeling of sadness to think when he was growing up he could have found his father and they could have met. The shock and emotional reverberations of these feelings led to very intense and vivid dreams: 'I've gone to some little pub or café or something. And there's somebody at the door who says "I think there's somebody you'd like to meet sitting in that booth over there." It's happened more than once as well. And I go over and there he is more or less as I remember him, shiny bald head with his pipe. And I get as far as going over and saying: "Excuse me, Dad?" Then I wake up; which is very frustrating. And he looks just the same of course.'

He was also forced to think about his mother's motives. He decided it was too long ago and too pointless to continue blaming his mother. He realised she had her own motives for this. Maybe she was doing it out of a misguided sense of trying to protect him. He realised she must have been driven by some horrendous sense of betrayal or loss of trust in his father. If he had created a charade of marriage in Lahore that turned out to be a cruel deception, he understood his mother's rage and lack of forgiveness. She was strait-laced, respectable, and decent. She was committed to the idea of fidelity and monogamy. Any discovery of his father's first parallel family and later affair and marriage with Alison would have appalled her and destroyed her sense of dignity and reputation. It would have been more than the point of no-return and he realised that she would have done absolutely anything to have protected him from the shame and humiliation of such scandal and discovery.

He recalled that she: 'set too much store by me I'm afraid. I was her blue-eyed boy. I could do no wrong; except when it came to girlfriends. "You're not good enough for my son." And she meant everybody and that included the lady I eventually married. It had to be done and dusted before my mother realised what was happening. But she did turn up for the wedding in Kensington; a very bleak November day. I remember it well. Mum was never really well off all those years we were together. She worked very hard all her life, bless her. She ended up as a civilian clerk with the East Riding Constabulary in Bridlington, South Yorkshire. Before that she had been a secretary to a doctor. She never let up. For a little woman she was very strong.'

Mike inevitably regretted the break-up of his parent's marriage because of the consequences that had in the mother and son relationship in the context of a one parent family: 'Part of the problem between my mother and myself was that she knew I adored my father and she knew that she could never have that kind of love of the same degree. I was very fond of my mother. I didn't always like her. We had fearful rows especially when I wanted to come into the business and the early days when I used to come home with girlfriends and she would slam the door in their faces so we had to end up in the local bus shelter or the local cinema, which did not please me.'

Dorothy was hugely protective of her son and the subsequent discovery of what she went through with her husband Alexander began to explain the difficulties Mike experienced in the mother and son relationship: 'When I got married, oh dear! Nobody was good enough for me. I think for a long time she was my chief antagonist. Being the single parent I think she found me too much of a sense of responsibility when I should have been taking on my own sense of responsibility. I was held back too long actually. When the wrench came it was worse than it need have been. I suppose when there is an only daughter, only son situation you are not sharing with another sibling. It's rather isolating. You are either not very much liked by your only parent or over-adored by them.

Either is equally bad in my opinion. And can be destructive.'

Mike fully understood that Dorothy hated his father Alexander Wilson. That hatred was entirely driven by her love for her son. She was determined to protect him from the truth about his father's duplicity and bigamy. He now understood that the more love, affection and respect he expressed for the memory of his father, the more desperate and threatened his mother became by the very thought of talking about him or saying anything that invited further curiosity, discussion and investigation.

From orphan to extended family

In 2007, the search for the truth about Alexander Wilson gave him a gift he never thought possible. He was introduced to Dennis and Daphne in Southampton- a half-brother and half-sister he never imagined he would discover later on in life. They immediately bonded. He discovered that Dennis was a practising poet and they soon exchanged letters in Sonnet form, as well as experiencing the joy of having their first collections of poetry published in 2008. He was delighted to discover that Daphne had been a dancer and actor and had run a successful theatrical costume and dancing shoe supply business. They had even performed at the same theatre in Exeter in the late 1940s. He then had the joy of meeting Gordon and Nigel, the sons from his father's third marriage with Alison and finally Douglas, the son from his father's fourth marriage with Elizabeth. They all discovered kindred spirits and were settled and exhilarated by finding themselves part of a wider family with so many common interests.

Mike was fascinated that his half-brother Gordon had had a longstanding and distinguished career in the Royal Navy and had become an expert in naval defence intelligence. He had had no idea his father had been in the navy when a young man. This all connected with his own strong calling to the sea: 'Before I had an ambition to go into the theatre, I remember for many, many years all I ever wanted to do was go to sea and join the Royal Navy. I loved it when we were evacuated to Bridlington. I learnt to swim and to sail there. It was magic. I still love the sea. I don't know why. Sadly, my eyes weren't good enough.'

Douglas introduced all the Alexander Wilson siblings to the Wilson clan tartan and when they gathered together, the men wore Wilson clan ties and Daphne a Wilson clan scarf. Extended family gatherings and events developed year by year. The theatrical and acting professional tradition in Alexander Wilson's wider family was enriched by the success of Nigel's daughter Ruth. Her multiple international acting awards for film, television and theatre and highly acclaimed profile has driven the successful commissioning and production of the three part television drama series, *Mrs Wilson*. This she has executively
64

produced and also performed the lead role of her grandmother Alison.

The fellowship and love Mike found for, from and with his brothers and sister helped him take all of the bizarre ambiguities of his father's life well into his stride. The past was not something he had any control over: 'I think the guy was extraordinary. He took more than just the bull by the horns. I still love him funnily enough. It seems rather a strange thing to say. How can you love a phantom, a vague memory? But I do.'

Mike's son Richard and daughter Kate observed that the discovery and welcoming into this wider family had transformed their father and he was more happy than they had ever known him. When he was diagnosed with non-Hodgkin's lymphoma in 2010, his newly found relatives gathered round him on his last birthday October 23rd 2010 at his home in Bromley giving him comfort, company and consolation. He passed away in December that year having discovered so many secrets and unravelled so many mysteries, but most important of all, having connected with the bigger family he never knew he had.

Chapter Four

Alison and sons

Their love blossomed dodging the bombs that fell on London during the Blitz of 1940 and '41. Despite the twenty odd years between them an intense mutual attraction developed in the MI6 bomb shelters during air-raids. He was the respected British Indian Army major whose fluency in Arabic, Persian, and Urdu made him a leading intelligence analyst eavesdropping on embassy and diplomatic legation communications in war-torn London. She was the MI6 secretary typing up and filing his 'special material' reports stamped 'Top Secret' for the eyes only of Prime Minister Winston Churchill, the war cabinet and intelligence chiefs.

So many people tried to warn her against the mysterious though charismatic charm of a man who self-effacingly showed reluctance in wearing his decorations and who claimed a family connection with the Marlborough dynasty. In 1942 after marriage and childbirth their world came crashing down around them. Disgrace and dismissal at the Foreign Office, hand to mouth existence, arrest and imprisonment, humiliating poverty. Why did they become destitute? Why did their first son have to be sent to a children's home and their second considered for adoption? How did they survive and stay together for 22 years? Why was Alison's love so blind? How and why did she learn to forgive when Dorothy had learned to hate?

There is much of Alison Wilson's memoir which could only be described as an excoriating attack on her husband's character. When describing the first weekend she had spent with Alexander Wilson in late January 1941 and in the same rented house in Hendon, previously occupied by Dorothy and Michael, she wrote: 'The devil is exceedingly subtle. It was not with my desire, not yet fanned to its full flame, but with A's [Alison used this initial to describe her husband] need that he trapped me. I have always known, but been reluctant to affirm, even to myself, that this very manifest need was the deciding factor. Thus does the devil wrap the evil deed in the guise of good. Not that weekend, but later, he completed his work.'

Alison is indeed, an impeccable eye-witness source to Alexander Wilson's life-story. She wrote it almost completely from memory. Perhaps it was her Secret Service training or her determination to protect her boys Gordon and Nigel that impelled her to destroy all the source records from the time she first met Alec. This even included ripping out and burning the remaining pages from her 1940 diary. When she was writing her memoir in 1986 she was perhaps not at all sure when she would reveal it to her loved ones. What she feared most was the distress caused had she 'not written this account.' Her husband's pageantry of lies and secrets was a source of hurt, confusion and human chaos. Somehow when she left Milton cemetery in 1963 after her husband's burial, she knew that what had been contained in the grief of that bizarre day might be released like demons and furies to haunt the lives of children and grandchildren who had no idea about their past.

She could tell the truth and leave a chronicle of integrity that could challenge the malignant legacy of her husband. All the particles of his deception could be drawn back like some powerful magnet into the crucible of their marriage and offer clarity and meaning. The writing is a sharply hewn diamond of intense honesty.

It is in its own way significant literature; perhaps better writing than anything her husband had been able to produce in 28 published and unpublished novels, and three academic volumes. She had been told at College that she had a talent for writing. But she would acknowledge with fierce premonition that she could never write fiction: 'To do so, would for me, have been a prostitution of the talent I knew I had been given and sooner or later would have to fulfil.' Alison McKelvie was somebody who could only write the truth: 'I revered truth, and rather than make a statement, the truth of which I am not sure, would rather remain silent.'

Their love had been set during the autumn and winter of 1940 when incendiaries and high explosive bombs rained down in those high intensity days of the London Blitz. She was nineteen when she first met Alec. She was twenty one and pregnant when she married him. In the spirit of some of the biblical tone of her memoir perhaps it could be said the first lie in the devil's grooming of his prey was that he pretended to be only twenty years older than her, when in fact he was 27 years her senior.

The frequent air raids meant that the formal ritual of office separation between the intelligence officer listening to espionage targets on ear-phones and the intelligence secretary typing up transcripts on a typewriter was reversed when the air-raid siren wailed. Working through the night they would eat together in the canteen and sleep together on the floor of the basement of the Foreign Office building when the bombs dropped and the ack-ack guns sent shells and shrapnel into the night sky.

People were working together for longer periods than when they were with their own families. And the necessary distance of polite acquaintance in the workplace collapsed into the intimacy of human friendship. Hand-shakes would linger longer than usual. A near hit from the Luftwaffe becomes a squeeze of reassurance, and later the grip of passion. What Alison described as 'mutual interest' began as enthusiastic conversation. This would eventually cross the boundary of public appearance and private confidence and then well up with all the emotions of a human relationship.

Alec made no secret of the fact that he was married, with a son, aged about ten, and that he was in the process of a divorce, his wife having walked out on him. Alison said she was unmarried and there was no secret admirer in RAF Spitfire uniform. It was Alec who was wearing the uniform of the famous British Indian Army 1/8th Punjabis regiment. Although the much older man he would have looked powerfully handsome and impressive if the famous 1940 war-time portrait of him bearing so many ribbons of military distinction is anything to go on.

The romantic introvert

Alison was a passionate and romantic 19-year-old writing poetry. When she first set eyes on Alec Wilson she had thought and written:

'…a stirring, throbbing anguish.

Known but only half revealed to man

To find expression through this hand of thine.'

She was Wordsworthian in sensibility as well as origin having been brought up in the Lake District. Her childhood bedroom overlooked Scafell Pike the highest mountain in England. Like her character, Scafell is particularly complex and mountain-topped with a roller coaster of rocky summits and 'narrow cols buttressed by a multitude of towering crags and deeply indented gills.'

She dreamed of 'beauty, truth, goodness and, above all, love - but only real love would do - eternal, unbreakable, prepared to suffer all the anguish without which love would not be love.' It was a love blended in with the 'ever changing kaleidoscope' of colour at sunrise and sunset in the Cumbrian landscape of hills and peaks. 'Greens, blues, browns, and mauves' continually nuanced by sun and cloud and light and shade enriched her intensely romantic imagination.

At the same time, she described herself as an introverted young woman. Making conversation would be 'untold and indescribable agony' if she could not think of anything to say, or her thoughts trite and stupid. She was an avid reader of good quality Edwardian novelists such as Hugh Walpole, Brett Young and Ernest Raymond. Heaven for her would be curled up in a chair, lost in the world of poetry and fiction, or to be shut up all alone in the drawing room, stretched out on the settee, listening to Handel's Largo, Tchaikovsky's Fifth Symphony, or the world famous American opera singer tenor of her childhood Richard Crooks singing 'I'll Walk Beside You.'

Alison was a tomboy whose father, a solicitor, was in his fifties, and her mother, in her fortieth year when she was born. The favourite in the family was her older brother, who read medicine at Cambridge University. She had wanted to go to university, but declined her father's invitation to do so in order to reduce the financial strain on his very modest middle class professional income. Instead she went to secretarial college in Piccadilly, London.

Alison was a creature of the Cumbrian hills, the natural beauty of which blended with her devotion to the beauty of words in poetry and literature, and the beauty of classical music. She 'related to animals', all of which she loved, much 'more easily than to humans.' An old black spaniel was the recipient of all her confidences. Horses were 'the most beautiful of God's creatures' and she loved everything about them. Of her parents she had the closest bond to her mother, a passionate and voluble woman who could 'dislike intensely and with vituperation.' Her future son in law Alexander Wilson would become the white-heat object of her outrage in future years. Alison recalled: 'It was she who prepared me for suffering, telling me when I was quite young, that I must learn to accept it, as it is the lot of every woman.'

Secret Service and Major Alexander Wilson

Alison had the perfect background to join SIS as one of the women secretaries employed in Section X to type up translations and transcripts of bugged telephone calls. Her discreet and quiet personality, secure and respectable bourgeois background from Whitehaven, and perhaps some other family Secret Service connections and involvement during the First World War, provided the ideal profile.

She first set eyes on Major Wilson when taken into the eavesdropping unit locked behind doors in some non-descript building in the St James's Square area of Westminster. It was April Fool's day 1940 when she first met Major Wilson, the middle aged man they called 'Buddha' with thinning hair beginning to turn grey. She was drawn to him because he was a writer. He would certainly impress her by giving her lunch and dinner at the Authors' Club in Whitehall Court on the Embankment.

They would return home late at night in the darkened streets, under a deadly and thunderous canopy of German planes releasing their incendiaries and high explosive bombs, and anti-aircraft batteries firing fierce salvoes of shells at bombers you could always hear but rarely see despite the bright light-show of tracking searchlights. Alison and Alec would often have to run for cover from the shrapnel as it bounced round them on the pavements.

Alison fell deeply in love with Alec. She told him she would have been content to step out of the picture had there been any hope of his wife returning. He assured her that there was no such possibility, that she had taken the child and returned to her parents in Yorkshire and that the divorce was grinding through its slow process. He proposed to her saying he wanted to marry her as soon as the divorce was through. She recalled: 'He was patient and never rushed anything. He taught me to love. He taught me the meaning of love by the depth of his demand; he was prepared to wait until I was able to commit myself irrevocably to the self-gift that went far beyond the sexual.'

In *The Sentimental Crook* Wilson's main character Michael Granville is clear that in love it is possible and perhaps inevitable to love several women and Granville states categorically 'I simply could not live without female companionship.' If Granville is a representation of the inner workings of Alexander Wilson's soul, there is an emotional logic to his falling in love and marrying Dorothy in India, and falling in love and marrying Alison in Blitz torn London. With Dorothy and Michael in Wensleydale in late 1940 and early 1941, with Gladys and Adrian, Dennis and Daphne remaining in Southampton when he travelled to India in 1925, a man who cannot live without female companionship is going to find it. Wilson, though, is an exception to the male way of doing things. Not for him a casual and short-lived liaison to satiate the passion. He would suspend reality and engage the full rituals of courtship, engagement and marriage. And it is important to realise that Alison's memoir shows it was he who proposed marriage to her long before any physical intimacy. The delay in marrying Alison when she was nearly 4 months pregnant with Gordon was not the indecision of a desperate two-timer being jemmied into a shotgun marriage. The cause had perhaps everything to do with his tortured conscience over entering a third-time parallel marriage without legal divorce or Vatican annulment.

Alison realised she had a major challenge introducing her boyfriend to her parents: 'Purporting to be twenty years older than me, but in fact twenty-seven, in the process of a divorce and of somewhat obscure background, with no home other than furnished accommodation to offer, he was hardly an ideal suitor, and it was nothing short of a miracle that my father made no difficulties.'

Alexander Wilson travelled to Cumberland with Alison to meet her parents and he performed his cover or second identity to its maximum extent and with the fall-back position when subjected to an attempt at verification by Alison's mother. He was not Alexander Joseph Patrick Wilson, son of a publican's daughter from Dublin and working class medical quarter-master who joined the army as a 15-year-old boy bugler at Aldershot. He was now Alexander Douglas Gordon Chesney Wilson, connected to the famous Marlborough family.

His putative father was killed heroically in Belgium at the beginning of the Great War while a gallant Colonel in the Blues and Royals. Gordon Chesney Wilson served in the Boer war at the same time as his real father Lieutenant Alexander Wilson RAMC. Lady Sarah and her husband had a second son Alan Spencer Wilson, born 1894, who died from a burst appendix in 1905. Wilson's first initial was, therefore, a near match. If challenged by anyone checking *Debretts*, he would explain that he was the illegitimate son of Colonel Gordon Wilson. His mother could have been Captain Gordon's glamorous widow, Lady Sarah Wilson, aunt to Winston Churchill, and the adventurer who during the South African War wrote dispatches for *The Daily Mail*. Lady Sarah was always gallivanting home and abroad and refusing to be the content and passive Victorian breeding horse.

Alison remembered: '...he seemed to be favourably accepted. He was in uniform, which gave him status, by then promoted to Lieutenant-Colonel, and it would be presumed, a reasonable income.' Along with his Chesney Wilson legend he also claimed to own a house, at Ringwood in the New Forest, which had been requisitioned and would therefore be unobtainable as a home until the end of the war. Alison's mother succumbed to her streak of snobbery and consulted her husband's copy of *Debretts* and realised that Alexander Wilson's account of himself did not tally with the facts. But he was not to be phased and had an easy explanation. He would confess to the awkwardness and embarrassment of being the illegitimate son of an illicit love affair with a member of the Marlborough family. All unverifiable and entirely plausible. Alison remembered Alec's 'extraordinary ability to make anyone believe anything.'

Alison believed she probably learned from his colleagues the false information that he had been awarded the DSO (Distinguished Service Order) and DSC (Distinguished Service Cross) in the 1914-18 war, but did not wear the ribbons on his uniform. So she persuaded him to put them up. She was aware their colleagues at SIS thought him someone rather special. He maintained he was a qualified air pilot and during the early part of the war said that he had joined the crews of RAF bombing expeditions. She would be desperate with worry and then relieved when he would return to her; on one occasion with a large, jagged wound across the top of his wrist, which he said had been caused by shrapnel.

Whenever the sirens sounded, she would see him take his tin hat and go out and help the Fire Wardens. He had the appearance of being a war hero. Across his chest she remembered it was covered with severe scarring, 'unmistakably the remnants of old shrapnel wounds from the First War.' He also had a leg injury, which caused a very slight limp, and claimed to have a plate inserted on one temple.

The combination of the uniform, and the Foreign Office employment gave him an aura of respectability which lulled her parents' suspicions. However, her father, a solicitor and registrar of the County Court, was by no means gullible, and, unknown to her at the time, had started making enquiries. But these would be tragically interrupted by his sudden death in January 1941 and never pursued to conclusion.

Alison's detailed and impressive account of Alexander's performance confirms his qualities in dissembling with cover and lies. If Alison's father had hired a private detective to check out his future son-in-law the credibility of the Marlborough connection would have crumbled. Lady Sarah Wilson or any of the siblings of the Duke would have been astonished and outraged by any suggestion they had been his siring parent. His promotion to Lieutenant-Colonel would have been exposed as a fraud. Any 'honorary' appointment would have had to have been sanctioned by somebody at the level of Generals Auchinleck or Wavell as it would have been wholly unorthodox. There is no surviving record anywhere of Wilson's presence in the British Indian Army or any official sanction of honorary Colonel status.

Wilson had no income or authority from any army whether by pension or emergency commission. It can be assumed he would have been paid at the civil service level of temporary clerk in the Foreign Office. The decorations Wilson 'allowed' himself to be persuaded to wear had no foundation in reality. They would, however, have enhanced his intelligence legend. Alison's direct eye-witness account of his spontaneous desire to help the air wardens was further proof of his patriotism. He was always willing to help in the war effort if given the chance and opportunity. And his knee injury was real. It was the major reason given in his War Office document for being invalided during the Great War.

The presence of the mysterious scars on his chest have been fully corroborated by other members of his family and official medical documentation. But there was no clear explanation how he got them. The presence of a plate in his temple can be added to the various other references to illnesses and injuries he told near relatives. They also include a serious blood disorder which he would tell Alison and his Southampton family necessitated weekend stays in private hospitals for blood transfusions.

There is no service record proving that he qualified as a pilot, and there is no corroboration of his crewing a bombing expedition. Only one reference to his flying career survives in War Office documentation and that appeared to have gone no further than crashing his plane in the Royal Naval Air Service. This paper confusingly sets out the R.N.A.S. acronym and also makes a reference to Royal Naval Auxiliary Service; not Royal Naval Air Service. While Ministry of Information, service media personnel, and accredited correspondents would be permitted to go on bombing raids, Richard Dimbleby for the BBC and Ed Murrow for the US CBS Network are two famous examples, it would be most unusual to allow an untrained 48-year-old middle-aged man to fly to Germany in a Lancaster, Manchester, Halifax or Blenheim bomber. Wilson's legend was a mixture of truth, fantasy and mystery continually shifting in and out of reality, intangible connections and associations like refracted illusions in a hall of smoky mirrors.

Near death experience

Harrington Gardens is very close to Gloucester Road underground station and in 1940 was situated in the separate borough council of Kensington. This borough along with its neighbour Chelsea merged as a result of local government reforms in 1963 and bore the brunt of the bombing in London's West End, largely because Luftwaffe pilots were aiming for warehouses and power station plants along the River Thames. German intelligence knew that the Lots Road Power Station powered the London underground and that the coal fired Battersea Power Station provided a significant contribution to the national grid of London and South East England.

Alison moved in with Alexander at a boarding house in the Earl's Court Road and they 'became lovers' in the Spring of 1941 after she had survived a near-death experience in the London Blitz. It happened when she was having supper in her room right at the top of a hostel in Harrington Gardens, South Kensington and the air raid siren sounded. By this time, she and her fellow residents took no notice. They had become acclimatized and nonchalant. The Luftwaffe's visits had been so frequent and the danger was now an everyday experience.

She was on her knees by her bed writing her diary entry about her developing relationship with Alec when she was enveloped by a terrific crash, followed by a rumbling and shaking of the whole house, and then total darkness. She rushed to the door, but it was jammed. She felt overwhelmed by 'a sickening terror.' She kept tugging violently at the door until it flew open and in the pitch blackness she felt the eerie rush of the outside air. Then clouds of dense smoke and the hot, flinty smell of burning. She recalled that she 'felt a blinding terror, because I thought that surely the stairs below me were on fire. I had one instinct: to get down those stairs, to run through flames if necessary. And so in pitch darkness and in the choking dust, I leapt down the stairs, scrambling over bricks and rubble.'

She could hear someone calling for help. After scrambling down three flights of stairs through the debris of bricks and shattered plaster she eventually saw some light in the hall and met a gathering group of survivors 'standing, silent, frightened and covered in white dust.' She joined them 'trembling from head to foot.' Alison's account of her miraculous survival at the height of the London blitz coincides with the records of bombings in Chelsea and Kensington during World War Two. The hostel building had been on the North East corner of Harrington Gardens at the junction of Courtfield Road and Ashburn Place.

The bomb had hit her building at an angle of 45 degrees, destroying the whole section under her room, which now jutted out at the top of the house with a void underneath. One girl was trapped with a badly crushed leg and foot, and they watched as the helmeted light and heavy rescue workers very gently carried her down. Alison immediately regretted that she had not made more of an effort to answer her cries for help, although she knew that by doing so she would almost certainly have fallen to her death or been severely injured: 'I felt it was a failure in time of trial, an occasion of cowardice and fear in which a primitive and all-consuming instinct for self-preservation had blotted out the power to act reasonably.'

This introspective honesty expressed in her memoir suggests one of the many reasons why Wilson fell devotedly in love with her. The depth of her anxiety over understandably saving her own life, but then wrestling with her conscience over whether she should have responded to what sounded like cries for help reveals an individual who would put the people she cared about before her own selfish interests.

Her other outstanding quality was the commitment of her loyalty and willingness to give Alec the benefit of the doubt even though circumstances and tangible clues suggested perhaps she would have done better to do otherwise. She was somebody who pledged her love for her husband and children well above any concern for herself. But her memoir demonstrates that she does not deserve to be labelled as gullible. Every one of her experiences involved an intense rational and emotional concentration on the implications of each of the dilemmas she had to face.

It is also significant that their relationship blossomed in the context of working in the professional world of intelligence. Alexander Wilson knew she was somebody he could trust and Alison knew that in the intelligence world nothing is what it necessarily means and truth is often more absurd and unbelievable than fiction. Her husband would push this understanding to its very limits.

Friends and lovers

Alison agreed to spend the first weekend with Alec shortly after her father died in January of that year. She joined him at the house in Hendon where he had been living with Dorothy and Michael. She recalled: 'I remember that as I stood waiting for the bus to take me there, I knew exactly what I was doing: I was going against every convention with which I had been brought up.' She accepted she was associating with a married man; not yet divorced, and that divorce in her upbringing had been an exceptionally rare occurrence, and 'a thing of shame not to be discussed in front of the children.'

Alison moved into the same boarding house in the Earl's Court Road after she was bombed out of her hostel. In due course they became lovers and before long she became pregnant. Alison later asked herself how she had arrived at this situation which for her was so out of character. Of course, she would later learn the extent of Alec's deception. But she knew that was only half the story: 'I was never coerced. What I did, I did freely, not impetuously, but after much deliberation. Only love could induce me to betray my better half. Once I had surrendered and admitted my love, I loved with intensity which enabled me to sacrifice everything I held most dear – goodness, truth, honour – an intensity that was to survive every onslaught except that of God himself.'

Marriage

The year 1941 was a truly tragic one for Alison's mother Mrs Annie McKelvie. She lost her husband George with a sudden and unexpected illness in January. And then in September her only daughter got married to a man old enough to be her father. It was not what you might call a society wedding. It was a Roman Catholic affair with no members of the groom's family present. Only the bride's brother Ian and her mother were there to give her away.

The ceremony was not even in what you might call a real church. For this was a Blitz ceremony. Our Ladies of Victory in Kensington had been gutted when almost the year before four incendiary bombs landed on the roof of the church and in the short space of two and a half hours it was completely devastated and burned to the ground. The Blessed Sacrament was saved and taken by the priests to the nearby Carmelite Church. This was used in a makeshift high altar first in the local Odeon Cinema and then in a more permanent arrangement in the basement of Cavendish's furnishings in Kensington High Street.

The ceremony on 8th September 1941 took place in this very basement and was very brief. Alison recalled that the priest Canon James Walton seemed disinterested. Regulations for mixed marriages were still very strict and only the minimum amount of ritual and celebration allowed. Alison fully converted into the

Catholic faith after her husband's death. She would later gain a theology degree with the University of London at the famous Heythrop College. Consequently, her memoir is a narrative and examination of her faith as much as family history. She said that at the time of her marriage she knew that as a Christian, the blessing from God, for which she had 'yearned had not been given. God, most certainly present in the Tabernacle, had turned his back.'

Alison said just after the marriage the 'most unpleasant thing she ever had to do in her life' was to tell her mother that it had been a shotgun wedding. Alison was nearly four months pregnant with Alec's child. Mrs McKelvie stood by her daughter 'to the best of her ability' though she made sure that Alison heard and felt the torrent of abuse she had for Alexander Wilson. The shame and anger brought forth 'a flood of indignation.'

Alexander Wilson had lied to her about obtaining a divorce from Dorothy. He had lied to her about obtaining the necessary annulment from the Catholic Church before being allowed to marry again. And he was lying to the Catholic Church. He had managed to make the arrangements in Kensington presumably with a priest completely unknown to him. When living with Dorothy in 53 Blomfield Road, Little Venice for six years, he had formed a close bond with Father Aydon at the Catholic Church of Our Lady of Delours and later St Mary of the Angels in Bayswater. Father Aydon testified to the War Office for his 'professional integrity, competence and reliability' and 'an upright character on all occasions.'

Alison's marriage and pregnancy meant she had to leave her job at the Secret Service. The head of their Department had been very opposed to the marriage. She had warned her against him. But Alison dismissed her advice.

Alison's dilemma: Secret Service Agent Husband, or Lying Fraud?

1942 proved to be as dramatic and catastrophic for Alison as 1941. She lived with the never ending and cruel dilemma of her love for Alec. She wanted to believe his explanations for their extraordinary bad luck when it came to finances. But inevitably her scepticism intensified as the poverty became humiliating. Her memoir charts a heart-breaking narrative of bewilderment. By the time of his death she became convinced his tales of intelligence and continuing service to the Foreign Office were an absurd fantasy.

It started after Gordon's birth in a private ward of the Lindo Wing of St Mary's Paddington and several weeks of puerperal fever and postnatal depression accentuated by the side effects of new life-saving antibiotics M & B. The first few weeks of married life had been conventional. He lived up to her expectations. He wanted to give a good impression.

Even before they married, he had given her a spectacular twenty-first birthday present of a beautifully graded pearl necklace. Her engagement ring had been a large sapphire surrounded by diamonds. She received a diamond necklace as her wedding present.

Her joy at giving birth to a beautiful and perfect boy with extraordinarily blue eyes and hair so fair that it was almost white had been masked by pain and illness. She needed to remain in hospital for more than three weeks, but already the money was running out. They had moved to a furnished flat in West Hampstead, but when taking baby Gordon to his weekly check-up at the post-natal clinic, burglars struck. All the jewellery was taken, family heirlooms and some of Alec's valuables as well.

Alec was dismissed from the Foreign Office: 'He explained it as a ruse to give an impression of discredit for S.S. [secret service] purposes.' Alison found that their living accommodation deteriorated in direct proportion to their income. They moved to a house in Hampstead Garden suburb. He appeared to be ill with a stomach ulcer and 'the occasional slight haemorrhage,' and started to disappear for twenty-four-hour periods. These were explained as going into hospital for blood transfusions. His second wife Dorothy would have found this story familiar and his first wife Gladys also.

Alison was terrified that the husband who was much older than her and now the father of her child might die. She was continually anxious about 'a sickening fear' of death, or premonition of disaster. What did come to her was humiliating poverty.

When he was not being treated for his blood disorder, Alec was walking the streets looking for work and less expensive accommodation. He was bringing in so little money the contents of their larder were reduced to one packet of dried macaroni. They had hired a woman to do some housework, but she left without saying a word after not being paid. And then they were evicted with all their belongings locked inside. Alison found herself out in the street only with Gordon in his pram.

A local clergyman gave them a roof over their heads for a night or two and they then moved to a boarding house in Paddington which Alison recalled 'was not as sleazy as one might expect. The occupants were a motley collection, including an R.A.F. officer and his wife, and a Pakistani doctor, with whom we sometimes played bridge in the evenings.'

1943- another year of debt and penury

Anything of value that had not been taken in the burglary went to the pawnbrokers. They never had any money to redeem what they had pledged. The boarding house landlady was a plump Irish Catholic woman who never missed mass and had a temper that rose in proportion to their rent arrears. She would kick up an awful and embarrassing row until the money was found. They borrowed from friends and family. Alec would borrow from her friends without her knowledge. Most were never repaid.

Alison took Gordon to stay with some cousins in a country house near Keswick for a holiday. One morning Gordon began to furiously scratch his head. She was mortified to find that they were infested with lice; most likely picked up in the squalid conditions of the Paddington boarding house. Desperate letters from her husband compelled her to surrender more of her dignity and self-respect by asking her relatives for a loan of £100, which was politely refused.

Unknown to Alison, her husband was still relating to his first wife and their adult children. He was meeting his sons Adrian and Dennis for lunch at the Authors' Club. They were also getting used to him asking for loans. Adrian would generously pay his club's membership subscription.

In 1944 Alexander Wilson and his daughter by his first marriage, Daphne, experienced close calls on the home front during the time of pilotless V1 doodlebugs and V2 rockets. Writing to Adrian on 26th June 1944, Wilson revealed: 'We were blasted on Saturday night, or rather Sunday morning, and I'm afraid I've lost a good many of my possessions in the mess, though something may be dug out. I'm all right except for a bump on the head and a damaged arm. I felt a bit shaky yesterday, but am not so bad today.'

Just over a week later he would add: 'Daphne's house was bombed, but she and Edith were at the cinema at the time and our dear girl saved all her possessions. She is now at home with Mummy. No, I have not recovered very much of my kit, the damage was too extensive. I don't feel too bad. My head is still bandaged but nearly well again and the broken arm is getting on as well as can be expected, especially considering my lack of white corpuscles!'

The severe injury to his arm is recalled by Alison in her memoir, but the destruction of his kit is not. As far as Alison knew they were still living in the Paddington boarding house. She was now pregnant with Nigel. Gordon was only two years old in 1944. Furthermore, Alexander Wilson by this time had been made a bankrupt with a full 'public examination' by the Official Receiver in February of that year.

Yet mysteriously no member of his first family had any knowledge of this at all. Similarly, Alison remembered the hand-to-mouth existence, but clearly had no knowledge of his official status as a bankrupt. This should have blocked him from gaining any kind of credit; even from pawnbrokers.

Arrest in Kensington Gardens

It was a Sunday in early October. They were returning from mass. Alison was pushing Gordon in his pram. They had been strolling happily in the park. Two men approached and took him to one side. Alexander Wilson was being arrested for posing as a Colonel in the Indian Army and wearing false decorations. He had been under surveillance for some time. The two detectives searched their room, but found nothing. They quickly became a 'sensation echoing all over the house' among the other residents. Alec was taken away for questioning leaving his seven month pregnant wife 'stunned, sick and cold with terror.'

She resorted first to ironing as some kind of meditation and then to something more spiritual in the form of praying on her knees and using a rosary he had given her. He returned just before midnight having been given police bail, but he was up before the Stipendiary Magistrate at Marylebone Police Court first thing in the morning. Alison never attended his court appearances. The following day he was remanded in custody for a week.

Alison was interviewed by a probation officer and explained that she had always believed he was entitled to wear the uniform and the decorations had been genuine. He returned to court from Brixton Prison a week later and was fined £5 for each offence. With no funds and having exhausted the lending patience of friends and family, he served the alternative of two months' imprisonment.

Alison visited him every week at Brixton Prison. She thought he was there for between four and six weeks. She would take him a 2 oz tin of his favourite tobacco, and became part of what she recalled as the saddest queue in the world of bedraggled, jaded and hopeless women with anxiety-ridden faces.

Alison's previously bourgeois and comfortable middle-class persona had to come to terms with the frightening and repellent 'cold sordidness' of the clanging bolts of huge metal gates, being searched by warders, and waiting to be called while sitting on backless benches. She was taken up to a post office style counter separated from her husband by bars and a glass screen with an awkward aperture to speak through.

On her first visit she said she doubted if there had ever been a divorce from Dorothy. His response shocked her. He lied to her that he was in fact serving a sentence for bigamy in relation to Dorothy's marriage. He maintained that his story about the divorce and annulment had been true. But these related to a first marriage, to a woman with whom he had had three adult children. He was still lying through his teeth. Alison had been led to believe that Gladys was Alec's sister in law. She was aware of her, but had never met her, or her children.

Alison said it was at this point that she saw Alec weep for the first and only time in her presence. Tears ran down his cheeks as he begged for her forgiveness and implored her not to leave him. He continued his sobbing protestation that the annulment for Gladys's marriage was true, that at one point he had the Vatican authorities in Rome searching for documents he claimed had been lost in the war. Alison recalled: 'It was a devastating shock. [...] I gave him my word. There was no alternative. I loved him and could not abandon him in his need.' When she walked away from the prison, she said she felt almost joy and had a sense of peace because 'there had been no temptation to abandon him; love had been tested and found to be true.'

At the same time Alexander Wilson continued to implicate Alison's appalling misfortune into the legend that she had become the unwitting player in an intelligence operation. He maintained that the arrest and prosecution were all part of a Secret Service plot to publicly discredit him so that he would be able to carry out an intelligence operation. He said he was unable to give her the details on the grounds of national security. This would continue to always be his defence in the face of the inexplicable. She recalled: 'Where complications or seeming inconsistencies arose he was always able to embellish his case with further inventions, until a vast fabrication was built up. He never forgot what he said or contradicted himself. He was extremely plausible, and many others besides myself were convinced by him.'

Alison later realised that he was always able to play this trump card. He had been in the Secret Intelligence Service. She knew this because that was where they had first met. They had worked together there. Consequently, his account of undercover intelligence work out in the field might just be true. Stranger things did happen in intelligence work, especially in time of war: 'To this I clung as to a lifeline. I wanted to believe him. I could not face the consequences of not believing. I loved him because of the good I saw in him.'

Alison was in a desperate social situation. She had no home, money, status, a two-year-old child to look after and another one due in two months. She turned to the Carmelite Priory where she was taking instruction in the Catholic faith, but was given no refuge or consolation. Her mother Annie had seen a report of Alec's prosecution and jailing in one of the London newspapers and came to her aid. She provided shelter for her and Gordon, but not for her son-in-law.

After his release from prison Alec lived in temporary digs for himself while Alison went to the Redhill Hospital in Edgware to give birth to Nigel. Gordon was sent to a children's home in Buckinghamshire. Alison was totally dependent on her mother's charity. The birth of her second son Nigel was a wholly different experience. She heard her screams bouncing off the walls of the delivery room: 'I had screamed with the full force of my lungs, in a rising crescendo, as each of the first contractions took hold of me, louder than any of my predecessors. I had succumbed to the grip of a primitive terror. I realised that for a little while I had been totally demoralised; I had descended to the purely animal. I had lost my human dignity - and I was overwhelmed with shame.'

The disasters overtaking Alison and Alec in 1944 had resulted in homelessness and imprisonment, public disgrace and depths of humiliation that had been unimaginable certainly for Alison. But they had also drawn them closer together and with a strength of purpose that resisted the insistence from her mother and brother that Nigel should be given up for adoption and Gordon left in the children's home. They had called their second son Nigel 'because he came out of so much darkness' and what Alison had hoped would remain the 'darkest period of her life, never to be repeated.'

Cinema management and temporary rehabilitation

After Alison came out of hospital, Alexander Wilson took up a new career beginning as an assistant cinema manager with one of the big picture house chains. Over a period of four years they moved from Lincoln to London, Purley, and Palmers Green. Dennis remembered visiting his father while he managed cinemas all over the Greater London area, including Balham and Hampstead.

Alison remembered moving from one set of rooms to another and was able to calculate that in seventeen years, they averaged one move per year. Alison realised how vital it was to learn that 'to get the best value for your money…you are unable to make a choice.' She would recall the lowest point when there were only a few old pennies left in her purse to buy a meal and she would walk up and down outside the greengrocers 'quite unable to come to a decision as to whether to buy some potatoes, which were more filling, or some carrots which, during the war were highly extolled for their vitamin value and which would have been better for the children.'

And so for four years things had gone comparatively smoothly. They began renting a furnished house and took in paying guests. Alison's confidence in Alec returned. She rebuilt her belief in him. But this happy equilibrium would soon come to an end. Gordon was six and Nigel was four. In 1948 their father would be arrested again. This time for embezzling the takings of a cinema he was managing in Hampstead. Thus, his career in cinema management was terminated with a three month prison sentence, and his young wife and boys would be plunged into abject insecurity yet again. Despite doing temporary secretarial work, and trying to let the garage of their rented house, complaints from neighbours made it impossible for her to keep the house.

When Wilson came out of jail he found that Alison and their two boys had moved in with one of her friends who was living in Barnes. He was not allowed to join them. Again, he had to live on his own after leaving the prison gates. He rented a room near them and would visit them, but she suspected that he never forgave her for this and always saw it as some kind of betrayal.

The last fifteen years in Ealing

Alexander Wilson found a job as the porter of the casualty unit of the Central Middlesex Hospital, in Park Royal, and found rooms for his third family in Ealing. For the next 15 years Alison would not encounter any 'major disasters.' All the time though she had to live with the spinning of his story of intelligence service trickery. He still insisted upon the original story of his family background and that what was happening was due to the Foreign Office discrediting him. He constantly raised Alison's hopes with promises that sooner or later he would be reinstated, with a large sum of back pay and that the house in the village of Ringwood in the New Forest would be handed back by the army.

All this would be embellished with detail and apparently supporting facts. Alison would not talk about her husband's legend to anyone. She feared that her whole life with Alec was a lie: 'I was forced to act a lie, to the children and to everyone else. It would have been impossible and too hurtful to have told the children the truth, and no part of it could be told without the whole. Rightly or wrongly, I always protected them from the disillusionment which I had had to suffer. I could not destroy the love and respect they had for their father and to admit their illegitimacy would have been far more traumatic for them than in today's conditions.'

Alison hated living a lie, but she felt trapped into it and there was no escape. One of Alexander Wilson's attractions was what appeared to be his exceptional and self-deprecating modesty. If what he claimed was true, if he was indeed a Colonel in the Indian Army, then to be prepared to work as a hospital porter without making any fuss or bother about it, would indeed be meritorious. Alison came to realise that this was inverted pride: 'I suspect that at work he gradually gave indications of who or what he purported to be so that his colleagues ended up admiring him for what he was doing.' Alison was tortured by the dilemma of never saying anything about it to anyone in case it was not true and never saying anything to anyone in case it was true.

During the 1950s both Alison and Alec worked to maintain domestic security for their boys though they were very much latch-key children, having to let themselves into an empty house on their return from school. Alison was 'basically happy' though feared every unexpected knock on the door in case she would find police officers calling. Her material life compared poorly to that of her successful brother who was a radiologist living in a high class area of comfort and security. She believed she compensated by almost obsessively scrubbing, scouring and excessively washing and ironing. She was ashamed of her 'truly vicious temper' that would let rip after an exhausting and frustrating day.

As was the case with all the other of Alexander Wilson's wives, she was the parent who wielded any necessary and heavy-handed discipline. He was the peacemaker supplying the gentle and loving element. But she remembered that he was 'a good husband' who endured her rages with patience. They were responsible together for a happy and stable home background and 'love for one another […] underpinned all our shortcomings and failures.'

There was no sign of personal extravagance in his character. The apparent instances of criminal conviction seemed entirely out of character. Alison wrote in her memoir: 'I loved him because of the good I saw in him. As a husband and in the home, he was good, kind, gentle, peaceful. He was a wonderful father, who adored his children, brought them up in their faith and fostered in them only the highest ideals, of which he appeared an exemplar. He was abstemious and spent hardly anything on himself: some tobacco for his pipe, an odd pint of beer and visit to a football match, taking the children when they were old enough, was his limit. He had immense courage, reinstating himself after his lapses and continuing to work to the end, in spite of severe heart trouble.'

Growing security and stability

In 1958 Alison's mother Annie died and an inheritance enabled her to obtain a mortgage on a house in Lancaster Gardens, Ealing so that after seventeen rootless years they were able to build a home of their own. Gordon and Nigel obtained free and assisted places at a local public school. The anxiety of debt diminished. Gordon entered Dartmouth to begin a highly successful career in the Royal Navy. He was oblivious to his father's early Royal Naval and indeed, substantial sea-going experience.

Nigel became head boy at his school and was accepted at Oxford. And Alexander Wilson claimed he had been reinstated at the Foreign Office and would no longer have to push casualties and cadavers around the local casualty unit. Alison was aware of some connection with the Sandersons wallpaper factory in nearby Perivale. She was not fully aware that he had got work there as a clerk in the management office.

When Alexander Wilson, the former Principal of a University College in India, a commissioned officer of the Great War, a celebrated and highly acclaimed popular novelist of the 1920s, 30s, and 40s, was working as a mere hospital porter at the Central Middlesex Hospital in the middle 1950s, he entertained his young son Nigel to lunch in the canteen. With the benefit of decades of hindsight, this mature and highly successful City of London businessman and much-respected father of four would speculate that he thought his father was probably in a state of some kind of mental or spiritual breakdown.

The precision and honesty of his mother's memoir would remind him of a curious incident at school, when he was called into the headmaster's office to be told that the retired Field Marshal Auchinleck had rung to ask if when attending a school sports day he might have spotted Alec Wilson in the crowd, a man he remembered from the Indian Army and his life in Lahore in the 1920s and early thirties.

Alison's disillusionment with her husband had been so great that Nigel was prompted to consider whether his father had actually impersonated Auchinleck in a phone call to his headmaster so that he could derive some inverted credit from a fabricated incident of personal aggrandisement. Yet the history of his father's documented life and service in India means it is entirely plausible that Auchinleck would have known his father professionally and socially. An examination of Auchinleck's biography indicates that the retired general was living in Mayfair, London when Nigel had been at school and had been an active sponsor of London boys' clubs and their participation in sports days with London schools.

It is apparent that Alison had a forensic moral acuity when judging her husband's behaviour, but she was equally unsparing in judging herself. This was her point of view and she had no idea of the wider context. She was not in a position to establish if her husband was still part of the intelligence world. He persisted in his story of going to the Foreign Office to work. Perhaps he actually believed in the illusion himself. By this time Wilson suffered heart attacks and needed hospital treatment and Alison feared for his life: 'Each time, after recovering, he went back to work, supposedly at the F.O. His statements and explanations became more exaggerated until, at the very end, they were so extravagant that they defied even my will to believe.'

Wilson had told Alison that she would find out about his true identity after his death because he had concealed the secret in a special compartment in his wallet. Needless to say, when he did pass away on April 4th 1963, 'there was no special compartment, and no verification.' Alison received letters of condolence from the wallpaper design and manufacturing business, Sandersons: 'It was then clear that that was where he was working right up to the end and had been for a considerable time. I knew nothing at all about the writers, the circumstances they mentioned, the place, the conditions, type of work he had been doing or anything else.'

Alison replied politely and did her best not to betray her own ignorance. It was clear to her that this was the reality and that all of Alec's assertions about the Foreign Office, the names of personnel, the little details thrown in from time to time, were all pure fiction. He had gone out every day, but to somewhere and to a life of which she knew nothing. He was writing another novel in his own head and extending the story telling to his immediate family.

All the time she wanted to protect her sons from the awful truth about his life; that most of it had probably been fabrication from beginning to end. She realised that there was not a single thing he had ever told her that she could put her finger on and now say 'that is true.' She knew nothing of his childhood, parents, family, background, schooling, his supposed time in India, in the Army, in the war, or what had actually occurred in respect of the Foreign Office decision to dismiss him as part of some secret intelligence operation. What appalled her most of all is that she did not even know 'of the twenty-two years of our life together.'

A final betrayal

On the night of his death 4th April 1963 Alison Wilson examined the drawers to his desk and discovered photographs and 'sufficient evidence to throw sickening light on previous incidents, making it clear that he had not been faithful.' She also found notes for a novel in which she recognised a very malign portrait of herself; something she felt was at her 'ugliest and most shameful worst.' She was appalled and crushed by the realisation it had been written with malice. She found notes attributing nasty intentions to certain actions of hers that had been entirely innocent. This was perhaps the ultimate betrayal. She formed the view that only malice could see malice where there was none: 'Love could not write such things, could not even think them [...] There was no love there, only a warped mind.'

Alison struggled to focus on what she did know about Alexander Wilson. He had written intelligence stories. She had seen correspondence with the publishers, had handled the books, had even watched him write a new one which was never published. But they were fiction and told her nothing of the true situation: 'This indeed was the supreme irony: the only reality in a mountain of fiction was fiction itself.'

The only things of which she had proof were his lies, and she had discovered enough to realise these were but the tip of the iceberg. She realised there was no memory of him that she could retain and know that it was true. Every conversation she had had, important and unimportant, had been a lie. If she had asked him to supply facts about himself so that she could become a Catholic, his answer would have been a lie; if she asked him what he had done that day, that was still a lie. He was one vast lie. He had not only died, he had evaporated into nothing. She came to a heart-rending and tragic conclusion: 'There was no one left, because where there is no truth there is no person. He had destroyed himself; there was nothing left but a heap of ashes; my love was reduced to a heap of ashes.'

In those words, Alison had unwittingly created the most tragic epitaph that could ever be expressed for the life of a secret agent. A secret agent for his country and empire and also a secret agent for himself. Wilson had been true to the lie at the centre of his very existence. His work for MI6 and any other intelligence body before or since was fully implicated in the multiple deceptions of his complex private life that had become their own sequence of Russian dolls each fitting into the other until, perhaps, he himself could keep no broad moral over-view of the full landscape of his duplicity.

Alison Wilson's words are truly Shakespearean in the way she defined the meaning of her life with him and his life with her. In her own way she was defining the ethical waste land that can exist sometimes in the real world of espionage, the ideological angst, existential loneliness, and despair of disillusionment scripted by John Le Carré for his *Spy Who Came In From The Cold* central character, Alex Leamas: 'What do you think spies are: priests, saints and martyrs? They're a squalid procession of vain fools, traitors too, yes; pansies, sadists and drunkards, people who play cowboys and Indians to brighten their rotten lives. Do you think they sit like monks in London, balancing the rights and wrongs? I'd have killed Mundt [an East German spymaster in the novel] if I could. I hate his guts; but not now. It so happens that they need him. They need him so that the great moronic mass you admire can sleep soundly in their beds at night. They need him for the safety of ordinary, crummy people like you and me.'

Alison was crushed by the deception and betrayal inherent in the context that she had married a man who was performing an intelligence legend most likely long after it served any real purpose. It was incontrovertible that he had served as an SIS intelligence officer for at least 3 years during the most desperate period of his country's struggle for survival in World War Two and the reality of that fact threw opaque shadows over what happened afterwards.

Forgiveness

Alison had identified the essential contradiction in Alexander Wilson's life and times; a contradiction that could always be explained in terms of his career as an intelligence agent and officer. Outside the intelligence legend that he adopted, Wilson's background could always be seen as honourable and respectable.

When they were alive and, before Alison discovered private jottings and documents suggesting infidelity and malice, they affirmed their love for each other in elegant and moving love letters to each other while they were in hospital. In late 1962, Alec may well have known that heart disease and growing infirmity meant he did not have long to live:

'Darling, what can I say to you? My heart is so full and there are no words which I can adequately express all I feel. First, I am so terribly sorry I have caused you so much anxiety and worry. I think, when things were as bad, I was affected most by all I saw in your face. Secondly, what can I say, from an overflowing heart, to tell what your love, your devotion, your fortitude and constancy have meant to me? I could never begin to say these things verbally to you; to find adequate expressions on paper is very difficult, but at least, neither embarrassing to you or me.

Oh Bunty, you have been so wonderful; you have done more than you can ever know to keep me going, and God can never have had more gratitude offered up to him than I pour out to him the gift of you. Our love is a marvellous thing, something to me precious beyond description. Looking back now how infinitely ridiculous our stupid quarrels seem; how completely out of character and utterly unnecessary. Forgive me for my part in them! When I love you so; when you are above everything and everybody, the one supreme person to me, disagreements are more than banal; they are– shall I say– bloody silly? And I feel a self-contempt for ever letting them occur.

All I live for now is to be back with you, and how wonderful it is to know that I am coming back to you. All along my patience has undergone a severe strain; the next week will be more than ever trying. But, at the end of it, to come back to you! To hold you in my arms; just look at you! Oh Darling!

Thank you for your great love, for your unremitting devotion; for everything!

God bless you my habib– sweety very much Habib-ullah as well,

Your always loving

Devoted Alex.'

When Alison went into hospital the following year for a serious operation, Alexander would write to her and reinforce his love and commitment to her: 'How I have – and am – missing you, my Habib. Now that I cannot even come to see you, I am more lonely than ever. I love you so, and, apart from you, am just empty and depressed. What a wonderful day it will be for me, when you come home again. But don't rush it, nevertheless. [...] God bless you, my Darling. All of me in eternal love and devotion to you. Your very own adoring Alex.'

What was also incontrovertible was that their relationship had been a love story on a scale that had dignity and beauty, and achieved another level of interpretation meriting the adjective Shakespearean. There was nothing sordid or shoddy about the love they had for each other. And there was something triumphant and supremely elevating in the way Alison was able to achieve spiritual forgiveness for her late husband and herself following her formal conversion to the Roman Catholic Church.

With her young adult sons by her side she went to her first communion: 'The first shock came when the priest announced from the pulpit that the Mass was being said for my intention. Almost immediately a strange thought entered my head: this is the one true fairy story. Whatever I ask for now will come true. With such an opportunity, what was my intention to be?'

Alison had to think quickly so that she could formulate it properly in her mind. It did not take long: 'I had only one wish, one concern, one prayer: for the forgiveness and salvation of A. However, I was not able to be entirely altruistic so, along with that my major, all-embracing intention, I pushed in a little, very secondary one for myself: that I would always progress in the spiritual life. I knew that if one stops advancing, one slides back, and I was afraid lest, having got where I was, I got no further.'

As she stepped into the queue forming in the aisle to go up for Communion she had a feeling she had never before experienced: something she could only describe as a sensation of perfect health, 'of total well-being.'

It cannot be imagined that anyone unable to share Alison's religious faith would want to begrudge her the right and joy in expiating the agonies of all that was wrong during her 22 years with Alexander Wilson. She had a right to remember and cherish the genuine love they had for each other. Her remarkable memoir written while 'in retreat' at the Carmelite Monastery at Dolgellau, Wales between January and February 1986 is a powerful expression of love for her husband and her God. It is a remarkable testament of Christian religious faith and makes a significant contribution to understanding what it was like to be Mrs Wilson as well as explaining at least part of the enigma of Mr Alexander Wilson.

Chapter Five

Elizabeth and son

It was the affair and marriage that many members of Alexander Wilson's family have found it hardest to understand or explain. It was the breaking point for Oscar Wilde's famous homily by Lady Bracknell on misfortune. One bigamy might have been an accident. A second perhaps a misfortune. But a third? Wilson embarked on the adventure of a fourth marriage and family only just over two miles away from where he was living with Alison and her two boys. How and why? They met while working in the early years of the National Health Service. She was the nurse. He worked in A&E bringing in and taking out the dead and living. Was it madness on his part? To Elizabeth this was a charming and exciting love that she cherished and protected to the very end. She took their young son Douglas to Scotland where she waited for the promised return to India. Where the Urdu language teaching books remained on the bookshelf. Douglas remembers receiving his father's presents at Christmas and the sad moment his mother told him of his passing away.

In photographs Elizabeth Hill is seen feeding the pigeons with a friend in Trafalgar Square. An attractive, thoughtful and intelligent professional young woman. When she married Alexander Wilson on 21st January 1955 she was a 27-year-old Hospital Nursing sister working at the Bethnal Green hospital in London's East End. Elizabeth spoke with a soft, respectable Edinburgh and recognisable Scottish accent.

She had been born in Bonnybridge near Stirling in June 1927, but spent most of her early life in Edinburgh. She had a twin sister who did not survive. Towards the end of school she developed the strong ambition to be a nurse. When going into the world of work at the age of 14 during the middle of the Second World War, her first job was in a chemist's shop. All she wanted to be was a nurse, and she pursued that with a single-minded determination. The proof of that professional dedication is that she pursued so many post-registration nursing courses so she could add to her range of nursing skills and qualifications.

She was in her early twenties when she moved to London in the early 1950s to take up the senior position of nursing sister which is the equivalent of a charge nurse now in the current NHS. Douglas remembers her telling him about how on the day of the Queen's Coronation in 1953 she came off night duty and immediately joined the throng of the London crowds with nursing colleagues: 'She loved every minute of that day.'

Betty- a smart and dignified woman

Although christened Elizabeth, she was known as Betty or Bett to friends, family and loved ones. Douglas remembers her as a discreet, reserved, polite and private person: 'She was smart, she was firm when it was needed, she was tidy, disciplined and organised, she was stoic and uncomplaining and dignified, she was warm, utterly selfless, generous and caring.' Is it any wonder that Alexander Wilson fell in love with her?

As is the case with Alison and Gladys, her Christianity was an important part of her life. She was dedicated to the large city centre Baptist church, Charlotte Baptist Chapel in Edinburgh and regularly attended a congregation that was 800 to 900 strong twice every Sunday. Douglas remembers she made close friends there, attended mid-week meetings, women's meetings, taught in Sunday school, hosted district meetings at home and contributed in so many other ways. She was giving back to the church and to the new generations of young people all that she had received there when young herself.

That selfless desire to help people less fortunate than herself, something she shares so strongly with Dorothy, most likely informed an ambition to go abroad perhaps to do missionary work. Douglas has a strong suspicion that 'she wanted to go overseas to a country where nursing would be a greater challenge. I also expect her strong Christian beliefs were part of this ambition.' The church she belonged to also had a strong missionary tradition and many international links. This may explain the evidence pointing to Elizabeth planning and hoping to go to Pakistan with Alexander Wilson after she moved to Scotland with Douglas in 1957 or 1958.

Elizabeth's granddaughter, Tamsin, remembers her as the caring and loveable 'grandma' who 'kept an immaculate and good looking house.' She was at her happiest when 'busied with daily chores or knitting or baking and happier still to be teaching me to be helping her.' One of Tamsin's strongest memories was that when going about the day 'she seemed to always be singing, quietly - a little more than humming, but not quite the full words and expression of the songs. The songs were majority hymns, but they were always being recited in a happy and busying type of way.' Elizabeth had 'a really happy disposition' whose presence on any hospital ward would have lightened the mood and turned patients' thoughts away from the pain and worry of their injury or illness. Elizabeth was the quintessential ward sister and grandmother: 'Warm and loving, and wonderfully calming and attentive.'

Marriage to Alexander Wilson 1955

Alexander Wilson's last marriage certificate from January 1955 was a bizarre expression of confusion and deception. He described himself as a bachelor and gave his age as 52, although it was likely he had been married three times before and his actual age was 61. He continued with his intelligence cover legend, giving his father's identity as Colonel Gordon Chesney Wilson of the Royal Horse Guards. He described himself as 'Alexander Robert Gordon Wilson formerly known as Alexander Robert Gordon Chesney Wilson.'

It seemed Wilson had an alternative address to the house in Ealing where he lived with Alison, Gordon and Nigel – 31 Kingsley Avenue in West Ealing, and Alexander and Elizabeth were later to live together at 29 Hanger Lane, Ealing. Hanger Lane is not far from Park Royal where the Central Middlesex Hospital was sited and where it is likely they first met.

This was a bigamous marriage with a young child maintained locally just about two miles away and over a period of two years. Alison in Lancaster Gardens had been suspicious about incidents, but had no idea of the full story at all. It is also certain that Gladys and Dorothy, Wilson's first and second wives were equally oblivious to this extraordinary onset of a fourth marriage and family.

When their son Douglas Bruce Andrew was born in late November of that year, Wilson resumed the identity that had got him convicted and fined in 1944: Colonel Indian Army (D.S.O) (Retired). He had spun a legend to Elizabeth and this included strong accounts and a sense of allegiance to Lahore and perhaps his academic career at the University of Punjab.

It is clear he was still working as a hospital porter though on the marriage certificate this had been elevated to 'Casualty Superintendent (Hospital) Retired Colonel (Indian Army). When a distraught Alison was searching her late husband's chest of drawers immediately after his death in Lancaster Gardens in April 1963 she said she came across clear evidence of his infidelity. Perhaps the photographs and documents directly related to his life with Elizabeth.

Elizabeth left no diary or written account of her relationship with Alexander Wilson. When Mike Shannon's family history investigation led to the children from his various marriages getting together for the first time in 2007, she was still alive- the only wife surviving. But by being so heavily afflicted with advanced Alzheimer's disease, she had no memory of her life with Alexander, and would pass away a few months before Mike Shannon in 2010.

Douglas expects she may have confided to some of her friends why she left London, and a marriage with a very young child, but he has not met or spoken to anybody who has this information: 'I don't think she even shared this with her second husband John Ansdell, who was known as Jack.'

Douglas Ansdell's Odyssey

Douglas Ansdell remembers the time his mother Elizabeth learned of his father's death. She revealed the news while sitting on the floor reading a letter. She had always spoken lovingly and positively of his father, but as mystery attended so many aspects of his life, so did the memory and representation of his life after his death in London.

A decision had been taken by his mother to move to Scotland some years before his death so Douglas has some memory of his mother receiving letters from him, but no visits. It is possible that the move to Scotland coincided with Alison and Alec obtaining the mortgage on their house in 1958 and his changing his job from hospital porter to clerk at Sandersons.

Douglas's earliest memories are of living with his mother and grandparents in a small house in St Stephen's Place in Stockbridge in Edinburgh. His grandparents were Elizabeth and Herbert Hill. He was told later that his grandfather would hardly speak to his mother as a result of her marriage and separation. But he was always good to Douglas and took him for long walks and sometimes to the cinema. At an early age he was told that his father lived in London but this was only a piece of information as, at that stage, he hardly knew what a father was nor what or where London was.

Douglas also has a memory of a specific and impressive present from his father: 'I can clearly remember receiving a model yacht from my father In London. It was far too difficult for me and so I needed my grandfather to build it and then we painted it red. I can clearly remember the yacht and I think there was a letter for my mother. There may have been other letters and gifts but I can't remember them. So, life went forward in Edinburgh and my father lived in London and that settled into my consciousness.'

When Douglas was three years old, he and his mother moved out of their grandparents' house. His mother was working as a nursing sister and had bought her own house, also in Stockbridge and not far from his grandparents. While living there Douglas has some memories of his mother saying to him that they would be going to India. He also had a much clearer memory of Hindustani/Urdu language learning text books and he can remember his mother teaching him to count in Hindustani, 'eck, do, teen, char, panj etc.' He was very young at the time.

At this time Douglas seems to have been using his full name of Douglas Bruce Andrew Chesney-Wilson. He can remember visiting friends of his mother, Robin and Grace White, who had four older children who used to chase

94

him round their garden chanting his full name.

Douglas believes he was about six or seven when his mother told him about his father's death. Sadly the impact of the news did not mean much to him: 'I had not met him, had never spoken to him and had not even seen a photo of him.' He does, however, have a clear memory of her holding the brown envelope containing the news.

In 1964 his mother remarried and a combination of things pushed any questions about his father to one side. Thoughts about his father did not surface again until he was in his early 20s. Elizabeth's new husband, John Ansdell, brought Ian and Stephen, two sons from a previous marriage, into the family, and then a year later David was born.

During his teenage years if the question of his father ever came up, it was quickly answered with the assertion that he died shortly after his birth. This seemed strange and incongruous. He could always clearly remember when his mother told him his father had died and he knew this was clearly not shortly after his birth. Douglas thinks the explanation may have suited the narrative that his mother was offering to his stepfather Jack.

She took on the Ansdell name after the remarriage. And she left nursing to focus on the home and larger family including the role of being a stepmother. Their son David was born with Down syndrome, or what is now described as serious learning difficulties, and he needed much time and attention. At a later stage she did return to work, with part time nursing, sometimes night duty, and she also ran a nursery from home. Douglas remembers how she loved family occasions and, in particular, took great delight in catering for and entertaining grandchildren: 'She always paid attention to younger people on these occasions and there would always be suitable food, treats and activities for children.'

Her granddaughter, Tamsin, remembers that her hands were always 'incredibly soft and warm. She loved me and stroked my hair and cared for us all and had an abundance of patience for us. She had a very calming atmosphere, she was never loud, or outspoken, she didn't shout, she seemed to me to be considered and calm and cheery and caring and as a result, she made me feel calm and I'm sure she will have for everyone around her.'

Tamsin's grandma was somebody who was very open and affectionate and 'had a quiet way of ensuring I didn't push the boundaries.' As a result, Tamsin felt proud to behave well with her, and could not recall any scolding from her at all: 'I can't imagine her angry at all.' She must have brought out the best in Alexander Wilson. Tamsin says she was an elegant woman: 'her clothes were considered and often included a pair of low heels, nice jewellery and a subtle swipe of lipstick. I'm almost certain all of her clothes were purchased in M&S

and that there was pride taken in doing that.'

Elizabeth first decided to confide in Douglas about her life with Alexander in the late 1970s. She came round to the house where he was staying and said that a play on television about the damage that family secrets could do had prompted her to pass on some information to him.

She revealed that his father had been the grandson of the Duke of Marlborough, that he was a Colonel in the Indian Army, that he worked with Lord Mountbatten in India, that he went to Repton public school and that he was one of the founders of the All India Cricket Club. She produced a Repton School leaflet that had been prepared for a school open day for former pupils. This leaflet commented on his father's family background and listed some of his achievements. Elizabeth gave Douglas the leaflet to keep.

Douglas remembered that at this stage: 'I did not have any reason to question the account my mother had offered nor the brief detail that was in the Repton school leaflet. The Repton leaflet was persuasive and had all the marks of a factual document with some sections of text that had been cut from a larger school publication.'

The Marlborough legend

Douglas set about trying to find out more detail from the clues given to him by his mother and the leaflet. He looked into the history of Colonel Gordon Chesney Wilson, and his father, the Portsmouth MP Sir Samuel Wilson. He researched the regimental history and obtained the wills of Colonel Wilson and his widow Lady Sarah. But all of 'these interesting enquiries and more led to dead ends.' It was perplexing that if his father had been the son of Colonel Gordon Chesney Wilson, why was there no reference to his father in the Colonel's will? Over the years, large questions and other lines of investigation ended up with no answers.

Douglas was fully encouraged by the interest and support of his three daughters, Tamsin, Bryony, and Rowan. His training as a historian and academic engaged a systematic approach with genealogical enquiries into births, deaths and marriages, enquiries at Repton School, The Indian Army, and a studying of the history of the family of Colonel Gordon Wilson of Horse Guards and Lady Sarah Wilson, a daughter of the Duke of Marlborough.

Douglas had discovered considerable amounts of factual information about his supposed grandparents, including the remarkable observation that Colonel Gordon Chesney Wilson was one of two Eton schoolboys who, outside Windsor Railway Station, had fought off with their umbrellas a would-be assassin of Queen Victoria.

The contrast in fortunes at the time of the 1901 census between the real

96

Alexander Joseph Patrick Wilson, aged 7, living with his mother Annie, older sister Isabella, and 2 year old brother Harold in modest lodgings in Purley, Croydon compared with 6 year old Alan Spencer Wilson who was being looked after at The Hall, Brooksby, Melton Mowbray, Leicestershire speaks volumes. Both had fathers serving in the Boer War. Captain Gordon Chesney was on Baden-Powell's staff at the siege of Mafeking. Honorary Lieutenant and RAMC quartermaster Alexander Wilson was provisioning hospital trains in Pretoria and Cape Town. Lady Sarah Wilson could afford to leave her two boys, 6-year-old Alan, and 8-year-old Randolph in the care of governess Agnes Simpson, maid servant Emiliene Gouland, domestic cook Rose Allen, kitchen-maid domestic Ellen Solhurst, housemaid domestic Emily Bodkin, housemaid domestic Florence Pouslin and Butler Geo Stickland. The real Alexander Wilson had no such domestic servant privileges in his family's very modest lodgings of a terraced house in Purley.

The 'Public School teams, Repton 26' document represents a sophisticated production of background cover/legend that would not have withstood robust forensic scrutiny by investigators even in the 1950s, but would serve the purpose of persuasion and impression on anyone willing to believe and take Wilson at face value. Present day scientific analysis discloses two scripts. Facing out are 'pasted' extracts of text in the form of a sporting panegyric to A.D.C. Wilson (Alexander Douglas Chesney Wilson): 'A.D. Chesney-Wilson was awarded his Colours for wicket-keeping at the early age of fifteen; then proceeded to celebrate his first match in the senior team by scoring 178 against Malvern, following it with 150 not out versus the Free Foresters. Established as a batsman, he was promoted to opening the innings with Jackson, a position he thereafter always held. Wilson's bat could be the daintiest of rapiers when he indulged in the finest of leg glides and most delicate of late cuts, a broadsword with those delightful cover drives of his, a bludge-on when he smote bowlers over their heads to the long-on boundary. As a Wicket-Keeper he was superb. Leslie Ames of Kent and England speaks of him as the finest wicket-keeper-batsman he ever saw, a tribute, indeed, from the most celebrated of that fraternity.'

The language appears to be in the fabulising style of a writer of fiction as well as a dissembler of self-fashioned autobiography. The interplay and juxtaposition of false modesty and fantastic boasting are characteristics that were soberly analysed by Alison Wilson in her memoir. Every pasted extract of text onto a light brown card had a reverse printing one of which through forensic analysis reveals a further manifestation of the 'Alexander Wilson' legend in the context of discussing Repton schoolboy casualties of the First World War: ' A.D.G. Wilson was so badly wounded that it was thought he would never play again, but he made a remarkable recovery. Alas! a regular soldier, he transferred to the Indian Army and more or less lost to country and English Cricket though he played for Sussex while on leave and once for the Gentlemen versus the Players at Scarboro.'

Douglas was surprised that the only thing his mother seemed to keep about her first husband was the forged Repton account of his fake sporting achievements: 'The Repton document is odd. It has all the marks of being something that is taken from a larger published document, but it is fiction. It is also odd that it does not mention some of his other achievements such as writing a number of novels and claims such as his involvement in secret service activity.'

The turning point in Douglas's odyssey came when he decided he needed some professional help. He was offered some help from a parent of a friend of his daughter Tamsin. She located his half-brother Gordon and agreed to make the approach on his behalf: 'This was an immense breakthrough.' All of this happened coincidentally when Mike Shannon was successfully reaching out to the first and second families.

He was able to come to terms with the fact that so much of the information that Elizabeth had about his father had been false. He was not a Marlborough, he had not gone to Repton, and he had not been a Colonel in the Indian Army and more.

Douglas does not know why his mother had taken him to Edinburgh and left Alexander Wilson behind in London: 'The explanation that seems to make most sense is that she discovered something about him and left London. Yet, if this was the case what she found out was very limited as when she came to tell me things about him, the narrative she had was still fiction. If my mother did discover something that brought the relationship to an end this did not extend to an exposure of the fictitious narrative my father had built up and had passed on to her.'

On the other hand, Douglas believes there is a possibility that their return to Edinburgh was only seen as temporary and only for a time until arrangements were put in place for them all to go to India. He has a vague memory of talk of their all going to India and, of course, there had been the Hindustani language learning. Douglas thinks it is most likely, something serious had been discovered that broke up the relationship. If there had been an India plan, he thought it would have been reasonable to expect photographs and visits to take place between them, but there was none of that. Elizabeth's granddaughter, Tamsin, also suspects Elizabeth's flight to Scotland had been triggered by the discovery of something devastating about her husband: 'My first emotions go towards her caring and beautiful nature and how heart-breaking it must have been for her to have come to some level of awareness of Alexander Wilson's deception. We don't know, because she kept this private, to what level she learned, but we do know the difficulties that coming back to Edinburgh as a single mother brought her.'

Douglas accepts that the extent of his mother's information on these things will never be known now, nor who wrote to his mother informing her of his Father's death. Either she was not inclined to keep things from her brief marriage or she decided to get rid of them when she remarried or later when her health was in decline.

It was in the last stage of her life that she was so cruelly afflicted by Alzheimer's. For ten years it robbed her of her memory and connection with her family and friends. The cruelty of this ten year period also took so many things from her son and granddaughters. Douglas says it denied him and her the chance to have a more mature relationship and 'it denied my daughters the opportunity to have a relationship with their grandmother at important stages of their lives.' Elizabeth died in 2010 and her funeral in October of that year took place in the church she loved so much.

Douglas asked her friends if they had known anything about her first marriage after she passed away, but this drew further blanks. Of all of Wilson's children Douglas has had the greatest challenge in trying to ascertain his identity in relation to this father. The main challenge had always been to separate the fact from the fiction in the representation of memory via his mother and this frustratingly limited amount of documentary evidence available to him.

The construction of narrative clarity was further obscured by the apparent collapsing of memory and time when his mother began to describe his father's death as occurring close to his birth in 1955. It was as though two sheets of mica had overlapped doubling the opaqueness.

Alexander Wilson's life with Elizabeth and Douglas

Douglas remembers his mother speaking about her life with his father as though they had a future and a significant connection with the Urdu speaking world of Pakistan. He also remembers stories of visits to the famous Veeraswamy Indian restaurant in Regent Street and this can be linked to the keeping of the Hindustani/Urdu language learning books at home during his early childhood.

He realises he should have asked her more questions but they 'developed a habit of not talking about these things and I don't think either of us had the determination to break the habit. So I started trying to find answers to questions about my father but I did not discuss these things with my mother.'

The Elizabeth marriage appeared so inexplicable and outrageous when discovered by members of Wilson's existing family. Gordon and Nigel would understandably reference the hurt their father had inflicted on their mother and inevitably reflect on the duplicity of their father's behaviour. It challenged the integrity and security of everything that they could recall in the memory of their childhood.

They began to question the integrity of his love for them. Suddenly they would double-check what they remembered of the day their father was marrying Elizabeth at Ealing Registry Office or the day of Douglas's birth.

Dennis observed that there was something almost pathological in the repetitive pattern of his father's behaviour. Romancing, marrying and fathering only two miles' away from his life with Alison, Gordon and Nigel was so bold and reckless Dennis wondered if subconsciously his father sought discovery and exposure. At the same time, he also acknowledged that Elizabeth would have been somebody his father loved and committed himself to and in his own complicated way he would have been as fully committed as he could be as a husband and father.

The last ten years of Alexander Wilson's life are in a way perhaps his most mysterious. His youngest son Douglas was born in the midst of the enigma. Yet everything that he can accurately recall from the earliest years of his sentient consciousness suggests that Alexander and Elizabeth Wilson had been very much in love.

Elizabeth left absolutely no trace of malice, hatred, or anger about her relationship with Douglas's father. She had only positive and romantic memories and information that constituted something to be proud of. What teenager or young man would not be fascinated when picking up small snippets of information: 'My father knew Winston Churchill, my father knew Lord Mountbatten, my father knew T. E. Lawrence and had worked in India. I also remember brief references to going to cricket matches with sandwiches.'

In his adult life Douglas found himself treading coincidental paths that were in phase with the life of the father he never knew, an experience shared by many of the half-brothers he had no idea existed at that time: 'I was engaged in charity work and my base was New Delhi. I did a fair bit of travelling around in India and Pakistan and was in Lahore on three separate occasions.'

When his mother gave him the fake Repton document, her mood was relaxed but serious and slightly apologetic that she had kept some things from him. There was nothing to suggest that she doubted the Marlborough/Repton/ Chesney-Wilson/Indian Army identity. It seems extraordinary that Douglas should have been walking the streets of Lahore, the very city that had been the centre of his father's dramatic life in Imperial India for eight years.

The Reckoning

Douglas is the only surviving child of Alexander Wilson who does not have a direct memory of his father's presence. His identity was constructed for him by his mother, a woman who so loved her son she was determined that that identity would be something to be proud of. There was no dark cloud or moral indictment enduring from this relationship, which is certainly the case with his father's marriage to Dorothy and Alison.

If Elizabeth had covered up the hurt and devastation of discovering her husband's other life with Alison and her sons so near to her in Ealing, she did not leave this as a legacy of regret and lamentation. The secrets may not have been hers. They may well have been conjured by this enigmatic man who performed and lived another human partnership based on love and respect. This relationship was strong and successful enough to persuade another intelligent and professional woman to marry and have a child with him.

Her grandchildren are immensely proud of her for being such a strong independent woman in an age where that was less expected and done. Tamsin is sad for her about what happened in her twenties, but happy for her that she forged a good and happy life with her first son Douglas and her second husband and family: 'She was such an amazing woman in our lives.'

If her narrative with Alexander Wilson carries with it the consistency of deception and unfaithfulness, it also carries a consistency of love and commitment, albeit impossible to fully achieve in all the circumstances of her life with him.

Chapter Six

The Buddha of St James's

This is the story of a brilliant spy novelist desperate to become a spy himself and getting an intelligence officer's job at the heart of MI6 in London during the Second World War. How and why Britain's leading spy-masters were convinced that he could be more useful in the 'hush hush' business rather than messing stores and munitions from Avonmouth, which is what he was doing in the Great War, remains a mystery.

We do not even know how and why he began writing espionage novels when he was teaching in British India in the late 1920s. And once he joined the Secret Intelligence Service, he certainly did not live up to the feats of derring-do of his fictional Sir Leonard Wallace of the Secret Service. From 1928 to 1940 the one-armed, pipe-smoking, master of disguise had been pitted against the evil shenanigans of Nazi and Soviet agents, and the corrupt designs of international organised crime.

Instead Alexander Wilson spent most of the day putting on earphones in some shady top secret surveillance centre in the St James's area of London listening to Arabic, Persian and Hindustani. He was systematically bugging the diplomats and the London embassies of neutral and friendly countries. There is no doubt he was a popular figure. The war-time chief of MI6, Sir Stewart Menzies thought he had 'first rate linguistic abilities' and 'remarkable gifts as a writer' of fiction. In his work, he may well have been known to the Prime Minister Winston Churchill.

After three years in the service his reputation was so high colleagues affectionately called him 'Buddha.' This was owing to experience in India and penchant for wearing the uniform of a British Indian Army major. He had also met and married his third wife Alison who had been working in the same secret unit as a secretary. But then in the autumn of 1942 the police decided a burglary at his London flat was something he had faked perhaps to claim on the insurance. He was summarily dismissed. And then the fall from grace was compounded by an MI5 investigation that would claim the 'Buddha' of SIS also faked his reports on the telephone calls of the Egyptian Ambassador and his Embassy in London. He was condemned as 'a great public danger' and the consequences of what followed would be very harsh indeed.

On the face of it this is a rather strange story of a government intelligence agency being fooled by a charlatan into taking him on, and when perhaps he got bored listening to banal small talk he turned his telephone eavesdropping into something more dramatic than even the spy yarns he wrote. Perhaps he wanted to inflate his importance. The truth, however, is not so simple. Wilson's reports that the Egyptian Ambassador, Hassan Nachat Pasha, was up to no good now appear to be fully grounded. And the authorities are still not prepared to release a key MI5 report which might explain the single and sensitive source that destroyed Wilson's credibility, even though it is 75 years after the events in question.

My father the spook

Mike Shannon always knew his dad, Alexander Wilson, was a spook. In the spring of 1938 in the middle of *Anschluss*, Nazi Germany's annexation of Austria, his father took him to the imposing old German Embassy in Carlton House Terrace overlooking The Mall. There he was introduced to a tall German who spoke beautiful English. He recalled: 'My mother, Dorothy, told me afterwards that I had been introduced to Herr Von Ribbentrop, the German Ambassador. My father and Ribbentrop spoke in a different language, which I later realised was German. Later I saw a portrait of Ribbentrop. It might have been at the time of his trial at Nuremberg. But I recognised him as the man my father had met at the German Embassy.'

The young Mike Shannon was used to mysterious meetings with foreign gentlemen speaking in strange languages. He recalled being taken along with his parents to have High Tea at the Savoy Hotel around 1938 or 1939: 'There were waiters wearing white gloves. We were all dressed well and there was a Palm Court orchestra. There my parents were the guests of a short squat German in highly polished patent leather black shoes and smelling heavily of eau de cologne. He exchanged pleasantries with my mother in English but then my father and Herr Otto Tinisch broke into rapidly spoken German.'

Wilson's publisher Herbert Jenkins made their author's intelligence connections plain to everyone with their blurb for his volume of three novellas *Chronicles of the Secret Service* in 1940: 'Major Alexander Wilson probably knows as much about the Secret Service as any living novelist.' Surviving letters Wilson had sent to the War Office in the late 1930s exclaimed that he believed he could serve his country in the area of intelligence.

In his May 1939 application for the Officers' Emergency Reserve he emphasised he had previously offered his services to intelligence. In 1937, the year before the Munich crisis, he had a Churchillian premonition of the dangers to World peace and the menace of the increasingly militarized dictatorships taking over in Europe:

'The desire to serve the country is uppermost in my mind, however. What the work is, where I am sent, or in what capacity I am employed does not matter so long as I feel I am performing duties of use to Great Britain. Personally, I believe my greatest use would be found in some branch of Intelligence Work, but, as I have said, I am anxious to do anything that is of service.'

> Your obedient servant,
> A. Wilson.'

Wilson's connections with the intelligence world before the Second World War will remain entirely speculative until such time the British authorities are prepared to release the files. These may or may not be held on him at MI5, MI6, India Office, and Metropolitan Police Special Branch registries. From about 1927 he began writing popular espionage novels and conjured a fictional global British imperialist secret service headed by Sir Leonard Wallace. There is no explanation how this came about. Wallace and his officers and agents became an imaginative talisman for the power and prowess of British intelligence in the world long before Ian Fleming started writing his high octane James Bond entertainments.

The Sir Leonard Wallace character bears close resemblance to the first 'C' of MI6 Captain Sir Mansfield Smith-Cumming. Many of the plots in the nine volumes published between 1928 and 1940 materialise propaganda messages and genuine anxieties and concerns of the SIS of the time. For example, the novella 'China Doll' in *Chronicles of the Secret Service* (1940) specifically communicates the fear of Japanese intelligence penetration of all parts of the British Far East empire. It recognises the quality and threat of the Japanese military machine and predicts the debacle that would overtake Hong Kong, Malaya and Singapore. These messages were not anywhere to be found in mainstream media or indeed in any other fictional platforms.

Was there an intelligence hinterland?

Did Alexander Wilson have any intelligence role in British India? The most anyone can say is that any European member of the Raj convening the British Indian Army university officer cadet reserve in the only all Muslim college of the University of the Punjab is likely to have been a useful informer. He was just the kind of ears and eyes on the ground that would be needed by Indian Political Intelligence in London and the Indian Intelligence Bureau in New Delhi. This is particularly so when as Principal of Islamia College he was living in a city rocked by violent terrorist intrigue for independence. A deputy commissioner of police whom he knew personally and often socialised with was assassinated by terrorist gunmen without mercy. He toured the Punjab and North West Frontier on behalf of the Raj serving on commissions investigating inter-communal violence.

During the 1930s he would write most of his espionage novels. Was he spying himself? The evidence is highly circumstantial. The speculation perhaps as much a flight of the imagination as the plots of his spy fiction. Why was he meeting Ribbentrop at the German Embassy during the annexation of Austria? It seems absurd to think that Ribbentrop was a fan of the Wallace of the Secret Service series and wanted Wilson to autograph one of his books. The meeting took place when there were two factions in the Foreign Office fighting over what should be done about *Anschluss*. The diplomat Sir Alexander Cadogan shared with his Foreign Secretary, Lord Halifax, the appeasement line. The hawks headed by Sir Robert Vansittart, and an ally of Winston Churchill, believed German Nazi militarism needed to be challenged. Vansittart had his own network of patriotically motivated and unpaid agents gathering intelligence for him all over the world. Wilson's son Gordon remembered how shocked and physically affected his father was when he told him of Vansittart's death in 1957 after it had been announced on the radio. Is it possible that Wilson was one of Vansittart's informants? The only other trace of Wilson's potential intelligence gathering behaviour in the 1930s is a letter his second wife Dorothy wrote to the publisher Longmans in November 1936 that her husband was preparing for a trip to Spain after the outbreak of the Spanish Civil War: '...he is awfully busy, I know, preparing everything for his visit to Spain.'

Putting aside all speculation and what are palpably circumstantial strands of information, by October 1939 it is clear he would have been interviewed by the second 'C' Admiral Hugh Sinclair, security vetted, and joined Section X of SIS to use his many language skills to bug the phones of London diplomats. His career at the Foreign Office in this secret service work lasted three years until October 1942.

We know this for sure, because the Foreign and Commonwealth Office released a file to the National Archives in 2013 detailing 'The Case of the Egyptian Ambassador.' The file from 1943 discusses the problem of an SIS language expert who MI5 claimed had fabricated his 'special material' reports on bugged telephone calls. It is highly likely this intelligence officer was Alexander Wilson. In the process of condemning him the file provides fascinating detail of his career and time in the service.

That can be calibrated with the first part of Alison Wilson's memoir 'Before' that she wrote in 1986 and later revealed to her sons and granddaughter Ruth. One of the main attractions of the middle-aged linguist known as 'Buddha' to the 20-year-old Alison McKelvie, working as a secretary in a top secret unit of MI6 in

1940, was that he was a writer. She said he had got his nickname on account of his 'supposed wisdom' and presumably his background of knowledge and experience of India. Alison recalled: 'I learned that he was a major in the Indian Army [...] The languages he claimed were about five, including Arabic, Persian, Hindustani, and Chinese. [...] He had had several spy stories published, the Wallace books under his own name and others under more than one pseudonym.' Alison had later pointedly given Dennis her husband's four unpublished manuscripts in 1963, including the one he had written in longhand and completed in 1961.

The SIS unit Alexander Wilson and Alison McKelvie were operating in was linked to Station X at Bletchley. It targeted the phones of embassies and legations of neutral and friendly governments. Wilson or 'Buddha' did the eavesdropping and translating. Alison typed up the reports for the 'customers', who would be SIS, MI5, the War Cabinet, Military Intelligence, SOE (Special Operations Executive for sabotage and subversion in enemy and occupied territories), PWE (Political Warfare Executive for psychological warfare and deceptive propaganda) and any other arm of government engaged in the covert and overt global war that would blight their lives for the next 5 years.

Professor Keith Jeffery's official history of MI6 gave more background on Section X which had been set up in the mid-1930s and worked in close cooperation with MI5: 'Section X [...] successfully listened into conversations to and from, and within, a large number of foreign embassies. These are variously said to have included, prior to the outbreak of war, those of Germany, Spain, Italy, Japan and the USSR. This produced quite a large volume of political, economic and military information. Conversations, for example, between the German military attachés In London and Berlin appear to have been particularly revealing, and included 'details of a reconnaissance that the former was to carry out of possible landing beaches along the South and West coasts of Ireland.'

Proof of working for the Secret Intelligence Service

Alison placed the location of this listening unit somewhere in the St James's area of Westminster. It could have been in the Broadway buildings that remained SIS headquarters during the Second World War. MI5, or the Security Service had been moved to Wormwood Scrubs prison and then Blenheim Palace, the country estate of the Duke of Marlborough. Alison said she got the job as a result of 'a combination of the right contacts and the right strings being pulled.' This would have meant that her father or another close relation may have been involved in intelligence during the First World War. She would have been 'tapped on the shoulder' or specifically recommended by somebody within the secret world's circle of 'enlightened nepotism.' Alison kept a family

107

photograph of herself as a teenager among the garden deck-chairs at her family home in Whitehaven with her father and brother. On the back she had scribbled the names of Colonel Reynolds and Colonel Shane in Room 126 of the War Office at Millbank and the telephone numbers Victoria 9876, 5221 and 3767. Perhaps these were the contacts she had been given in 1940 for the vetting process and interviews preliminary to joining the Secret Service?

Alison gave her head of department a description that fitted the characterisation of Connie from John le Carré's novels about George Smiley and 'the Circus':

'The day came (1st April 1940) when, after being carefully vetted and having signed the Official Secrets Act, I went along to a well-known and seemingly banal branch of the F.O near St. James' Park, but which proved to be a camouflage for more intriguing activities. The head of the department, to which I was to belong was a very masculine woman. She was short, unattractive, very tubby, a chain smoker with heavily stained fingers who, when amused, chuckled rather than laughed, and who was, I am sure, very efficient at her job, having ten to fifteen men and three secretaries under her direct control. She took me up a narrow back staircase and, as we ascended, I had a strong sensation of walking towards my fate, which indeed was the case. At the top of the stairs we were confronted with a locked door, which she opened with her keys. On entering I saw that we were in what looked like a vast telephone exchange. A mechanic was working in an area where there were rows and rows of wires and plugs, whilst all-round the large room were men seated at desks, each wearing earphones, manipulating a receiving instrument on his desk and obviously taking down what he heard. [...] Each operator was an expert in several languages.'

Former Assistant Director General of MI5 Peter Wright would identify Millicent Bagot 'the legendary old spinster in F Branch who kept tabs on the International Communist Party for decades' as 'the model for John le Carré's ubiquitous Connie. She was slightly touched, but with an extraordinary memory for facts and files. Potter and his successors in the Registry despaired of Millicent. "I only hope we get the files back when she retires," he would mutter to himself after a particularly heavy file request from F Branch.' There is, in fact, no shortage of candidates for the mythical character of 'Connie' in the British intelligence world. A BBC *Timewatch* documentary on the early history of MI5 featured an interview with the femme formidable, Catherine Shackle, who had a long career in the Security Service between 1934 and 1963, and had a surname that was wholly appropriate for someone who served as head of MI5's Registry files. There was a hint of menace in her voice when she observed that she and her ladies were regarded as 'the lowest form of life'. She also paid homage to the first woman head of registry, Miss Lomax, the First Lady Superintendent, whose black and white portrait indicated she would be more than a match for Boris the Bolshevik or Fritz the Hun in a dark alley.

And Alexander Wilson himself had contributed to the characterisation of the formidable 'Connie of MI6' in his unpublished post Second World War novel *Out of the Land of Egypt*. It is clear he used his experiences at Broadway to found a new representation of the Secret Intelligence Service: 'He had then been introduced to Miss Venables [...]The Admiral had told him that the somewhat austere-looking lady was almost the corner stone of the department, and that, unlike two of the famous monkeys, she saw all and heard all, but, like the third, said nothing, adding: "Except to me, and she generally says far too much then. In fact, she bullies me, and I go in fear of my life, when she starts getting critical."

But Wilson's Miss Hilda Venables was a much more sympathetically drawn legend than either Alison's description of their respective MI6 line manager, or le Carré's tragic and predatory Connie. Wilson's new SIS chief Admiral Sir Brian Lease appears to be based on the second 'C' Admiral "Quex' Sir Hugh Sinclair who ran the service between 1923 and 1939 and is likely to have interviewed him in 1939. Hilda could have also been a blend of Sinclair's sister, Evelyn, who operated as an unofficial secretary/companion and housekeeper to the Chief at 23 Queen Anne's Gate. Wilson gave his character Hilda the ability to give out 'a disgusted cluck' and an encyclopaedic mind for filing useful information: 'There was nothing apparently she did not know about the Service and its personnel, and she was a goldmine of international information, with a photographic memory for faces and events. Her mind was as efficient as her filing system, and just as orderly. She had, it was reported, once been in love, but nobody seemed to know when or with whom, or why her little affair had not blossomed. But there was nothing of the sour embittered spinster about her. On occasion she could expand to a surprising degree, and friends who had the privilege of being invited to her well-ordered but cosy flat in Knightsbridge to tea or to the exclusive little dinner parties she gave, every now and then, spoke enthusiastically of her charm and flair as a hostess.'

This is very realistic writing by Wilson. There is a sense that in this unpublished fiction he was providing near mirror portraits of people he worked with and knew in MI6: 'She was tall for a woman, and rather angular; had once been good-looking, but, though she still retained evidence of comeliness, and her features were regular and attractive, her skin was now sallow and a trifle parchment-like, her eyes behind her glasses a faded blue, and her hair, which she wore drawn tight in a bun, an unattractive mousy grey. She was always well dressed, and favoured tailor-made suits which were made for her by a fashionable costumier, her shoes were hand-sewn, and her stockings the sheerest of sheer silk. She abominated nylons. Strangely enough, however, for such a neat person her umbrella, which she invariably carried, rain or shine, always looked untidy. It seemed that she had never mastered the art of rolling it, or rather them, as she possessed quite a collection.

Her office, as spick and span as herself – an example of pure, orderly efficiency – adjoined that of the Chief. His had no separate entrance and as, consequently, he had to pass through hers on his way in or out, she always knew when he was present. There was quite a spacious recess in one corner, hidden by a curtain. In that was a small electric stove, and a shelf containing cutlery and table ware. Daily she made coffee in the mornings and tea in the afternoons for herself and Sir Brian; occasionally cooked a meal there for him, when he was too busy to go out to his club, where he usually lunched. She was adamant in her insistence that he should never miss a meal, and, apart from her secretarial duties, kept a watchful eye on his comfort and well-being. But she was never obtrusive.'

Long before his rival and more successful spy writers Alexander Wilson was characterising, acknowledging and reporting a much more powerful and equal role for women in the espionage business. Hilda Venables is neither a mere secretarial cipher, nor a domestic slave or quasi work wife. Wilson's prose contains precise and corroborative detail of women figures in the real history of British intelligence whose intellectual and leadership abilities had made a significant contribution to the services, and combined with his positive representation of women front-line agents marks him out as a male spy author who was pioneering and long before his time.

The Secret Intelligence Service at Broadway during World War Two

While Alexander and Alison Wilson were working together in MI6 between 1940 and 1942 a new war-time Chief was in charge, Stewart Menzies, who had taken over after Admiral Sinclair's death in 1939. Nigel West's description of the war-time Broadway headquarters in *At Her Majesty's Secret Service* chimes with passages from Alison Wilson's private memoir: 'Although not a university man himself, Menzies placed no restrictions on assembling the hired help – they came from academia, Fleet Street and just about anywhere else where suitable skills might be found and harnessed. Christian names were preferred to military rank, and the informality of the pre-war era continued during the conflict, even if Menzies himself rarely ventured from his red-carpeted office on the fourth floor, into the maze of frosted-glass cubicles, corridors and flimsy partitions in which his subordinates worked on the fifth and sixth floors above. The club-like atmosphere was enhanced during the war years by the roster, applied to everyone, for fire-watch and night duties, which were performed either on the roof or in the basement bar where some staff preferred to spend the night during the air-raids. Regardless of rank or experience, SIS officers and their pretty secretaries met for pre-dinner and pre-theatre drinks in the bar, in preference to The Feathers across Broadway, and during the Blitz sometimes remained there until dawn.'

In his unpublished novel Wilson described his central character Gerald Graham, a major in the Coldstream Guards, stationed at Wellington Barracks, being interviewed by the Chief of the Secret Intelligence Service and engaged in induction training: '...he had been entertained to tea, during which Sir Brian had questioned him in a desultory sort of manner about his ambitions, his ideas, hobbies and leanings, his likes and dislikes, and even his inclinations for or against the other sex. But though the questioning appeared trivial and spasmodic, Graham realised he was being cleverly and systematically pumped. [...] ...and thus was Graham initiated into the secret world of the Intelligence Service, deep under Whitehall, where he met some of his future colleagues. There were monitoring rooms, decoding rooms, wireless rooms, containing the most intricate and powerful radio equipment Graham had ever seen, and rooms seemingly devoted to an endless variety of maps and international directories, guides and reference books. There was even a rest room, which was generally only used by men waiting for their instructions to go on some assignment or other. Those off duty preferred their homes or clubs, though the amenities there were good, and the whole place was thermostatically treated, the air atmosphere being as fresh as in the upper air.'

Wilson continued in a very evocative and detailed description of MI6 induction and training: 'Right away commenced the rigid course of training which it was imperative Graham should undergo, in order that he should become thoroughly conversant with all phases of Secret Service work. During the following two or three weeks, he learnt such a variety of things which had never before come within the orbit of his knowledge and understanding, that at times he felt confused, but always he proved an apt pupil. The subtlety of methods of judging character, anticipating the other fellow's reactions, thinking with the mind of an adversary were all part of his curriculum. He learnt to see without being seen, to hear without being heard, to walk on the most difficult surfaces without sound and was even given instructions in the art of tracking. Not the least of his experiences was training in the more brutal methods of defence to counteract brutal methods of attack. As he had undergone a course of commando training there was little additional he could add here to that which he already knew. It was impressed upon him that this part of his training was only, as his instructor put it, "in case." Men engaged in the sort of work he would be called upon to perform rarely meet trouble of the kind necessitating commando methods of attack or defence. Finally, he was shown how to recognise colleagues abroad whom he had never met, how to deal with contacts not a hundred per cent reliable without committing himself, and even the fundamentals of lip reading.'

This description resembles an account of real-life MI6 practice by the SIS official historian Professor Keith Jeffery: "The recruitment process continued in practice to involve a mixture of the informal and formal, as recalled by one officer who joined SIS in 1947. Having served in the Guards during the war, ending up with the rank of major, he had spent eighteen months in business before he started to investigate the possibilities of a career in the Foreign Service. Told by a friend "that a special department of the Foreign Office was looking for new entrants", he expressed interest and was approached by an individual who took him to lunch twice at his club, Boodle's in St James's Street, and quizzed him generally about his life and background.'

Wilson's depiction of the London SIS mess-room in *Out Of The Land Of Egypt* matches Professor Jeffery's description of the reality: '...from 1948, senior members of the Service could use 'the slightly more salubrious, waitress-served (and more expensive) facilities of the Broadway Club', which operated as a kind of senior common room within the headquarters building where colleagues could discuss Service business with comparative freedom. For younger officers a mark of favour was to be invited in the first instance to be an 'evening member' of the club, allowing them to meet their seniors informally over drinks.'

Wilson's espionage prose presents an ethos of professionalism and hard work. Kim Philby during his exile in Moscow recalled a dialogue between two Secret Servicemen indicating war-time needs meant the Secret Service had been recruiting too many 'doubtful sorts' from the wrong clubs about town:

'Leitch: "An amazing amount of crooks seem to have got into SOE, SIS and all those outfits during the war, don't you think?"

Veteran: "Well, have to take what you can get in wartime, don't you?"

Leitch: "They seem to have got most of these chaps out of the bar at White's, so far as one can see."

Veteran: "Yes, well you wouldn't find anything except crooks there, would you?"

Leitch: "Where were you recruited?"

Veteran: "Boodle's."

Intelligence products created by Alexander and Alison Wilson

Certain files at the National Archives give some idea of the kind of work engaged in by Alexander and Alison Wilson during the first few years of the Second World War. The bulletins emanating from their eavesdropping and surveillance operation would be known in the secret world as 'Special Material.' MI5 Deputy Director General Guy Liddell's diary would make many references to the kind of valuable intelligence. It was a rude breach of international treaties and diplomatic immunity.

This was a time of war and as Prime Minister Winston Churchill rather cynically put it: 'In wartime, truth is so precious that she should always be attended by a bodyguard of lies.' Sources prone to be somewhat critical of the intelligence services complain that MI6 and its decoding and deciphering evolution, GCHQ, have continued the spying on diplomatic communications in and out of London ever since; not even sparing its EU allies and 'Our American Cousins.'

The significance of this bugging was highlighted by Nigel West in his introduction to Volume 1 of *The Guy Liddell Diaries*: 'When referring to "special material" Liddell inadvertently reveals the countries, including France, Eire, Persia, Finland, Sweden and the Soviet Union, which were the subject of regular telephone monitoring. [...] Liddell's comments prove at least the telephone communications of certain embassies were recorded on a regular basis and circulated to senior intelligence officers. They were also an extraordinary daily commentary on what was truly happening behind even the most *sub rosa* of scenes. For example, on one occasion an SIS officer asked Liddell to record in his diary a prediction, to see if it would come to pass, and on another Liddell noted a request for a particular issue to be omitted from the official minutes of the meeting.'

Alexander and Alison Wilson's secret SIS telephone bugging unit was even engaged in eavesdropping on Vatican diplomacy as Guy Liddell's MI5 diary reveals in January 1940: 'Special Material has now been extended to cover the Papal Nuncio. It seems that he has been visited by the mysterious St. Clair Grondona who has been making the rounds of neutral embassies on what he describes as a semi-diplomatic mission.' Proof that US diplomats were being bugged as well is revealed by the entry for 18th May 1940: 'Stewart [Stewart Menzies- 'C' the WWII head of MI6] told me an amusing story which came up on Special Material. The Americans ordered 25 camp beds from Harrods, but as these were described as cots in America, 25 baby cots arrived at the embassy. An irate official told Harrods that he was talking from an embassy and not from a crèche.'

The entry in Liddell's diary for 20th May 1940 may have been a 'Special Material' bulletin translated and typed up by Alexander and Alison Wilson at SIS Broadway: 'The Latvian Minister has proposed to the Afghan Minister that they should go fishing. The Afghan Minister has invited the Chinese Ambassador to join them. The latter has accepted with pleasure, remarking that there is nothing like fishing for the deep contemplation and discussion of grave issues and events.'

A fuller explanation of how the SIS embassy bugging operation dovetailed with double-cross and active intelligence operations is very well illustrated in Liddell's MI5 diary entry for 10th October 1942. The objective was to mislead Fleet Street about 'Operation Torch'- the invasion of southern Italy: 'The Chiefs of Staff have been in consultation with the Ministry of Information and appear to think that the leakages in Fleet Street can best be dealt with either by talking to certain selected journalists and asking them to take a definite cover-story line or by taking the press fully into their confidence. Personally, I think that either line would be a mistake. As regards getting at leading journalists here, I suggested that this could better be done through embassies such as the Spanish and Turkish. The information would then leak back to journalists such as Poliakov, Litauer and Kuh. It was proposed that we should make a concerted attack on Alba and also on Orbay, the Turkish Minister. I think the line would be to start with two minor indiscretions by people who might be slightly in the know, and follow this up with a major indiscretion by somebody obviously in the know. Alba would be bound to report this to Madrid and the information would go direct to the Japanese and Germans. I thought it necessary, however, that whatever story went over it should be different to any of the previous cover stories.'

Liddell was outlining the classic intelligence deception strategy of 'boomerang'. For disinformation to reach your target, it needs to be spun to the outside and then to be received by your target as a journalistic or intelligence 'discovery.' The monitoring of Embassy communications via 'Special Material' would provide the necessary quality control assessment of the operation's success.

A few examples of embassy and legation intercepts from the Second World War have been released by GCHQ to the National Archives. These relate to the flurry of cables from London after the Luftwaffe's resumption of bombing in February 1944, which became known as the 'The Little Blitz'. They are marked with the highest classification of 'Most Secret'. These intercepts are likely to have been deciphered/decoded radio messages. Whilst references to diplomats having to find alternative accommodation after their buildings had been hit by high explosive would have been of mild intelligence interest, analysis by the

114

Iraqis, Saudi Arabians and Iranians of Jewish terrorism in Palestine and the British military response would have had greater value.

'MOST SECRET TO BE KEPT UNDER LOCK AND KEY: NEVER TO BE REMOVED FROM THE OFFICE: JEWISH TERRORIST ACTIVITY IN PALESTINE: REPORT FROM SAUDI CHARGE, LONDON. No. 128516

Date: 22nd February 1944

From: Saudi Arabian Chargé d'Affaires, LONDON

To: The King, Riyadh, Date: 19th February 1944 [Cable: and W/T: IID]

The air raids on ENGLAND last night were among the strongest and most ----- raids since the beginning of the war. There was much destruction but God was kind to us, and protected your Majesty's Legation with His care and attention while the Iraqi Legation suffered great damage.   The Jews in Palestine have begun a vigorous terrorist movement against British officials and have already killed three of them. Their papers in PALESTINE have begun to support the terrorist movement and to say It Is the only way to open the gates of PALESTINE to Jewish immigrants. Although the terrorist movement is strong and is directed against the English themselves, the papers here have not written a single word of comment on it.   YUSUF SALAMA

Director (2).F.O. (3).War Office (4).Colonial Office. Air Ministry.MI5.'

Alison and Alexander were in the front line of Britain's intelligence war when the country was on its own. Their service in this SIS unit was through the worst of times: the ill-fated invasion and retreat from Norway; the German invasion of Denmark, Holland, Belgium and France; the evacuation from Dunkirk; the Battle of Britain; the fall of Hong Kong and Singapore; defeat and ignominious retreat in Greece and Crete; the fall of Tobruk and Rommel's advances in North Africa.

Alison's use of the shorthand acronym 'S.S.' in 1940 coincided with the scribbling annotation on Alexander Wilson's War Office file. Her mention of signing the Official Secrets Act means that she must have known that when she wrote her memoir many years later she knew she was breaking it. Her reference to 'careful vetting' raises the question of the extent to which her future husband had been investigated prior to joining. Perhaps his vetting process would have been much more exhaustive. Wilson's references and qualifications for MI6 would surely have been carefully checked. He would have needed the support and validation of somebody whose word the Service trusted and respected. Alison talked about languages that Alexander 'claimed' he could speak and understand, but it would have been absurd for an intelligence officer to have been employed in such a unit for three years without genuine fluent and effective linguistic ability. In the translation field, the fraudulent and incompetent do not last long.

On the 17th of March 1940 Alexander Wilson wrote from Woodlands, Golders Green to his oldest son Adrian, a serving soldier in the Hampshire Regiment in Palestine. He was living there with his second wife Dorothy and six-year-old Michael: 'I have no time to write now, though I am feeling the urge badly. My job is not quite that of Wallace, but it is in the same line, and I am generally kept very busy.' Wilson's relations with Herbert Jenkins were by this time rather strained, which is evident in his remark: 'Jenkins still have some manuscripts of mine to publish. They are absolute outsiders, but Nemesis is approaching them. I am shortly going to get a lawyer to investigate.'

On the 19th May of that year the German blitzkrieg had stormed into France and Wilson wrote to Adrian: 'I intended writing to you last Sunday, but the invasion of Holland and Belgium came along to give me such a dose of hard, almost continuous work, that I have hardly had the time to eat or sleep since it started, let alone write letters. […] Still, I suppose I must try and accustom myself to the belief that I am doing something worthwhile, though my inclinations and feelings are not here but in Flanders. I have had the satisfaction of knowing that the hours upon hours of work without rest were a necessary, if tiny little part in the big job. It is a little bit soothing, that reflection. Still my inclinations are elsewhere. I suppose you have heard as much about the big battle as is allowed to filter out to the public here. At present the news is very vague. But I think that Hitler has made a big blunder. The pocket or bulge which the Germans have driven into the Allied lines may very possibly prove their doom and the end of all Hitler's hopes and dreams of World domination. We shall see by the first or second week of June.'

Dennis was amused that his father's assessment of the military situation demonstrated his usual excess of optimism and poor judgement.   However, some military historians have argued that the British tank action at Arras if supported strongly by the French, could have exploited the over-extended charge by General Guderian's panzers to the French coast.

A Dramatic Fall from Grace

Alison and Alexander Wilson were married and lived together for 22 years. Throughout that time Alison experienced a never-ending and agonising dilemma. Her love for the man she called 'Alec' meant she always wanted to believe his explanations for their extraordinary bad luck when it came to finances. She wanted to resist a growing sense of scepticism as the poverty became so increasingly humiliating. Her memoir charts a heart-breaking narrative of bewilderment. By the time of his death in 1963 she became convinced his tales of intelligence and continuing service in the Foreign Office were an absurd fantasy.

116

The long and downward spiral of disillusionment started after Gordon's birth in a private ward of the Lindo Wing of St Mary's Paddington in early 1942 and several weeks of puerperal fever and postnatal depression. They appeared well-off enough for her husband to make sure she was treated with the new life-saving antibiotics M & B. But her depression was not helped by the drug's unpleasant side effects. And then in 1942 her twenty-first birthday present of a beautifully graded pearl necklace, her diamond necklace wedding present, and large sapphire engagement ring surrounded by diamonds disappeared in a burglary along with other valuable heirlooms. This awful blow of losing these irreplaceable treasures coincided with a dramatic change in their everyday fortunes: 'About this time Alec was dismissed from the F.O. He explained it as a ruse to give an impression of discredit for S.S. [secret service] purposes.' As became clear long after her death, this grave duality of misfortune was no coincidence at all.

Alison found that their living accommodation deteriorated in direct proportion to their income: 'The Paddington boarding house was not as sleazy as one might expect. The occupants were a motley collection, including an R.A.F. officer and his wife, and a Pakistani doctor, with whom we sometimes played bridge in the evenings. Problems with the rent continued. I don't know where Alec got what little money there was. I understood that for some months the F.O. had continued to pay him, but by then that must have ceased.'

Chapter Seven

'A Great Public Danger?'

The Foreign Office file on the Egyptian Ambassador released to the public in 2013 makes clear that MI6 sacked Alexander Wilson in October 1942 because the police had investigated him for faking a burglary. But it went much further than that. FO1093/263 'Case of the Egyptian Ambassador' explains that subsequent to his leaving, MI5 concluded that Wilson's embroidering of his interpretation of telephone calls by the Egyptian Ambassador and others had led to them wasting their time investigating a fictitious espionage group. It is presumed the Egyptians were spying for Nazi Germany (though this is not explicitly stated) in return for independence should Great Britain and its Empire lose the North African campaign. There are six key authors for the documents contained in the file.

'C' of the Secret Intelligence Service (MI6) Sir Stewart Menzies. He was the third chief from 1939 to 1952. As we know, Wilson had been recruited and most likely interviewed by Sir Hugh 'Quex' Sinclair, the second Chief of SIS from September 1923 to November 1939.

There is reference to 'Kellar' as the author of the MI5 report [not included in the file]. Kellar is Alex Kellar described by MI5 historian Professor Christopher Andrew as 'flamboyant, thought to be the inspiration for the "man in cream cuffs" in John le Carré's *Call for the Dead,* played in the film by Max Adrian wearing a dragon-patterned silk dressing gown with a purple handkerchief and a rose in his buttonhole. In the summer of 1947 he suffered a breakdown after being diagnosed with suspected amoebic dysentery and returned to London.' Andrew also refers to Kellar's 'rather camp manner.' Kellar carried on his career as a very senior MI5 officer in the E Branch- overseas intelligence in the colonies and finished his career as Director of E Branch [wound up in 1971]. He was active in East Africa, but mainly in Kenya (anti Mau Mau operations).

Sir David Petrie was Director General of the Security Service MI5 from 1941 to 1946 during the Second World War. Petrie (1879–1961) worked in the Indian Police from 1900-1936, serving in a variety of police intelligence roles. He headed the Delhi Intelligence Bureau of the Indian Police and served as the Chairman of the Indian Public Service Commission until 1936. He joined the

Army Intelligence Corps after the outbreak of the Second World War. In other words he was very much 'an old India hand.' Professor Andrew said Petrie was 'an outsider' and had to deal with 'the Service's difficulty in responding to all the demands made on it, poor morale and lack of leadership.' He used the military title 'Brigadier.'

Sir Alexander Cadogan was the Permanent Under-Secretary of State at the Foreign Office (the top civil servant) throughout the Second World War. He had succeeded Sir Robert Vansittart in 1938 and served in this role until 1946. Vansittart had a without portfolio role of 'Diplomatic Advisor' only until 1941. Cadogan and Vansittart were usually at daggers' drawn.

Peter N. Loxley was another senior civil servant in the Foreign Office (Cadogan's private secretary.) It is worth mentioning that there was a bitter turf war between MI5, MI6 and the later SOE during the Second World War. SIS was subject to considerable pressure, criticism and attack over the quality of its intelligence, and reasons for having officers and infrastructures in places that MI5 and SOE thought were theirs.

Patrick Reilly was 'C''s personal assistant between 1942 and the end of 1943 based at Broadway Buildings in Menzies' office.

Essentially the issue in this report is that MI5 said they wasted their time investigating an espionage operation supposedly directed by the Egyptian Ambassador in London and a network of his agents from his staff which did not exist. The problem is defined as a result of the invention/fabrication by Wilson when listening to telephone communications in and out of the Embassy. Wilson is the person taking all the blame. Petrie, Cadogan and Loxley are very angry (not quite apoplectic) and want revenge on him in terms of his never being employed in any official position again without the sternest warnings (i.e. negative references to any future employer). One gets the impression Wilson's boss, Stewart Menzies, actually liked him and he defends him as well as acknowledging what can be described as the margin of appreciation and interpretation when live translating (without electronic recording) of telephone conversations.

Cadogan says: 'I am sorry that your people (MI5) should have been put to such trouble in killing this wild goose.' There is a fascinating additional piece of longhand by Cadogan to the left of page 3 'I put this by mistake in box for SofS! I have explained the case to him, and he doesn't want to see the report.' This means that the whole affair and Wilson's involvement was read by Sir Anthony Eden, Foreign Secretary between 1940 and 1945.

Loxley added: 'We should be indeed unlucky to run up against another such master of fiction as Wilson. Cadogan would, incidentally, be glad to know what

Wilson is doing now, and whether he is employed in any official job. If so it would seem desirable to warn those concerned of his utter unreliability.'

Reilly replies: ' "C" has asked me to thank you for your letter of the 30th June about Alexander Wilson and his invented telephone conversations. Wilson has no official employment now, and "C" thinks it very unlikely that he will get any. If he did, those concerned would certainly be warned about him.' Cadogan in longhand on the letter from MI5 DG Petrie adds: 'An astonishing story. And 'S/S [Secretary of State] wishes to read at weekend.' Cadogan also scribbles in longhand on the letter from "C" to DG of MI5 Petrie: 'We shall, be indeed unlucky to run up against another such master of fiction as Wilson.' On the letter from Petrie he adds in longhand: 'An astonishing story. (Incidentally it is a very good piece of work and well written).'

Petrie's covering letter for the report to Cadogan makes a number of key points. The alleged activities of the Egyptian Ambassador had been 'exercising our minds since the early days of the war.' The investigation by Kellar was 'careful and delicate,' and the Ambassador's activities and his 'reputed agents' have 'been pure fiction.' The fact Wilson left SIS last October (42) 'is perhaps some small compensation for the amount of trouble to which his inventive mind has put us all. A fabricator, such as this man was, is a great public danger.' Kellar's report contains information of mainly political interest and Petrie implies the point that they, meaning MI5, can be more helpful on such matters than SIS: 'If you should wish to make any use of it, I know you will bear in mind the very delicate source from which it has been derived.' In other words Kellar's denunciation of Wilson may be on the basis of only one source.

'C' 's apology to Petrie, the Director-General of MI5 is three pages in length and very detailed. He says he feels 'bound to accept the conclusions' in Kellar's report that the Egyptian Ambassador's intelligence activities and his agents circulated to all SIS clients in 'Special Material' 'have in fact been pure fiction.' Alexander Wilson is named as the only officer who recorded and translated these allegations. 'This officer joined my organization in October 1939. He was of course vetted in the usual way. He was taken on as an interpreter of Hindustani, Persian and Arabic, and he passed the usual tests. Another officer of the Section concerned, who was an examiner of Hindustani, Persian and Arabic and who sat next to him for some time, said that Wilson was the finest natural interpreter he had met.'

Wilson was not dismissed for incompetence or deception in his work but because 'He was found to have staged a fake burglary in his flat. He had subsequently been in further serious trouble with the police'.

It could be argued that 'C' is doing his best to be fair about Wilson but goes along with MI5's wish to have him tarred as the inventor and fabricator: 'Wilson had previously been a professional writer of fiction. When some of his reports were questioned, toward the end of his service here, the possibility that he was embroidering on what he heard was taken into account and he was given a very serious warning that he was not to report what he thought was meant in the Egyptian conversations but to keep to the literal translation of the words used. From this time all his reports were carefully scrutinized, and he was questioned consistently to ascertain if he was sure his interpretation was accurate. On no occasion would he admit any doubt. Another officer, who sat next to him listened in to the Egyptian conversations on several occasions, but heard nothing that was not reported substantially correctly. While, therefore, we must admit that a great deal of what Wilson recorded was pure invention (though I think it probable that in many cases he did no more than embroider on what he actually heard), I do not think that we can hold ourselves to blame for not having discovered earlier what was happening.'

Menzies talks about Section X having '230 separate lines on the boards. Three-quarters of the calls are purely social ones or calls between servants, which are of no interest to anyone.' He said they did not have enough recording machines for every line. There may be some kind of admiring back-handed compliment from 'C' when he says: 'I do not think it at all likely that we shall again have the bad luck to strike a man who combines a blameless record, first rate linguistic abilities, remarkable gifts as a writer of fiction, and no sense of responsibility in using them!'

He says his staff's 'nerves are naturally strained by the very nature of their work. Wilson is the only person against whom there had been the 'slightest suspicion of having faked or written up reports. In general, I think we can claim that an extremely difficult and trying job has been consistently carried out with meticulous attention to the accuracy of the reports.' And the letter is signed famously in green ink 'C'.

It is rather unlikely that Wilson would have had any employment in any form by any Great British intelligence agency after this investigation, report and conclusion. The lack of a reference and indeed determination that people should be warned about his unreliability might account for his difficulties getting any kind of professional or official employment during the rest of the Second World War, reverting to the uniform and decorations he was not entitled to wear, and going to the Authors' Club whose membership fee was paid out of the kindness of his oldest son Adrian in 1944.

This report may also account for the destruction of his career as a published author as MI6 and MI5 could well have briefed against him to Herbert Jenkins and all the other main publishing houses. Wilson, despite his significant success and literary talent, and completed manuscripts was never published again. *Out of the Land of Egypt* fictionalizes Nazi, Gestapo and SS connections to Egypt as a refuge for an Odessa organization style sanctuary. He refers to Egyptian collaboration with Nazi missile scientists and speculates that Hitler is alive and well in post war Egypt, which at the time was a credible rumour encouraged by the Soviet Union. Despite its anti-Semitism and racist depiction of Arab stereotypes, it is a stunning novel for its time and it is astonishing it was never published.

Petrie makes no reference at all to any previous knowledge of Wilson, which for somebody having such a huge role in the Indian Police, suggests Wilson had no contact or involvement with the Indian Intelligence Bureau in Delhi or Indian Political Intelligence in London. If he had been informing as an agent in his role at Islamia College, it would be very unlikely Petrie was unaware of this. Petrie wrote the seminal Indian Civil Service book on communism in India. The affairs and events in the Punjab would have been on his radar in Delhi. But on the other hand, it would not be in Petrie's interests to reveal such knowledge, particularly if Wilson had rendered good service. MI5 were seeking to discredit him utterly (for justifiable reasons if the evidence is credible) and embarrass MI6.

The lack of concern or interest in the position of Alison and her children shows the cruel hand of an unforgiving bureaucracy that will always exploit a convenient scapegoat. It would not have crossed the minds of these men how in making it very difficult for Alexander Wilson to earn a living, they were plunging his family into the depths of desperate poverty and hardship in a war-time society with very limited welfare provision. It is understandable why he began borrowing from money lenders in the East End of London that led to his bankruptcy at the end of 1943. There may even have been a disturbing coincidence in Wilson's dismissal from SIS in October 1942 being the very time that the Battle of El Alamein was taking place, and the cruel deception played on Mike as a 9-year-old boy that his father had been killed in action during that very battle.

Evidence supporting Alexander Wilson's reports on the Egyptian Ambassador

Alex Kellar's report may be inaccurate and wrong on the basis of other files released into the public domain and available at the Public Record Office. There are files which demonstrate that the Egyptian Ambassador, Hassan Nachat Pasha, was intelligence gathering with his staff in establishing contacts and obtaining information from the Ministry of Information, discussing post war alignment with the Soviet Union's Ambassador in London, and obtaining information from foreign correspondents based in London about the Allied leaders' war conference in Casablanca.

One file demonstrates that in the early part of 1944 Nachat [in documents his identifying name is presented as 'Nashat'] was recalled to Cairo and in only a matter of weeks was plotting an overthrow of the pro-British (described as Anglo-maniacal) regime. The British ambassador in Cairo, Sir Miles Lampson, (later Baron Killearn) sent to Sir Alexander Cadogan intelligence reports of Nachat's mischief and urged Cadogan to engineer Nachat's recall to London: 'Nachat is being a political nuisance and his early return to London would be a blessing'.

Killearn reported Nachat's intention 'eventually to become Prime Minister'. He observed: 'It will be remembered how effectively in 1925 Nachat organised the absolutist regime for King Fouad not only against the Wafd but against the Liberals and democratic independents. It was only our intervention which brought about the removal of Nachat, and the end of his attempt to establish Palace rule in the country'.

Hassan Nachat Pasha had been described as Egypt's Rasputin in the 1920s and was strongly associated with Anti-British imperial political elements. He was Egyptian Ambassador in Berlin for 10 years before taking up the post in London in 1938. He was said to have had an affair with a German Princess, entertained the Nazi elite lavishly, and although diplomatically polite and courteous to the British when in London, part of an Egyptian elite that hoped for Axis Power victory and allied defeat in North Africa.

A secret declassified FO file indicates his counterpart in Tehran, Zulficar Pasha, was in secret negotiations and intelligence gathering for Nazi Germany. A United Nations file in 1948 reveals German intelligence and Foreign Office files proving the Egyptian diplomatic service was playing a double game with the British even after the defeat of Rommel at El Alamein in 1942. Plans were discussed to smuggle King Farouk into exile in Berlin; and bomb Tel Aviv. Hitler and Ribbentrop exchanged secret overtures of support and hopes for British defeat in Egypt with King Farouk's governments and diplomats.

Major AW Sansom of Egyptian field security in Cairo published his memoirs in 1965 and stated that the majority of the Egyptian elite and armed forces were pro German and Italian; actively working against the British. Prior to 1942 'Under an almost openly pro-German Prime Minister Aly Maher Pasha, for nine months the Egyptian government gave our enemies all the aid it possibly could'. Egyptian forces had to be withdrawn from Allied operations in the desert in 1940 on the order of Winston Churchill because they were known to be reluctant to fight for their effective military occupiers.

At the end of 1940 General Sir Henry Maitland Wilson, examining papers captured in the Italian HQ in Libya, was surprised to find a complete set of British plans for the defence of the Western Desert. They had been supplied by Egyptian Army Chief of Staff, General Aziz el Masri. Sansom described forcing a plane carrying General Aziz el Masri to crash land on take-off in 1942. It was being flown by Egyptian Air Force Squadron Leader Hussein Zulficar Sabri to Rommell's headquarters. There was a plan to establish a 'Free Egyptian Army' on German occupied territory. The Germans had been in contact for the previous two months and this was his third attempt to escape after previous attempts by U-boat and German plane disguised with RAF markings. The British forced King Farouk to dissolve a pro-Axis power government in 1942 by surrounding his palace with tanks and deposing the Prime Minister, to be replaced with pro-British Egyptian politicians.

Did the Egyptians fake their London spy-ring as counter-intelligence?

It Is entirely conceivable that Alex Kellar's investigation and conclusion could have been wholly legitimate and Alexander Wilson's 'Special Material' reports had also been entirely accurate. Hassan Nachat Pasha was a veteran diplomat with ten years' experience of serving in his country's embassy in Nazi Germany. It does not appear to have occurred to either MI5 or MI6 that an Egyptian patriot seeking proper independence for his country from the oppressive imperialist control of Great Britain would have surely suspected the British were listening to his telephone calls. It is a classic counter-surveillance and intelligence technique to generate false information and anticipated actions and activities to flush out the malign attentions of British intelligence. Hassan Nachat Pasha and his staff may well have been the inventor of what Sir Alexander Cadogan described as 'the wild goose' that put the MI5 people to so much trouble. It was classic decoy and chaff on the part of the Egyptians.

It could be argued that the Egyptians were perfectly entitled to play whatever double game was needed to achieve an understandable aim of wresting themselves from the influence and control of the British Empire. A large swathe of their territory and their biggest geographical asset, the Suez Canal, were effectively occupied and owned by the British and the French. For the first three years of the Second World War, Nachat was diplomat to a country that had been losing every battle to the Axis forces.

It was not easy being in a city hammered during the blitz by the German Luftwaffe. His embassy, Bute House, in South Audley Street, Mayfair, took a direct hit on 28th December 1940, killing a British telephone operator, a maid, the longstanding butler, and injuring many of his Egyptian staff. The diplomatic legation evacuated to the Dorchester Hotel next door until returning to the fully restored building in February 1942. Throughout Nachat's tenure he had a reputation for living and entertaining ostentatiously. He and his entourage defied war-time rationing and shortages with lavish parties and he was known as 'the grand seigneur' about town. He was chauffeured around London in top of the range Mercedes and American Studebaker limousines. He was also courting a British Royal connection. He would eventually marry the Australian-born Patricia May Marsh in what was regarded as the Society Wedding of the year on 24th October 1944, which coincidentally was Alexander Wilson's birthday. She was thirty-two years his junior and niece to General Robert Priest, Queen Elizabeth's doctor.

Whatever was being said when his calls on Grosvenor 4641 and 4642 were being bugged by Alexander Wilson, Nachat was busy investigating the twists and turns of world affairs and how this affected short and long-term Egyptian interests. His intelligence was sophisticated and well sourced. On 1st February 1943 Bletchley Park intercepted a coded radio message to the Minister for Foreign Affairs in Cairo that Nachat had picked up from Russian and American correspondents in London that Allied chiefs had examined a German peace proposal via the Papal envoy at the Casablanca conference offering an alliance against Soviet Bolshevism in return for the maintenance of German frontiers as they stood in 1939. Nachat sent another cable to Cairo on the 16th February 1943 describing an overture from the Russian ambassador in London for Egypt to diplomatically align with the Soviet Union and China. Sir Alexander Cadogan briefly noted in handwriting that Nachat's cable contained 'a bad remark.'

When the British Ambassador in Cairo, Sir Miles Lampson, cabled Cadogan in early 1944 to urgently expedite Nachat's early recall to London, he emphasised his suspicion that : '...Nachat is banking to a considerable extent on his high stock at home in England; and in anticipation of getting good solid backing from many influential quarters there.' Cadogan was very defensive in his reply: 'Nachat has not influential support here of which we are aware; and suggestions which he may make to the contrary will be largely bluff.'

MI5 and MI6 may have foolishly decided that as Alexander Wilson's character had been called into question with the fake burglary allegation, his special talent for imaginative story-telling as a novelist somehow qualified him for 'embroidering' the banality of everyday chitchat to and from the Egyptian Embassy with a new spy novel he did not have time to write for Herbert Jenkins. The correspondence between Cadogan, Petrie and 'C' suggests that the

Alexander Wilson case gave them as much amusement as consternation. They seemed to be competing with each other to coin the *bon mot* that defined the unfortunate narrative. Phrases such as 'wild goose', 'master of fiction' and 'great public danger' pepper the correspondence. In the light of long-term history if there is any mirth to be gained from this affair, the Egyptians had reason to be the most amused. And they would continue getting the better of the British in matters of intelligence as the events of Suez 13 years later were to prove.

It could be argued that there has been a racist presumption at play here that the Egyptians were so inferior that nobody at MI5 or MI6 could have conceived it possible that they had used their imagination and guile so creatively and cleverly to deceive the British and waste their time and resources.

The legend of the fabricated network, is, in any case, a time-honoured operational performance genre in espionage. The British 'Ace of Spies' Sidney Reilly was successfully lured back into Russia in 1925 by Felix Dzerzhinsky's Soviet secret service, the OGPU. They had conjured a fake anti-Bolshevist front organisation called 'The Trust'. Once over the Finnish border Reilly was arrested, interrogated and executed.

There is also the celebrated MI5 D-Day deception operation involving Agent Garbo, whose real name was Juan Pujol. Pujol was a Spanish businessman expert at creating a fake network of German agents operating in Britain and who radioed his reports by Morse code to the Abwehr and helped convince Hitler's intelligence establishment that the allied landings in June 1944 would be in the Pas de Calais and not Normandy.

Graham Greene's most celebrated spy novel, *Our Man In Havana,* is entirely based on mocking the inherent risks and consequences of fabricating spy networks and not realising the subterfuge. The successful film version made in 1959 had Alec Guinness starring as the vacuum cleaner retailer James Wormold, and Noel Coward cast as the MI6 case officer Hawthorne seeking to employ his services. Wormold needs money to pay for his daughter's education and his dalliance with the murky world of British Intelligence leads him to fabricate a network of agents based on people he knows in the Cuban Capital. The comedy turns macabre when unpleasant things start to happen to his agents, including assassination.

Greene had been inspired while working as an MI6 case officer in the Iberian Peninsula during the Second World War and learning that German agents in Portugal were sending back to the Abwehr fictitious reports based on fake networks of informants, which garnered them expenses and bonuses to add to their basic salary.

It is also possible that Alexander Wilson did have an intrinsic inability to delineate aspects of fiction and fact when working in the real world of intelligence. A mind so tuned to brilliant espionage story-telling may have been prone to 'filling the gaps' in fast telephonic dialogue heard in his non-native language of Arabic. And it is a bitter-sweet irony that while the imaginative guessing was proven mere fantasy when subjected to the objective correlative of MI5's investigation, the Egyptian Ambassador and his staff were still intelligence gathering against Great Britain's interests in the different ways elucidated by the other files now available in the National Archives.

The Alex Kellar MI5 report from 1943 that alleged Wilson fabricated his phone tapping reports is being withheld for 'security sensitivity.' This decision has been challenged seven times at the Foreign and Commonwealth Office, the Information Commissioner, the Information Tribunal and a separate appeal to the Foreign Secretary using Parliamentary channels. Kellar based his devastating indictment against Wilson on the word of 'one delicate source.' Why are the intelligence agencies holding this information back when like with the Egyptian Ambassador file they could easily redact identities?

The Security Service, MI5, who debunked and discredited Wilson's work, relied on the Soviet spy Anthony Blunt for penetration agents at the Egyptian Embassy. Thus, the accuracy and reliability of phone intercepts could be measured against the observations and information obtained by Security Service agents gathering human intelligence. They included the ambassador's chauffeur and Lady Dalrymple-Champneys, wife of Sir Weldon Dalrymple-Champneys, who was permanent under-secretary at the Ministry of Health.

Perhaps MI5 and MI6 would not be so content if they had known that Blunt was telling his Soviet controller in Moscow that Lady Dalrymple-Champneys '... is useful only in one way, namely through her contact with the Egyptian Ambassador, but she is only able to get gossip from him. She moves in a circle where she also meets a number of undesirable people, like Prince Letislan, men such as Busch and also Queen Geraldine of Albania. In general, however, she is not useful'.

There was nothing sacrosanct about the 'diplomatic bag' being secretly plundered by British intelligence. It is possible Anthony Blunt was also aware of the contents of the Egyptian ambassador's diplomatic bag going to and from his government's foreign ministry in Cairo. We know this because the translation from Russian of analysis and files passed to the NKVD/KGB during World War II by Anthony Blunt when he held a senior position in MI5 revealed the existence of an operation called 'Triplex'. Nigel West and Oleg Tsarev wrote in their 2009 book *Triplex: Secrets from the Cambridge Spies*: 'Triplex was, and remains, one of the most closely guarded secrets of the Second World War. No reference to it has ever been published, and the official multi-volume history *British Intelligence in the Second World War* contains absolutely no mention of this source, which is still highly classified in Britain. Ironically, the only documents to describe the source are to be found in Moscow, where they were sent by Anthony Blunt, one of the very few Security Service (MI5) officers entrusted with the task of supervising the XXX (TRIPLEX) operation and distributing the intelligence product: material extracted illegally from the diplomatic bags of neutral missions in London.'

What is being covered up?

The surviving children of Alexander Wilson have fully supported a Freedom of Information Act battle to have the Kellar report released. It was rejected by the Information Tribunal (first tier) in 2016, and even after the Foreign Office agreed to carry out another sensitivity review when the matter was raised in Parliament in 2018, the decision to keep it under wraps 75 years later endures. The refusal is altogether perplexing when the Information Tribunal observed in their ruling: 'The report was written during the Second World War. Ordinarily, as Professor Crook indicates, it might have been expected that the report would have been transferred to Kew. It is, however, plain that this has not occurred. Having regard to the age and subject matter of the information, we are puzzled by this fact.'

Nigel Wilson says: 'The refusal to disclose has caused enough suffering. Where is the fairness or justice in a partial disclosure of Kellar's report but a continuing refusal to tell the other side of the story? What is being hidden more than 70 years after the events in question? All we want is the truth, if truth can ever be revealed in the murky world of intelligence. As things stand our father has been left in a FOI limbo, as unreliable and a public danger. I think he was better than that, but if the files are released and prove otherwise, so be it. That would be a better conclusion than the current stench of concealment.'

His brother Gordon argues: 'The indications are that my father was unjustifiably discredited for his reports, described by a superior as 'fabricated', on the pro-Nazi activities of the Egyptian ambassador in order to protect the reputation of a British individual. If this were indeed so, the presently redacted files would reveal the extent of the miscarriage of justice, since subsequent events seem to have brought to light documentary evidence that the Egyptian ambassador in question did indeed have links to the Nazi regime'.

Gordon and his brother Nigel have powerful reasons for demanding access to papers and files that can bring clearer understanding about how and why their father was cashiered and condemned as a 'great public danger' by the intelligence world. The Egyptian Ambassador's file reveals a high level government plot to ruin Wilson and stay on his back. Perhaps it is no coincidence that after being cast adrift as a public menace, Wilson's career as a published novelist came to an inexplicable end. A man who had been a successful Professor of English literature, with three prestigious academic publications and Principal of a university college in Lahore, who rescued it from the academic and sporting doldrums, who could speak several languages, became virtually unemployable.

A patriot always bursting to do his duty wandered about London, borrowing from friends and money lenders, who in today's parlance could be called loan sharks, and masking his shame with the costume of a British army lieutenant-colonel's uniform and decorations he wishes he could have had the chance of winning. It was a pathetic picture. There is evidence the eyes of MI5 and Special Branch may also have been on him.

As he would tell the Stipendiary Magistrate at the Marylebone Police Court it was foolish vanity that made him do it. He was desperate to be allowed back into uniform and to do his bit for his country. The court heard the police had been following him for some time, perhaps as long as six months; a somewhat excessive surveillance operation for a case where there was no evidence at all of the uniform and medals' performance being put on for the purpose of fraud.

So many facts in this case throw up contradictions and paradoxes. The third 'C' of MI6 talks about Wilson being dismissed from the Secret Service for a fake burglary at his flat in Hampstead. But his third wife Alison, who lost all her precious family heirlooms and treasured jewellery in the raid, makes no mention at all of any such suspicions that her husband was responsible, or that the police gave her any indication that it was other than a burglary by somebody else. Sir Stewart Menzies says that Wilson was in serious trouble with the police in 1943, but there has been no other reference to this, particularly in newspaper reports of his two subsequent trials for the uniform matter in 1944 and theft from a cinema in 1948.

How could Alec have been investigated by the police for the fake burglary without his wife Alison having any idea about the inquiry? It is fairly obvious that Wilson would have needed a substantial amount of money to pay for Alison's medical treatment, the use of pioneering, expensive, and life-saving new antibiotics six years before the National Health Service. It makes sense that pawning or selling the jewellery was the quickest way of raising these funds. Faking the burglary by calling in the police would mean that Alec did not have to take the blame for disposing of Alison's precious heirlooms without her permission.

If he tried to claim on any insurance, suspicious loss adjustors could well have called in the police. It is entirely plausible to imagine a deal worked out between MI6, the police and insurers. The Spooks would have wanted the embarrassing affair kept well under wraps and out of the courts. The police would have been content for any money Wilson obtained fraudulently to be paid back and the knowledge he was going to be sacked. MI6 would certainly not want him working for them anymore and Wilson could have squared an assurance that nobody would tell Alison that it was her husband who had been the Raffles in this part of Hampstead. If there was no insurance claim, then it was a virtually victimless crime. Wilson had been selling their jewellery to save Alison's life. He had fabricated the 'burglary' and called the police to simply cover up the fact he was not earning enough money to pay for the antibiotics.

It is equally possible that Wilson had absolutely no idea about Alex Kellar's MI5 investigation into his phone intercepts and the accusation he had been making up his phone-tapping transcripts. He was long gone from SIS by the time Kellar's 'Case of the Egyptian Ambassador' report landed on the desks of the chiefs at MI5 and MI6. There is no evidence in the report that he had any chance to defend himself, put his point of view, or challenge the truth and reliability of the unknown 'delicate source' and Kellar's analysis and conclusions. It is quite conceivable that Kellar had not spoken to Wilson about the alleged fabrication at all. Why would he need to?

What a sad and tragic vista this must have been. A middle-aged patriot tramping the streets of London looking for employment, calling on publishers' offices with increasingly dog-eared manuscripts of unpublished and rejected novels, and completely oblivious to the fact that the country's security establishment had branded him a very great public danger. Even worse, MI6, MI5 and the Foreign Office had instigated a plot to make sure he never got any kind of official work again and this insidious hounding may have extended into the publishing world and beyond. The poverty and destitution for Wilson and his young family in War-time and immediate post-War London begins to make sense. It is extraordinary that a famous and previously successful author, fluent in several languages, a former successful Principal of a University College, rewarded with a University Fellowship for his service, a former Professor of English Literature, and newspaper editor could not get any work at all.

Paradoxes and ambiguities

The Egyptian Ambassador's file states Wilson was dismissed by SIS in 1942, yet the bankruptcy directory *Stubbs Weekly* for February 1944, some sixteen months later, stated categorically that he was still 'temporarily employed in a government Dept.' When he was prosecuted for falsely wearing a lieutenant-colonel's uniform and decorations such as the D.S.O., D.S.C., and Croix de

Guerre in October 1944, he was not prosecuted for his wearing of the full-set of medals for service in the Great War. Yet, his War Office records categorically declared he was not entitled to wear any of the First World War medals because he had not been posted overseas.

Even more perplexing is the fact the prosecution told the Marylebone Police court he was entitled to wear the First World War medals. Wilson told Alison that his arrest, prosecution and jailing were all part of an intelligence operation. In the light of the Egyptian Ambassador's file, this explanation seems risible. Yet, there is something not quite credible about the false uniform and medals prosecution.

His son Gordon, who had a long and successful career in the Royal Navy, reaching the rank of Captain, has not been able to make head or tail of the uniform and medals fiasco. The D.S.C. was a naval only decoration and it seemed absurd that as an army man he would ever have worn that during the Second World War. Equally confounding is the fact that on the basis of the picture of him in Lieutenant Colonel's uniform, he has the false ribbons sewn on in the wrong order. It was as though he were performing and wearing a costume for an audience that could not tell the difference.

He went to Brixton prison because he said he was unable to pay the fine of £10 and so he would serve two months in the alternative. Alison's memoir indicates he was released after four to six weeks imprisonment for good behaviour. He received his sentence on 9th October 1944, after seven days in custody on remand. He was expecting to meet his sons Adrian and Dennis at the Authors' Club on the 16th October. They did not turn up because they did not want the awkwardness of discussing his court appearance. Adrian received a letter from him on Authors' Club letter-headed paper from 2 Whitehall Court dated Monday 30th October 1944 which would just coincide with his release after serving four weeks in Brixton jail. But if he had been in prison for six weeks, how could he have sent the letter from the Authors' Club?

It seems somewhat incongruous that on the day he gained his freedom he would go to the Authors' Club to write letters rather than return to his home with heavily pregnant Alison and infant Gordon. Equally perplexing is the fact that despite the existence of many letters he wrote on Authors' Club letter-head, his sons Dennis, Adrian, and Michael having lunch with him there, along with Alison when working with him at SIS, there is absolutely no trace of Alexander Wilson in Authors' Club membership records. The Club's membership files do disclose full details for MI5's legendary spy-catcher Maxwell Knight, and SIS intelligence officer and novelist Graham Greene. During the time in question, Knight had only two books to his name and Greene only a handful. By 1944, Alexander

Wilson had written and had published 24 novels.

Impact on family and questions to answer

The full extent of Alison and Alexander Wilson's private destitution and public humiliation from the end of 1942 raises a number of disturbing public interest issues. Their right to family life had been devastated and very nearly destroyed. The consequences could have been irreversible and deeply tragic. The situation was so bad Gordon had to be sent to a children's home for a time. Alison's family pressured her into thinking about putting up Nigel for adoption. The question remains. Truly what steps and interventions were applied by MI5 and their Special Branch colleagues to prevent Alexander Wilson ever being published again, and forcing him to end his working life as a hospital porter and lowly clerk in a Perivale wallpaper factory?

Gordon Wilson is appalled by the contrast with the Second World War MI5 head of section who may have directed Alex Kellar to target Alexander Wilson: 'It is ironic, is it not, that an official in the same department was one, Anthony Blunt, who, after being subsequently uncovered as a Soviet agent, was quietly moved aside to the prestigious appointment as the Keeper of the Queen's Pictures? The discrepancy between his treatment and that meted out to Alexander Wilson for producing what, to all intents and purposes, appears to have been an accurate report, which however raised some uncomfortable side issues, could not be more marked. I would go so far as to say that, in an historical perspective, it is an outrageous difference that now alas can never be redressed.'

Outrageous indeed when on the basis of the evidence suggested by all the other National Archives files available, Wilson was properly and accurately tracking the intelligence gathering mischief of the Egyptian Ambassador. Outrageous also that Anthony Blunt was carrying on his pro-Soviet Union treachery. Between 1941 and 1945 Blunt smuggled 1,771 documents out of MI5 offices in St James's Street, Mayfair to hand to his Russian case officer. Gordon quite rightly points out that 'there is no doubt that the miscarriage could be partly alleviated by the release of the files under questions which would redress the stigma of fabrication so cavalierly, and indeed deviously, expressed by Alexander Wilson's superior.'

Dennis Wilson is another surviving witness of the period. He was undergoing his training as an infantry officer in 1943-44 and had fought in the Battle of Normandy, been severely wounded and evacuated by the time of his father's bizarre prosecution for the uniform and medal offences in October 1944. Dennis has not been able to understand how Sir Alexander Cadogan could have been one of the architects of his father's dismissal and ruin when his father referenced him so strongly as the person to go to should something happen to him: 'In the Spring of 1943 I was posted for eight weeks to a pre-Officer Cadet Training Unit (OCTU) training camp in Wrotham, Kent, during which time I met father several times in London at the Authors' Club, and on at least one of those meetings he told me that if anything happened to him, I would be able to learn the truth by making contact with Lord Cadogan. Although he never told me anything about his work or what he was doing, the very fact of his secrecy indicated that he was doing some sort of Secret Service work. He once told me that he had had a conversation with Churchill which, if it was true, would indicate that in 1943 he was still employed by MI6.'

Dennis is convinced that his father could not have been responsible for the MI5 charge of fabricating the 'Special Material' telephone bugging reports. Otherwise 'he would never have told me to contact Cadogan (somebody completely unknown to me) for fear of the possibility that by doing so I would learn something shameful or detrimental to him.' Is it not painfully ironic that Alexander Wilson was proudly and respectfully assuring his son that Sir Alexander Cadogan was the man to go to if in this desperately dangerous and ghastly World War he should not survive. Ironic and troubling indeed that it should be the very man who had instigated the plot to ruin him and make sure he paid the price for a charge of negligence and incompetence he had never had the chance to defend or even be aware of. Dennis believes the confidential advice to go to Cadogan means his father was completely innocent of Kellar's allegations. To this day Dennis is appalled about 'this ruthless and inconsiderate treatment of someone whose loyalty and patriotism could never be doubted.'

The denial of access to papers and files that could shed light on Alexander Wilson's activities in all dimensions of intelligence is thoroughly mean-spirited and an added cruelty to all the emotional distress that members of his many families have had to contend with. After so long what is being achieved by keeping the key locked on these chambers of memory? Is it possible that these registries are in fact empty and the state is guarding archives devoid of any useful information and historical meaning? The British bureaucratic obsession with secrecy has been mocked and condemned by Malcolm Muggeridge who famously observed: 'Diplomats and Intelligence agents, in my experience, are even bigger liars than journalists, and the historians who try to reconstruct the past out of their records are, for the most part, dealing in fantasy' and 'Secrecy is as essential to Intelligence as vestments and incense to a Mass, or darkness to a Spiritualist séance, and must at all costs be maintained, quite irrespective of whether or not it serves any purpose.'

The circumstantial evidence through the 1920s and 1930s, combined with the content of Alexander Wilson's books indicates a knowledge and role in intelligence gathering that is much more extensive than public records have hitherto confirmed or revealed. There is clearly information about his surveillance of the Egyptian Embassy during the early part of the Second World War that the authorities want to continue to hide more than 70 years later. Trying to make sense of Wilson's intelligence work is like navigating a maze blindfold. The integrity of the state's determination to maintain these secrets has to be called into question when three years after the first edition of his biography the file on the Egyptian Ambassador is released to the National Archives without any explanation. Perhaps the impact of the BBC television series will lead to further oblique revelations. The public and historical interest certainly justifies wider and fuller disclosure of files and documents about these events of so many years ago.

Chapter Eight

'One of the best' – Compton Mackenzie

Compton Mackenzie was a British writing superstar of the first half of the twentieth century having authored more than one hundred books, including *Whiskey Galore* and *The Monarch of the Glen,* been admired by Scott Fitzgerald, Max Beerbohm and John Betjeman, and influenced George Orwell and Cyril Connolly. He was also the literary critic of the country's best selling daily newspaper The *Daily Mail* and in 1935 wrote that Alexander Wilson's new romantic comedy novel *The Magnificent Hobo* was 'an ingenious fairy-tale' and that 'I should be prepared to bet that the vast majority of readers will find "*The Magnificent Hobo*" one of the best of the season.'

This was praise indeed from an author who had been an intelligence officer in the Great War, and who turned his hand to writing spy novels himself from time to time. Mackenzie was not a fan of 'unconvincing imitations of Puss in Boots and Dick Whittington,' but he was very pleased to say 'it should be evident that nobody who enjoys best-foot-foremost fiction can afford to overlook '*The Magnificent Hobo*.'

The novel *The Magnificent Hobo* contains some of the funniest examples of Wilson's novel writing. He was able to describe with a knowing eye the joy, agonies and hilarity of provincial touring theatre in early 20th century Britain. The characters from the touring Bigglesworth Repertory Company and their adventures on the road through the Hampshire towns and villages of the 1920s and 1930s represent a charm and hilarity that would sustain a modern television sitcom in the standard and genre of *Dad's Army*, *Fawlty Towers*, or *Some Mothers Do 'Ave 'Em*. Alexander Wilson had trodden the repertory boards and such was the affection and fun spinning into comic prose from his memories, there was every reason to suppose that his life on the thespian road with his first wife Gladys had been among the happiest, most carefree and enjoyable of his life.

Wilson's life writing

Alec and Gladys's touring drama company days took place between his being invalided out of the army during the First World War in 1916, service in the merchant marine around 1919, and teaching in British India from 1925. Their second son Dennis believes entire plots and pages of dialogue have been directly drawn from reality: 'We know for certain that the comedy *Double Events* (1937) is based on a holiday that father and mother had in Kimmeridge, Dorset, while he was on convalescent leave, together with several friends who would later join their theatrical company. In fact, it is likely that one purpose of the holiday was to discuss what they would produce and where they would perform their shows.'

The Magnificent Hobo included many of their actual touring experiences and the characters they worked with. The climax of Chapter X *'Music Hath Charms–'* features the rescuing of a chaotic production of Napoleon by the inspired piano playing of the character Rupert Revelstoke: '...With a few exceptions, the audience would far rather have sat listening to the inspired playing of the musician who seemed to have dropped from the clouds. They listened quietly without overmuch interest to the dialogue, raised a sympathetic murmur over Josephine's search for Napoleon, grew mildly thrilled when the latter ordered the treacherous general to be taken out and shot. Unfortunately, Charley's method of executing himself left much to be desired. When he had quitted the stage under escort, he picked up a mallet, and hit a sounding thwack on a block of wood. Even the yokels could not believe the noise representative of the discharge of muskets.

"They must ha' lost their rifles," came an audible voice from the rear of the hall," "'cos they've 'it 'im on the 'ead."'

Dennis broke out in a huge grin when he recalled: 'Well that was said by my father himself at a performance of the same play at the Grand Theatre in Southampton by the famous Denville Repertory Company to the great amusement of the adjoining audience. He actually said it and raised his voice "They must have run out of rifles because they've hit him on the head with a mallet!" It's very funny and it's something of a family legend though mother said the scene did give her considerable embarrassment at the time.'

The Call of Hollywood

Such was the success of *The Magnificent Hobo* Wilson's agent, John Farquharson, regarded as the best in Britain with a client list of the country's top authors, was negotiating a film option with Hollywood. Farquharson told the War Office in 1939 that Wilson was 'an author of considerable ability [...] I would say that he is honourable and reliable in anything that he undertakes. He is also pleasant in manner and invariably courteous.' Wilson talked to his first family and wife Gladys about moving everyone over to Los Angeles and living the Californian life. Perhaps he said the same to his second parallel family in London—Dorothy and their son Michael who would have been two when the novel was published.

Wilson's twenty four published novels between 1928 and 1940 received critical acclaim throughout the world in tiptop reviews from New York to Singapore. He was a leading seller for Longmans and P.G. Wodehouse's publisher Herbert Jenkins. He was a versatile story-teller commanding the genre of spy novel, romantic fiction, crime thriller, and comedy. He could tackle abortion, child abuse, and rape, and fashion pioneering depictions of betrayal and treason at the heart of espionage. Why did this brilliant and successful author never have anything published after the Second World War? Another four unpublished novels never saw the light of day. Just how good are they? Wilson is now acknowledged as the missing link in spy writing between Buchan and Fleming- some say without Wilson there would never have been Bond or Bourne. What did this country lose when Wilson's brilliant writing career was unaccountably shut down?

It is a complete enigma that an author such as Alexander Wilson could have such a consistently strong reviewing press across the world and simply disappear after 1940. He hardly features at all in thriller, crime and spy writing anthologies published since then. Recognition of his ability spanned literature periodicals, broadsheet 'qualities', provincial and mass circulation popular national titles. For example, The *Daily Mirror* described *Murder Mansion* in October 1929 as 'Very well constructed and extremely well written, this is a detective story of distinction. It concerns the cunning and desperate moves of a gang of crooks countering the Scotland Yard men who were trying to find Christine Van der Frean.' In June 1937 the *Mirror* conferred a 'Good' rating for Wilson's Leonard Wallace thriller *Microbes of Power* and described it as an 'Exciting thriller about British and foreign spies and Secret Service agents who are the last word in heroism.'

It is difficult to understand why Wilson's tribulations with fake telephone intercepts while working for MI6 should have been any reason to stop this talented, popular, and much respected author from ever being published again. The rule of the Official Secrets Act at the time meant the public should never know about it. And there is no evidence whatsoever that apart from his third wife Alison whom he met at SIS, Wilson said anything to anybody about what he did, what had happened to him when he had been there, or indeed that he had any idea himself that he had been condemned as the fabulist of the Secret Service eight months after being kicked out.

Wallace of the Secret Service series

The clearest mark of Wilson's success in popular fiction is that for twelve years his Wallace of the Secret Service series set the public imagination on the global reach and power of the British Secret Service. To that extent he was a massive agent of propaganda as well as a great publishing hit and sensation. When the march of military dictatorships cast their menacing shadow across the world and ignited the Second World War, the rollicking fantasy of Wallace and his agents offered so much consolation and hope as reading entertainment.

Wilson developed a formula that became so predictable his eldest sons Adrian and Dennis liked making fun of them. Dennis actually wrote a parody and sent it to his father who was not amused. A letter to Adrian discussing the 1937 Wallace novel *Microbes of Power* shows his sensitivity: 'Your criticisms of 'Microbes of Power' were more the type I should have expected from Dennis than from you. I cannot understand why you and he think it your bounden duty to pick holes in my books. I appreciate and welcome fair criticism, but I do resent obvious attempts to search for flaws. I should not mind if they were flaws when you found them, but some of Dennis' remarks, and, I regret to say yours also in this case, were petty and in poor taste.'

The affectionate spat between father and son prompted Wilson to explain how he went about plotting the Wallace novels: '(1) Secret Service men are human, and as likely to fall in love as anyone else, and there is no objection to their being married so long as they always put duty first. Readers, the great majority that is, like a love interest in a story. (2) The Intelligence Department, the actual existing one I mean, consists of a Head and four men who do the jobs I delegate to Sir Leonard, Cousins, Shannon etc. From that you will see I actually make use of more individuals in pukka Secret Service work than the real Intelligence Service. There is Sir Leonard Wallace himself, Cousins, Shannon, Cartwright, Hill and now Foster and Willingdon. At the Foreign Office there is a large research, decoding, scientific and clerical department. I also talk of that in my books under Brien and Maddison. Then there is the Naval branch, the Military branch, and the Special Branch at New Scotland Yard, all of which I talk about from time to time. In short I have studied my subject, and it tallies almost identically with the existing Intelligence Service. You would be surprised how parallel it is. Naturally, as a novelist I am compelled to deviate in certain particulars; otherwise I should find myself getting involved in the Official Secrets Act.'

Alexander Wilson's oldest son by his third marriage, Gordon Wilson, had a real opportunity to evaluate the research and knowledge that his father had of Rome which is a key location for Microbes of Power. He was himself familiar with all of the buildings, roads and routes used as the exotic and dramatic backdrop for the Secret Service adventure: 'I was impressed with the accuracy of the detail. It was all authentic and credible and it struck me that this level of integrity in the research was of a much higher standard than some contemporary novels and factual treatises I had been reading when re-reading my father's novel."

When republished by Allison and Busby in 2015-16 the Wallace books could still sell in their thousands. The very fact that nearly ninety years later so many people were interested in reading them is a sign of his enduring and universal appeal. But this point has to be qualified by the fact that Wilson's prose is of his period and clouded by all the baggage of the racism, anti-Semitism, homophobia and patriarchal sexism of his age. Many readers of the present are not prepared to understand or contextualise. They find such prejudices expressed so explicitly in writing offensive and disgusting.

He was highly acclaimed in *The Times Literary Supplement* when they were first published from 1928. The TLS reviewer said of the second novel *The Devil's Cocktail* published in the same year: 'The author strives conscientiously to provide a thrill on every page.' By 1933 the TLS gushed with enthusiasm for the Herbert Jenkins series. On *The Crimson Dacoit* the reviewer said: '...Mr. Wilson has the gift of storytelling: and, unlike some storytellers, he evidently devotes time and thought to the working out of details. The result is a thriller which is very good...' Wilson was marked out as producing a thriller 'among the best of its class.' In September 1933 the TLS said of his *Wallace of the Secret Service*: '...the novel is not merely sensational, but a genuine piece of forceful story-telling, which carries the reader into strange lands where courage and daring are to be met, even if misguided in their objects."

The 1933 *Wallace of the Secret Service* volume is a collection of ten self-contained short stories in which Wilson's fictional British Secret Service spans the world meeting the many threats to national security. In one story he is up against Lenin. In another, 'East Is East', Wallace has to tally with Mahatma Gandhi during the struggle of Indian independence.

'East is East' was perhaps the most journalistic blend of espionage fiction and current affairs reality in Wilson's India prose. He pitches the fictional Sir Leonard Wallace, Chief of the British Secret Service, into a direct intelligence gathering, shadowing role for the real life Sir John Simon Commission investigating the growing campaign for dominion government, self-determination and eventual independence. Furthermore, Wilson dramatises his secret service chief targeting Mahatma Gandhi for intelligence gathering through undercover infiltration. He produces a thoroughly political, entertaining and ironic representation of a figure who would become an icon for passive resistance and the eventual success of civil disobedience.

'East is East' is one of Wilson's more successful Wallace stories because of the layers of dramatic irony and surprise he weaves into action that is politically acute and mischievous. His characterisation of Gandhi is as authentic and fascinating as the famous Sir Richard Attenborough biopic of 1982. Wilson's representation of Mahatma is so sympathetic, admiring and accurate that readers could be forgiven for thinking he had known the real man through direct acquaintance or even friendship.

Wilson deftly explores the ethics of espionage in the realm of politics. What is the point of spying in the heart of the body politic? Wallace suggests there is something noble about maintaining surveillance on potentially violent subversives and heading them off. Gandhi dismisses such a preoccupation as a paranoid exaggeration of a phantom menace. The so-called extremists are no more than over-enthusiastic left-wingers whose bluster is being blown up out of all proportion.

In 'East is East' Wilson has Wallace unashamedly returning to the pursuit of deception when he adopts the identity of a sadhu complete with naked arm stump so that he can re-infiltrate himself into the heart of Gandhi's Ashram.

'East is East' ends with a passage of fine dramatic irony and a subtle ambiguity of meaning:

"Ah, yes," replied Gandhi; "it was an unfortunate accident. Strangely enough the sadhu had also lost his left arm. Now, if you could have brought yourself to adopt a disguise of that nature, even I might have been deceived."

"God forbid!" returned Wallace fervently.

Gandhi laughed.

"You Englishmen are a lot too fastidious," he declared. "It would do you good to experience some of the wretchedness and poverty that is so prevalent in India. I could almost wish to see the immaculate Sir Leonard Wallace transformed into a religious mendicant, if only for a day."

"I don't think that is very kind of you, Mr. Gandhi. Well, goodbye. I am delighted to have made your acquaintance."

"But not so delighted, I imagine," returned the Mahatma with a sly smile, "as you would have been had you succeeded in imposing on me, and perhaps discovering thereby rather more than it is good for you to know at present."

Wallace shrugged his shoulders.

"That is a matter of opinion," he said. "I shall always treasure the remembrance that I have been a welcome guest at your Ashram."

Wallace was being recognised as a British imperial espionage action-hero, spanning the globe to disable international conspiracies against Rule Britannia. Wallace and his Secret Service was an undoubted precursor to Ian Fleming's James Bond. He aggrandised a fantasy of British imperial power between the

World Wars which in reality was far from the truth in the same way that Fleming created a post war fantasy of 007 whose exploits against Soviet backed master criminals exaggerated the role and power of Great Britain in the Cold War.

The TLS review for Wilson's 1934 novel *Get Wallace!* described a plot rattling with 'breathless pace' and 'brisk entertainment.' Alexander Wilson had created the intelligence officer/agent and Secret Service Chief combined, the intelligence superman waging war against the Comintern, terrorist insurgents of the British Empire and the Kaisers of organised crime. The villain of *Get Wallace!* was even an actor trained and practised in the art of disguise, deception and assumed identities, thus highlighting the performance artifice in espionage. Wilson was clearly conjuring original spy narratives that entertained the imagination of English readers who believed in the British Empire and the legend that the British Secret Service was the best in the world. Like Fleming he was constructing cultural propaganda.

The Scotsman clearly recognised Wilson's place in spy fiction by making its review of his novel *Get Wallace!* on November 19th 1934 the lead item: 'Major Wilson tells an exciting tale of international espionage on a grand scale, the bartering of nations' secrets among rival nations, and the successful efforts of the British Secret Service, under Sir Leonard Wallace to foil the gang. The words Secret Service have about them an arresting glamour, of which effective use is made in this instance in lending colour to the background of the story, lifting its less richly endowed brother, the crime novel. Sir Leonard Wallace returns to Britain from a holiday in America to find the members of his staff in the midst of a first-class mystery. National secrets, embodying plans and documents, have been acquired by a gang and offered to the highest bidder among rival countries. Britain is perturbed; France is scared. The solution of the mystery involves Sir Leonard and his assistants in 48 hectic hours of action. From the first attempt to kill Sir Leonard on the quayside, dramatic situation follows dramatic situation in orderly but rather breathless fashion. The reader has just finished a palpitating prowl round a sinister house in the Isle of Sheppey, recovered most of the stolen documents, and bolted the crooks from their lair on to a yacht, when he finds himself in Camden Town abruptly interrupting an underhand piece of business between Stanislaus Ictinos – gorgeous villain, worth every letter of his name – who is one of the two principal partners of the gang, and a Russian emissary. Then he finds himself in a raiding party on the gang yacht and chasing the escaping Ictinos, suspecting the end is near. But the author has one or two situations to work off before the grand climax is reached in a dénouement not unexpected, but nevertheless entirely effective.'

The reviewer has realised how Wilson has distinctively embedded the conventions of espionage fiction with the crime genre and identified that in real life the secret intelligence world would eventually have to recognise that global organised crime was as much a threat to national security as enemy spy agencies.

Wallace At Bay was published during 1938- the feverish and nervous year of Munich. The novel was hard-boiled. The anarchist/communists sponsored by the Soviet Union were villainous 'others' from Poland, Italy, Yugoslavia, Bulgaria, Czechoslovakia and Germany, who spoke in cod accents and awkward broken English. There was physical demonization that was reminiscent of the depiction of 'evil' foreign spies in *Bulldog Drummond* movies that would have been playing in the cinemas of London in the 1930s like the modern James Bond franchise. There was a John Buchan style character in the form of one of the lead anarchists and assassins, Ivan Modjeska, who had the power to control his enemies through hypnosis; a device central to the Richard Hannay and Sandy Arbuthnot novel, *The Three Hostages*, first published in 1924, and whose central villain Medina applied his malevolent skill of hypnosis to manipulate his victims.

Through the Wallace books Wilson could always touch on something urgent and journalistic. This was certainly true about *Wallace At Bay* in which the central plot concerned the planned murder of King Peter the Second of Yugoslavia on a tour of Britain. Only four years earlier his father, Alexander the First, was shot dead by a Macedonian gunman in Marseilles. There had been speculation that Croatian nationalists and Mussolini's secret service sponsored the King's assassination, and when Hermann Goering attended King Alexander's funeral in Belgrade he may well have been masking the fact that Nazi Germany had also enthusiastically supported the regicide.

No tears would have been shed in Moscow where the Soviet Union had resented King Alexander's harbouring of two hundred thousand White Russian exiles and his public association with anti-Bolshevist leaders who had been sentenced to death in their absence. Wilson extended this degree of malevolence to fictionalize the Soviet Union's commissioning of King Peter's murder on a visit to London to pay his respects at the Cenotaph on Remembrance Day.

Wallace At Bay could also be seen as an early version of what would become known as the James Bond style novel. Very much in the style of the later Ian Fleming, he conjured the existence of a sinister international gang of nihilists, orchestrated by an ugly caricature of a rasping dwarf master anarchist/ communist called Ulyanov, the Principal of the Council of Ten, who spewed evil venom with the malignancy of hydrochloric acid and molten lava.

Ulyanov was a prototype human Dalek whose revolting personality was contained in a dwarf-like and bald physiology and Vulturine features that expressed the predatory ruthlessness of some ghastly half bird, half reptilian monster. Even Ulyanov's favourite adjective for murdering people was the Dr. Who Dalek execution cry 'Exterminate!' His metallic voice resonated with all the menace of Joseph Goebbels, or the high-pitched mesmeric rants of Adolf Hitler. The money, terrorist ideology, and orders emanated from Moscow. The headquarters of this regicidal 1930s Al Qaeda, or ISIS lay half-buried in the suburbs of Vienna and were equipped with fortified underground radio communications and a concealed aeroplane runway and hangar.

Sir Leonard Wallace, Wilson's heroic chief of the British Secret Service, found himself captured, tortured and abused with a degree of violence and sadism that Fleming would certainly have been proud of. Wallace was subject to torture that involved ripping open the skin of his face, branding the flesh on his chest with a red hot poker accompanied by the description of burning flesh, and gun-fights that did not skip on the detail of bullets entering skulls and brains and convulsing and dying bodies.

The terrorism novel

Wilson put all his experience of British imperial rule in India into his 1933 novel *The Crimson Dacoit*. He was able to draw upon his eight years of participation in the elite of the Indian Raj, and his intimate involvement in the Urdu and Arabic speaking higher educational Muslim community. The focus of the novel was on the mentality of political terrorism. Although harking back to events of ninety years ago, Alexander Wilson's observations resonate acutely with current causes and motivation of Islamic terrorism.

The novel opens with the characterisation of Ram Chandra Jawaya Pal, who would choose the way of violence rather than Mahatma Gandhi's pacific creed of civil disobedience. Pal would not be a devotee of Gandhi's maxim: 'Nonviolence is the law of the human race and is infinitely greater than and superior to brute force.' He is Hindu like most of the insurgent independence activists in North West British India who had chosen violence over negotiation.

The two main Indian characters in the novel are Hindu and Sikh. At the beginning of the novel the villain of the peace is undoubtedly the Hindu terrorist, Ram Chandra, and 'the good Indian' is the Sikh, Rai Bahadur Sardar Gopal Singh: 'This gentleman – that rare type of person, a Sikh without a beard – was a very prominent member of the Indian Police, a man whose successes were legion and whose fame had spread throughout the whole of northern India. He also was a superintendent, attached to the Criminal Investigation Department, and practically worked on his own.' North West India's Muslim community is not subject to any slights of pejorative representation; it has a silent background presence and if its members are to be depicted as anything they would be the implied victims of the massacring and brutal Dacoits in 'The Raid on Dalhousie': '...Half a dozen bodies were stretched lifeless on the ground, and the roadway was littered with scraps of cloth, shoes, bottles, empty provision tins and other remnants of the wholesale pillaging that had taken place. [...]

Continuing his way up Terah Hill an even worse scene of desolation spread itself before him. Quite half the houses were burning ruins; blazing beams and spars were still falling and, in places, masses of masonry littered the way. People were sitting amidst the pathetic remnants of their property, women sobbing and men wearing the grim look engendered by the sudden swift catastrophe that had befallen them. There were others attempting to salvage lost treasures from smouldering heaps of ruins of what had so recently been dwelling-places. A few – lucky ones – whose homes had not been destroyed, or who had managed to overcome the flames, were doing their utmost to render assistance to their stricken neighbours. Ian counted no less than fourteen bodies lying in various parts of Terah, and there were several men and women being attended to for wounds and other injuries by two doctors and their volunteer assistants.'

This British imperialist novel, hardly the fashionable focus of contemporary literary studies, turns out to be suffused with the narrative of betrayal. For Gopal Singh is the 'clean-skin' mole within the circus. He is in fact 'The Crimson Dacoit'; something not fully unveiled and discovered until the intensely dramatic and murderous final chapter appropriately titled 'The Final Ordeal.' It is intriguing how Wilson had fictionally investigated the potential for ideological disillusionment and moral dislocation at the heart of the Oxbridge educated elite at the very time the Soviet Union was about to realise its recruiting potential with the notorious Cambridge apostles: Blunt, Burgess, Philby and Maclean. Through Gopal Singh he had presaged the idea of enemy infiltration into the heart of an intelligence establishment, in this case the British imperial police force in India.

His characterisation of Ram Chandra is a complex and original study of a terrorist's motivation and social psychology. His rhetoric and political ethics enunciate the ideology of Al Qaeda, ISIS, and insurgent Taliban. It is also a novel addressing the acute political and journalistic agendas of the early 1930s and generates and resonates multiple layers of ideology and power relationships as well as representing a literary device of popular propaganda.

Action Women

Wilson's enthusiasm for portraying professional women agents in the field rather than sexist Mata Hari stereotypes was evident in the 1937 characterisation of Barbara Havelock in *Microbes of Power*. Havelock is the British Secret Service's undercover agent in Cyprus, held in high regard in London: '...He walked to his desk, and sat down. Unlocking a drawer, he took out a small, leather-bound book, and commenced to turn the pages. "Number Thirty-Three," he murmured to himself, "Barbara Havelock, teacher at the Nicosia High School for girls. She's the girl for whose education you took responsibility when her father was killed, isn't she?" Brien nodded. "She seems to have done pretty good work out there, Bill. Have you ever had any reason to suspect any lack of efficiency on her part since you obtained the job for her?"

"None at all. Why? Aren't you satisfied?"

"Quite. I was only thinking that in a high school her activities are bound to be rather limited. Make a note to get her promoted to an inspectorship of schools, will you?"'

Microbes of Power is a spy novel pioneering in its representation of the technology and science of secret warfare as well as a progressive acknowledgement that women intelligence agents and officers are equal in ability in the field as men. Wilson describes in detail the applications of electronic microphone bugging as well as plotting the scenario of biological warfare.

Agent Barbara Havelock is not spared any amount of danger and falls victim to death by stabbing in the chapter entitled 'In Her Country's Service', a fate he spared his woman agent Rosemary Meredith in the 1939 novel *Wallace Intervenes*. Havelock's demise is full of melodrama and rather Flemingesque In terms of depicting the impact of the woman agent's demise on the developing romantic interest with Wilson's James Bond equivalent Captain Hugh Shannon. It is possible to detect seeds of *Casino Royale*: 'Mrs Malampos gave a triumphant cry.

"The girl is dead – kill the man!" she screamed in Greek. "Death to all spies!"

A dreadful laugh – icy, terrifying in its timbre – broke from Shannon. He drew the revolver from his pocket, and fired rapidly at them both. The man went down with hardly a sound; the woman gave one piercing shriek; then pitched forward, and lay still. Shannon put away his weapon.

"I have avenged you, Barbara," he whispered, looking down at the still, pathetic little form at his feet.'

Wilson's female agents and detectives such as Havelock, Meredith and Coverdale in *Microbes of Power*, *Wallace Intervenes* and *Mr Justice* respectively give him a unique position in the cultural history of the spy and crime genres. He promotes a vision of women beyond that of auxiliary spouse, secretary or sparring partner, which is unusual in a male writer of that period.

Siren calls from intelligence

The final Wallace volume *Chronicles of the Secret Service* was published in 1940 when Wilson was now working at MI6. It consisted of three novellas: *The China Doll, Noughts and Crosses,* and *That Bloody Afghan.* In *The China Doll* Sir Leonard Wallace recognised Japanese intelligence penetration of Hong Kong: '…I must admit to a feeling of admiration for the Japs. They have chosen their time well, and with amazing nerve and skill, when Europe is staggering about like a drunken man from one crisis to another…I shall rout out, lock, stock and barrel, the nest of the Japanese spies here.' Wilson's fiction warned that Japanese armed forces could successfully invade the British Empire in the East and overrun the defences of Hong Kong to Singapore. This seemed like a conduit for the expression of real fears of British intelligence experts. Was its publication in 1940 some kind of siren call? Prior to the fall of Hong Kong and Singapore in late 1941 and early 1942 the British media carried no stories of any threat from Japanese intelligence and military. The Japanese had been dismissed in racist terms as monkeys in trees. The British or Australian warrior was depicted as being the equal of ten Japanese soldiers. *That Bloody Afghan* was a spy thriller set in the North West Frontier in the same genre as *The Four Feathers* by A.E.W. Mason. It could also be described as a Lawrence of Arabia for Afghanistan. The story showed a respectful understanding of the political and religious complexities of Islamic culture and how these can emerge in an Islamic insurgency against foreign and Western imperialism. Again, it was another example of Wilson's popular fiction being rooted in some kind of direct knowledge and specialist understanding.

Membership of the 'Clubland heroes'

Was Sir Leonard Wallace one of the 'Clubland heroes' of espionage fiction? Any reading of the books proves he was more than a clubland hero. He ran the professional spy infrastructure in St James's and Wilson should be recognised for bridging what former MI5 Director-General Stella Rimington has described as the romantic and realist traditions of spy fiction genres. Rimington was commissioned to write a new introduction to Graham and Hugh Greene's classic 1957 *The Spy's Bedside Book.* Without referencing Wilson's books it could be argued that Rimington provides an excellent description of Sir Leonard Wallace's place in spy fiction: '… there is the geopolitical spy, nourished on the British side in the struggle to keep the Russians away from the Indian north-west frontier – the world of Kim. This strand of spying, with its long-term strategic focus, its professionalism, its ideological undertones and its large-scale organisation, has gradually, through the Cold War and modern terrorism, absorbed all the others.' Wilson's Wallace fulfilled the criteria of the geopolitical spymaster, and he was also addressing in most sophisticated terms, the actual phenomenon of terrorism in the 1920s and 30s, its root causes, ideological and political mischief, with realistic, psychological and romantic writing.

Rimington also offered an elegant and precise answer to the question of when a spy story is not a detective story: 'A detective story classically involves a puzzle, something happens and the contract with the reader specifies that the questions "Whodunnit? And "Howdunnit?" should be answered. A true spy story is not concerned with such matters. "Who", is often given at the outset; there is not necessarily any puzzle, and if there is, the questions to be answered are more likely to be "What?" and "Why?" In this, a spy story resembles human life, being more concerned with situations and psychology.' In some respects Rimington is also commenting on Alexander Wilson's life as if he were a spy story. On one level we knew who he was. But we are also asking 'What' and 'Why'. We are trying to understand his life situations and unravel the psychology of what lay behind them.

In Alexander Wilson we can find a complex blend of genres, styles of expression, cultural and political representation, and qualitative writing. His prose style, literary ability, and style and range of expression are wider than those of John Buchan, Ian Fleming and much of Compton Mackenzie. His representation of tradecraft and political intelligence is more sophisticated, relevant and journalistic/historical than the left-wing Eric Ambler and more direct and positive than the pessimistic John le Carré. Wilson challenges issues of representation and ideology within the ritual of the spy genre and he also takes risks in shedding formulaic skins to experiment not in high cultural self-indulgence for the Bloomsbury set but for the popular reading audience. It is not being suggested for one moment that Alexander Wilson was a better writer than Buchan, Fleming, Mackenzie and Ambler. But there is an argument that Wilson in his own right made an original and important contribution to espionage and crime fiction. He also represents a straddling of high and popular cultural expression in the literature that helped fashion and serve the imagination of readers at this time.

The established canons of spy fiction criticism have neglected an author who in his novel *The Sentimental Crook* (1934) uses first person narrative to characterise the bold, naked and exciting life of an international hobo ducking and diving in and out of the shady world of crime and professional theatre. The writing is in turn existential, realistic, cynical and romantic. It has the evanescence of autobiography as does the more modernist and socially realistic version written under the pseudonym Geoffrey Spencer *Confessions of a Scoundrel* just one year before. And then there is the geopolitical dimension drawing on the experience and challenge of Great Britain's 20th century Empire. Through *The Mystery of Tunnel 51* and *The Devil's Cocktail* (1928) and *The Crimson Dacoit* (1933) Wilson explores the origins, motivation, and psychological consciousness of terrorists and terrorism, sometimes in the context of Islamic fundamentalism. He is an invisible writer from the past who has a message and relevance for us in the present.

Chapter Nine

Killing the Author

Wilson's *The Death of Dr. Whitelaw* (1930) is not spy fiction, but is characteristic of the detective genre of its time and this earlier title published by Longmans indicates his strengths and originalities as a crime fiction author. The central character Jack Armitage was: 'A magnificent specimen of young manhood, he was twenty-four years of age, six feet two inches in height, and as straight as a ramrod. Not particularly handsome, he possessed a good-humoured pleasant face, the attractiveness of which was enhanced by the deep bronze colouring which a life spent mainly in the open air had produced. His grey eyes had a peculiar habit of screwing up into mere slits when he laughed, with the result that tiny wrinkles showed at each corner. He had a large mop of unruly brown hair surmounting a broad forehead which was indicative of the brain power which he undoubtedly possessed. Altogether Jack Armitage was as clean-limbed, as typical an example of the athletic Englishman as any who had ever played cricket on that most famous of the world's great grounds.'

At the beginning of the novel he was resonating with the glory of 'a flawless century in each innings' in a test trial at Lords having come 'down from his varsity, where he had obtained a cricket "Blue."' His family was rich, with a seat in Aylesbury where his beloved father, a retired general attended to his estate. This was the quintessential upper middle class celebrity hero and aspiration for every public schoolboy mesmerised in the culture of *Boy's Own* adventure stories. Armitage represented the safe and secure values lauded by the novels of William Le Queux, Phillips Oppenheim, John Buchan and Sapper. There was certainly the touch of the British Aryan *gravitas* in Wilson's central character; a world apart from the hard-luck and flawed flotsam and jetsam of an Eric Ambler novel, the sad *ennui* and corrupt morality of Somerset Maugham's *Ashenden*, or the twisted guilt and tragedy of a Graham Greene 'entertainment'.

But the direction of Wilson's ideological narrative was as cunning as a googly bowled by the England spinner Wilfred Rhodes at Lords in the 1920s, or Thomas Bignall Mitchell for Derbyshire in the 1930s. Critics of detective and spy fiction seem altogether trapped into making comparisons within a low-cultural frame. For example, if they had come across Wilson's work, like most popular detective fiction anthologies, he would have been labelled Buchanesque, in the style of Le Queux or Phillips E Oppenheim, or if he dabbled in any modernist expression or blended in touches of realism he might have been dismissed as a quasi-Ambler or mini Graham Greene.

It is a fact that there is a high and low popular cultural divide in most literary criticism. Oppenheim and Le Queux and their ilk are excluded from *The Oxford Companion To English Literature* and *The Cambridge Guide to Literature in English*. Buchan, Maugham, Mackenzie, Conrad, Greene and Le Carré are in. Ambler only gets a mention in the Oxford Companion. A close examination of *The Death of Dr. Whitelaw* by Alexander Wilson challenges the notion that we are dealing with low-cultural, popular, and what was referred to in the early part of the 20th century as 'shocker' literature; some kind of grubby evolution of the Victorian Penny Dreadful. Graham Greene sought to make a distinction between novels he wanted to be considered as English Literature and books he preferred to be regarded as entertainments.

When Wilson writes sentences such as 'At first he was inclined to let his thoughts run riot in mordant acrimony of the doctor's behaviour, but calmer reason prevailed at last,' and 'The girl must be made to speak and to remove for ever the stain of perfidy and concupiscence which, by her silence, she had cast upon him,' this is neither the style nor language of junk literature or pulp fiction. Wilson's book turns on an interest in the parallel and contrasting fortunes of a family divided, and the problems of justice and injustice; themes that are central to the plays and novels of John Galsworthy (1867-1933). Wilson's novel challenges the security and comfort zone of Edwardian values within the middle to upper-middle classes. Jack Armitage is plunged into a narrative of horror based on the terror of false accusations, social humiliations and conspiracies hidden behind the cloak of status and respectability. The crime narrative is a journey of moral and social insecurity; an abiding preoccupation of twentieth century literature.

There are, of course, many tropes in Wilson's work. His patriotism is unshakeable and consistent, and consequently naïve. Every novel seems to end with a bonfire night of marriage or marriages even if the road to romantic fulfilment might have been a little rocky. He is no less subject to the cultural influences and prejudices of his time than any other writer. But his work exhibits the expression of tensions and ideological struggles that were no doubt troubling many of his readers and he is not afraid to challenge the status quo in politics and social values.

Unpublished novels- promise unfulfilled

Murder in Duplicate, Out of the Land of Egypt, and his final handwritten and untitled novel disclose a level of research and access to information that must have been surely beyond that expected of an A & E hospital porter or clerk in a wallpaper factory. While Wilson's prose is blighted by out of date values, it is also elevated by a pioneering sense of social and political awareness of themes and ideas that would take root in mainstream culture many years later.

Out of the Land of Egypt was perhaps created by Wilson in the late 1940s or early 1950s and marked a Cold War development in his espionage writing. His characters and plotting derive from the new world order defined by Checkpoint Charlie and the Berlin Wall. He successfully describes the *modus operandi* of Special Branch and the Secret Intelligence Service. He reveals the interior and operation of the secret Kingsway tunnel installations of surveillance and communications. He discloses the culture of recruitment and training of MI6 intelligence officers during the Second World War. He captures the immediate post war anxiety and suspicion on the part of Western and Soviet intelligence agencies that Hitler had not died in his bunker in April 1945. He reveals the secret Odessa network of former SS officers, agents and scientists evading their culpability in war crimes, and their covert missile weapons of mass destruction programme provided to Egypt's dictatorship under General Gamal Abdel Nasser. He presents the paradox of Germany's Nazi police state elite reinventing itself as the totalitarian head lock on the freedoms and liberties of those Germans unfortunate enough to be living in the Soviet zone of occupation.

If Wilson was not participating in the Great Game as an agent his writing imagination showed every sign of being connected to research resources and information fully concealed from the public domain. His son Dennis found the novel rather disappointing in parts. He was uncomfortable about his father's racist depiction of Egyptians and instances of anti-Semitic characterisation although he acknowledged that the book had been imagined and created during the politically wrought years of Britain's engagement with the Palestine Mandate and Suez.

This novel represented an attempt to create a prototype for a new post war fictional Secret Intelligence Service with new characters, a new 'Chief' based on Admiral Hugh Sinclair and a new writing identity, Colonel Alan C Wilson, drawing closely though not exactly on his earlier intelligence legend. However, Wilson was not wired into the Zeitgeist of disillusionment with the decline of the British Empire. Politically he was not counter-mainstream and appeared to have sided with the losing and discredited position in Suez. He had not understood where Great Britain was going and had not grasped the implications of the Fleming and James Bond formula of fantasy and escapist materialism.

He belonged to an older generation of espionage story-telling and was disconnected from the new generation of post war agents and officers recruited from the public schools, Oxbridge and Swiss language academies, who with privileged insouciance arrogantly mocked the older generation's ideological and operational failures in a style suffused with the atmosphere of paranoia and corrupted cold war realpolitik.

Eric Ambler and Graham Greene became literary superstars. John le Carré became the fashionable ventriloquist of a deeper understanding of the moral relativism of the post war Great Game. It is possible that Wilson must have felt *passé* and irrelevant with every return of his manuscript from the leading publishers accompanied by the standard rejection letter.

Wilson's two unpublished crime novels *Murder in Duplicate* and *Combined Operations* were again meticulously researched and pioneering in the advancement of social criminology and the challenge to counter-intelligence posed by organised crime. *Murder in Duplicate* suggested it was also written in the late forties or early fifties. Wilson tapped into the political anxiety over the reliability and justice of capital punishment that would precipitate storms of moral panic in the cases of Derek Bentley in 1954 and Ruth Ellis in 1955.

Wilson advanced a positive representation of women in the professions of journalism and law, and extended his counter-stereotyping with the characterisation of a suave, confident and public school educated detective inspector at New Scotland Yard. Not for him the homely Jack Warner of *Dixon of Dock Green*, or working-class sons of greengrocers and butchers made good. He was advancing the future recruitment of a higher class of secret service super agents into a professional, public school educated graduate generation of detectives deploying strategic management, science, and concentration of intelligence and resources that would begin to dominate New Scotland Yard towards the end of the century. No question of patronising depictions of one dimensional 'PC Plods' promoted well beyond their ability.

Wilson twisted the political sympathy for the cry of the innocent to construct a paradoxical discourse where the reader is confronted by ambiguity and the unexpected. He realised that the most plaintive and plausible submissions in capital murder cases often originate from the guilty.

But his unique understanding of the loneliness and vulnerability of judges who try capital cases represented a more daring and original direction of plotting in the thriller genre. When he developed the psychological distress and isolation of judicial sensibility into the sociopathic and homicidal, Wilson's popular detective fiction collared an establishment shibboleth and shook it to its foundations. The idea of a High Court judge being a deranged killer was certainly original and unusual in the crime fiction of the 1950s. Even today the popular imagination seems incapable of associating Her Majesty's judiciary with corruption and criminogenic performance rather than the disposition of punishment.

In his last novel, that he did not have the time or resources to have typed up for manuscript submission to publishers, Wilson crafted a thriller with breath-taking pace and suspense. His story advanced the notion that the modern state's reliance on traditional infrastructures of policing was inadequate and insufficient in facing off the threat and menace of global organised crime. Wilson's solution was to combine the forces of pensioned off army, naval and air force intelligence and use the tactics and skills of counterespionage to roll up organised networks of brothels, drug trafficking and protection rackets. As with some of his earlier novels he was plotting policy and ideas thirty or forty years ahead of his time. It has the pace and verve of the 1958 novel by John Boland *The League of Gentlemen* which was adapted into the successful 1960 film comedy by Brian Forbes. But instead of constructing a caper about hard-up army officers plotting the perfect bank robbery, Wilson writes a far more sophisticated political crime novel using the frustration and disillusionment of retired military intelligence officers to reinforce and rescue society and democracy from the tentacles and corruption of gangsterism and racketeering.

Dennis Wilson was given the handwritten manuscript of this untitled novel by Alison in 1963. He read it for the first time some 45 years later, and discovered that his father's ability to write original and successful thrillers had not waned in his final years and so long after he had last been published. Indeed, Dennis believes it is one of his best books. With the admiration of a son who was always proud of his father's talent and ability as a writer, he took pride in giving it a title that gave justice to its content. And so *Combined Operations* remains in its neat copper-plate fountain pen manuscript awaiting perhaps some future publication as the last novel of a remarkable writer somehow mysteriously lost to history during the Second World War.

Assessing Wilson's writing prospects after the Second World War

The post Second World War social and cultural context would provide the springboard for the accelerating success of Ian Fleming's *James Bond* spy novels and they were also helped by the popularity and promotion of the Bond character as a strip cartoon in the *Daily Express* from 1958.

Fleming's *James Bond* brand discovered multi-media merchandising. Leonard Wallace, disguised as a Bavarian nanny or Corsican nun, would hardly have had the same appeal in a strip cartoon on the back of the *Daily Sketch*.

Continued sales of Wilson's books would not have been helped by his 'apparent death' in 1942. In Wilson's absolute departure from his life with Dorothy and Michael he had also lost the family and world that had given birth and nurtured his writing career. Letters to the publisher Longmans indicate clearly she acted as his secretary and business manager; notwithstanding that he had Curtis Brown and then John Farquharson representing him as literary agents.

It may be no coincidence that his writing career thrived after his marriage with Dorothy in Lahore in 1928 and then abruptly terminated with their separation in 1941 and the decision to 'kill him' in regard to his responsibility and relationship with his son Michael in 1942. It was in April 1940 he had first met 19-year-old Alison McKelvie at MI6 and their affair blossomed soon afterwards. He married Alison in 1941 when she became pregnant with their first son Gordon. Only four unpublished manuscripts have survived from the 22 year period Wilson was married to Alison between 1941 and 1963. Dorothy may well have been his professional and very productive muse. His life with Alison was blighted with a pretty humiliating downward spiral of employment from being sacked by MI6 for being in trouble with the police, sacked from cinema management for cooking the books, and then scratching a living as a hospital porter and factory clerk. Four unpublished manuscripts in 22 years and a pile of publisher's rejection slips is an ignoble end to whatever identity of writer he had ended up with in his own mind.

It is highly unlikely he was going to gain any income or kudos from the books he had had published before 1940. Publishers tend to make more of an effort to promote the work of an author who is contracted to write more and better. He was not only yesteryear's writer. He was a writer from a bygone age. It is hard to imagine interest in his novels continuing beyond the war. Many thriller writers of the 1930s found it difficult to create entertainment about a murder whodunit in a country mansion in England when millions had been slaughtered in the Nazis' system of concentration camps. Solving the riddle of a poisoned retired Colonel or the stabbing by paperknife of an eccentric governess on the croquet lawn somewhat pales into significance in the shadow of Auschwitz chimneystacks and the burial pits of Bergen-Belsen. Although it has to be said Agatha Christie's formulaic thrillers never lost popular appeal after 1945.

Dorothy L. Sayers decided to retire her much-loved amateur sleuth Lord Peter Wimsey by 1945. Indeed, she would direct her literary talent during the war years to dramatising the story of Jesus Christ in the hugely popular and influential radio series directed by Val Gielgud *The Man Born To Be King*.

Bulldog Drummond and Colonel Blimp had no role in the new script of *totaler krieg* (total war). Perhaps it was inevitable that Wilson would have had difficulty finding a post war role for Leonard Wallace. Many perceived the fall of Singapore as the beginning of the end of British imperial power in the East. The significance of signals intelligence, and computerised deciphering of codes at Station X made Wallace and his disguises redundant. The gangsters of global organised crime that Wallace, Cousins, Shannon and Brien had fought in the 1930s had been upstaged by the destructive and malevolent power of a Nazi gang whose actions had been beyond the imagination of the world.

The Second World War had threatened to lay waste the fictional writer's creative imagination on the subject of murder. For millions God had died and so had the logic and normative terms of fairness and justice in the struggle of good over evil. Science had ended the war against Japan, but only in the nihilistic splitting of atoms that destroyed the souls of hundreds of thousands in less than a second of chemical reaction. When the scientist Primo Levi emerged from Auschwitz, if, as one of his biographers suggested, he had died there, what was his status as a survivor endeavouring to create literature out of his experience: the living dead? Levi conveyed how the Nazis had murdered thoughts before they had snuffed out the breathing of their victims: 'They crowd my memory with their faceless presences, and if I could enclose all the evil of our time in one image, I would choose this image which is familiar to me: an emaciated man, with head dropped and shoulders curved, on whose face and in whose eyes not a trace of a thought is to be seen.'

The Cold War had no use for an intelligence man with a wooden arm and a pipe. No, the proper place for Wallace in the cold winter of 1947 was perhaps running a boarding house in Cromer where he could shuffle in his slippers and reminisce about his adventures in Hong Kong and Shanghai while sipping Bovril, or Ovaltine. The brilliance of Fleming's literary imagination was sizing up a new fantasy for the spy in post war Britain. And Fleming's creation would be younger, fitter, leaner, and meaner. Agent 007 was not in any mood to drink Horlicks.

The Bond thriller was framed with a muscular and pungent symmetry of opening and closing precision: 'The scent and smoke and sweat of a casino are nauseating at three in the morning. Then the soul-erosion produced by high gambling – a compost of greed and fear and nervous tension – becomes unbearable and the senses awake and revolt from it.' [...] '"This is 007 speaking. This is an open line. It's an emergency. Can you hear me? Pass this on at once. 3030 was a double, working for Redland. Yes, dammit, I said 'was'. The bitch is dead now."' Fleming's literary art was a cut diamond for the pocket paperback. It could be worn in the casino at Monte Carlo, or a branch of Woolworths in Bognor Regis.

Wilson's opening and closing symmetry belonged to a world where young men met their fathers for lunch at Boodles, or Whites in St James's and expected their debutante sisters to find husbands after learning grace and favour at Swiss finishing schools: 'A young man sat moodily in the comfortable depths of an easy-chair of dark green leather, and gazed round him, from time to time, with an air of complete boredom.' [...] "'What about Sophie and Bernard Foster," accused his wife with a smile. "You certainly were responsible for bringing them together, Leonard." "Yes; I admit that," he nodded. "Ah, well! Blessed are the matchmakers, for theirs is the pleasure of making others happy-sometimes.'"

Wilson's prose is an Edwardian tiara in danger of falling off as soon as the band plays swing for a jitterbug at the Chelsea Arts Ball. In operations Wilson's secret agent has time to interrogate the ethics of making love for King and Empire. By contrast Bond only has time to kill quickly for Queen and NATO. If there are any regrets, the taste of bitterness is quickly washed down with a dry martini in a deep champagne goblet. Fleming directs the theatre of the cruel. Wilson directs a theatre of the kind.

Wilson's quaint romanticism, already challenged by the modernist experiment in the depiction of sexual consciousness and identity by James Joyce and Henry Miller, would have been somewhat passé after a war that had separated millions of husbands and wives, had made divorce respectable, and had shattered the social ethic that enjoyment of sex had to wait until the wedding night. There is a spirit of sentimentality in Wilson's writing, which is out of place in the age of *James Bond*. Ian Fleming realised that the new Zeitgeist was cynical materialism.

However, Wilson's contribution to the culture of spy writing does not deserve to be invisible. While it can be argued that Fleming's prose was more sinewy and heated, Wilson's characterisation plumbed greater depths in the ethical doubts and moral insecurities of his characters and to that extent he was reflecting the crisis of power and ideological authority in the British Empire. He encoded the ambiguities and complexities of contemporary espionage in a world that was hurtling towards war.

It can be argued that Wilson's plots were more exquisite and suspenseful, his prose more humanitarian and politically astute. Wilson propagandised and entertained. He directly commented on and intersected with contemporary politics and world affairs. But perhaps a process of comparison that scores points is missing the point. Fleming and Wilson are literary compatriots and companions, not competitors.

They belong to a regiment of writers in the 20th century that constructed and guided the social imagination of millions of readers to engage with the secret world, a struggle for power fought in the shadows, a great game of spying, deception, betrayal, disillusionment, subterfuge, subversion, and double-cross. This was the new literature of the sociological occult; black magic anthropology and grand guignol *in camera*. The spy writer fills a black box theatre with parables of amorality, and millions of readers are consequently drawn to this black hole of popular escapism because of the licence it gives to glorify in *schadenfreude*, voyeurism and homicidal empathy. Spy novels are created by the imagination of *Dr Faustus*. And in the history of real-life espionage the contractual terms of Mephistopheles are ever-present.

While there is a compelling argument that Wallace would have been well past his sell by date in the post war years, *Wallace Intervenes* indicates that Wilson had sown seeds of literary insight and social psychology that would have enabled him to continue the fictional history of MI6 and associated agencies. There is the supposition that had Wilson lived beyond his pretended death at El Alamein in 1942 and his writing career continued, his secret agent character Rosemary Meredith, and many like her, would have had a place in the Special Operations Executive, to be flown into occupied countries to derail trains, blow up heavy water reactors, and high technology plants supplying the Nazi's V2 rocket and nuclear weapons programmes.

His characters Bernard Foster and Sophie von Reudath had a role to play in war-time espionage in neutral Switzerland, Spain, Portugal, Sweden and Turkey. Wilson would have had an opportunity of charting the development of women agents in the field and the growing and significant role women had in intelligence across MI5, MI6, SOE and the black propaganda agency, the PWE (Political Warfare Executive). Wilson's optimism and romanticism could have absorbed the implications of total war, Hiroshima, Nagasaki, Nuremberg, Indian independence, and the catastrophic upheavals to the social institution of marriage and sexual values brought about by six years of global conflict during which millions of wives and husbands were separated by service overseas and traumatised by a closer breach at the swing door between life and death during the blitz on the home front. Much of the British Empire remained intact for Wilson to reinvent the spy novel in post war Hong Kong, as well as the postcolonial conflicts in Palestine, Malaya, Korea, Vietnam, Kenya and Cyprus.

Furthermore, the defection of Hilda Zeiss and Colonel Schönwald from the Abwehr in *Wallace Intervenes* could have been the foundation of a narrative rooted in the new secret war fought on both sides of the Iron Curtain after the construction of the Berlin Wall in 1948. Wilson's covert understanding of Nazi dissidents hints at zu Putlitz's actual defection when an air attaché in Holland in 1940 and the quiet though effective double-game played out by the actual head of the Abwehr, Admiral Canaris, until his dismissal in February 1944. Canaris faced house arrest and eventual execution in April 1945 after evidence of his duplicity accumulated; particularly after the plot to kill Hitler failed in July 1944 (Operation Valkyrie).

Wilson may well have been in a position to plot more cheerful narratives to rival those of le Carré's gloomy circus rivalry between George Smiley and Karla, moles, and double agents. Indeed, who among Wilson's merry band of characters: Wallace, Cousins, Brien, Shannon, Carter, Foster and Batty had the potential for being a Burgess, MacLean, Blunt, Cairncross or Philby? In all honesty it is hard to think of any of these stalwart patriots ever being hooked by the bait of Comintern allegiance. But the ideological complexities of the Cambridge spies would surely have given Wilson some inspiration to develop his secret service narrative with a new generation of officers and agents.

Perhaps Rosemary Meredith could have been the first female 'C' of MI6, decades before Stella Rimington took the helm of MI5, and then characterised the impressive Liz Carlyle as a fictional role model for the intelligent, effective and modern woman intelligence officer.

In reality Alexander Wilson did have a new Secret Service, a new Chief and plot for the post war intelligence agenda. But *Out Of The Land Of Egypt* was not taken up by British publishing as the successor debut of a new spying series. Wilson submitted under a new legend: Colonel Alan C. Wilson. His new 'C' was based on Admiral Hugh 'Quex' Sinclair. The story telling was full of adventure, mystery and modern military technology: helicopters, rocket programmes, but politically it touched the wrong nerve. His theory that the SS and Nazis had been reinventing themselves was close to the truth. But the idea that Hitler was alive and well in Egypt and Gamal Abdel Nasser was his ally and the Führer of the Middle East became the wrong politics.

Politics of economic justice in *Mr Justice*

In *Mr Justice (1937)* Wilson constructs the perfect crime novel. It is taut, disciplined, political in its subversive depiction of vigilante justice, and pioneering and revolutionary in its gender representation. Many of his novels would have been brilliant British films had they been produced in the 1930s or 1940s. Intriguingly some could be made now with little need for substantial modernisation in terms of adaptation. The quality of *Mr Justice* was fully recognised in *The Scotsman*'s review of 1937: 'A skilful and daring thief, who selects as victims only those whose wealth is ill-gotten and distributes his plunder to the deserving poor – such is "Mr Justice," a modern and piquant "Raffles." His exploits are few, but meticulously planned, and battle the best brains of Scotland Yard, even though Alan Cunningham – the young detective inspector in charge of the investigations – has a suspicion from the first as to his identity. The reader will probably have an equally shrewd but equally erroneous suspicion of the slim young figure who so consistently eludes all pursuers. There are some false clues which will undoubtedly confuse all but the most skilful sleuths; but the unexpected dénouement is not impossibly difficult, and the scenes leading up to it are vibrant with excitement.'

The climax to *Mr Justice* carries a punch and surprise at the end of the plot that renders most of Agatha Christie's efforts as the work of an unqualified apprentice.

Wilson presents a close circle of friends any one of whom could be the romantic 'Robin Hood' figure who in the dead of night delivers a non-violent vigilante restorative justice against greed and financial exploitation. The prime candidate is Bruce Coverdale who begins the novel with the expression of opinion that reads like a confession through prophesy:

"'...The English law may be as good as any in the world, but that doesn't prevent It being unjust. Every day something happens to show it up as the unstable thing it is."

The speaker's eyes flashed a challenge at his five companions. [...]

"...If it is impartial, how do you account for the numerous discrepancies that are constantly occurring? Quite recently a bank cashier absconded with a thousand pounds. After several months of freedom he gave himself up. The defence made out some fantastic story about his mind being unhinged by a death in his family. The money was said to have been spent, the poor fellow being unable to account for it. He was sentenced to six months in the second division. Almost at the same time, a young girl, who had barely left her teens, was sentenced to a year's imprisonment for obtaining goods from various stores by fraudulent representation. Yesterday I read of an unemployed man who, rather than see his family starve, stole twenty pounds. He was given eighteen months' hard labour. None of the three had been previously convicted, so they can be said to have started level. Yet the man who had stolen most and, in addition, had betrayed a trust, escaped with the lightest sentence. In a few months he will be released, and be free to enjoy the money which he is supposed to have spent while mentally deranged, but which, I wouldn't mind betting, he has planted nice and snug, so that he can enjoy it when he comes out. If you can prove to me, Alan, that those three convictions are in accordance with fair and impartial justice, I'll say no more.'"

Bruce Coverdale is addressing directly his friend Alan Cunningham, a detective sergeant and later promoted to inspector at New Scotland Yard. They are in a group of six friends meeting for dinner in a private room for a farewell party to Bruce due to leave for India the following day. When Bruce returns from his teaching job on leave and rich and undeserving public figures begin to be robbed and humiliated, Wilson's prose leaves the reader suspecting any one of the characters: 'Coverdale, Cunningham, Willard, and Templeton had been at school together, and the friendship then formed had grown deeper as the years went by. They all felt that Coverdale's imminent departure was marking a regrettable transition in their lives. Hitherto, they had never been far apart and, living within easy reach of each other, were accustomed to use each others' homes almost as their own. They were all more or less of the same age, Bruce Coverdale being the youngest, but Willard, the eldest, with his twenty-six years, could only give him ten months. Templeton and Cunningham came in between. The latter, like so many well-bred and well-educated men of to-day, had entered the police force as a constable, had quickly proved himself an exceptionally gifted young man and, sent to the Criminal Investigation Department, had risen rapidly to the rank of sergeant. Willard, pale-faced, dark-haired, tall and thin, had taken to journalism, and had become a well-known columnist on one of the great dailies. Templeton, round and jolly of countenance, stoutish of body, an unnecessary monocle always in his right eye, did nothing particular, and did it rather well. His father had left him far more money than he could ever spend. He was the only married man of the party, being ideally mated to a girl with a temperament and disposition very similar to his own.

Myra Templeton, fair and fluffy, offered a striking contrast to Diana. Extremely pretty, she was, nevertheless, overshadowed by the other girl, whose beauty and personality rather eclipsed her whenever they were together. Myra knew it, but did not mind. She was entirely without envy and, in fact, being very fond of Diana, was extremely proud of her friend.'

Wilson established the attraction and love interest between the Detective-Sergeant Alan Cunningham and Bruce Coverdale's sister Diana:

'...Few men could resist the charm and beauty of Diana but, having known her since they were both children, he had learned, in addition, to appreciate and admire the sterling character of his friend's twin sister. As he returned her look, he marvelled once again at the beauty that was hers, and his heart grew hungry within him. He felt he would have given his soul to have glimpsed some reflection of his love in those wonderful blue, almost violet eyes. Slowly his gaze travelled to the delicately-shaped eyebrows, which, being perfect in form, needed no artificial plucking to aid their symmetry, thence to the broad white forehead, the mass of glossy chestnut hair. Then his eyes sank to the lower part of that patrician face, glorying in the straight little nose with its sensitive nostrils; the sweet mouth, now half open in a smile, showing two even rows of tiny, white teeth; the beautifully-formed but determined chin; the creamy softness of a neck that spoke eloquently of the divine skill of the great Sculptor. Truly, he reflected, Diana was well-named. Only a goddess could possess such perfections both of body and mind. A little blush began slowly to mantle her throat and face and, realising the effrontery of his intense regard, he reluctantly tore his eyes away.'

Mr Justice can be seen as an intensely political novel; not in the sense of advancing the aims of the Independent Labour Party with George Orwell style writing, but in articulating an anger and revenge fantasy for economic justice. Alexander Wilson's 'victims' are not necessarily the hunger marchers and unemployed working class miners and shipbuilders of Jarrow and Ebbw Vale, but equally the hard-working and meritocratic middle classes losing their savings in failing banks. Wilson's book addresses a crisis more of social ethics rather than party politics. He cleverly explores through his fiction how a 20th century vigilante 'Robin Hood' can conspire with the new world of mass media in the empowerment of the legend of 'Mr Justice' in the letters and messages left at the scene of 'his' criminal outrages:

'You have risen to prosperity by fraud and through the sufferings of the men who worked for you. Justice demands that a percentage of your ill-gotten gains should go to those in dire poverty through no fault of their own. The gems I am appropriating will raise a fairly large sum for this purpose. Later I may extract more from you.'

'Mr Justice' designed 'his' own insignia to leave on 'his' devastating calling cards for the selfish and avaricious. The invisible social vigilante targets individuals whose wealth has been derived from the exploitation and unfair embezzlement of others:

'Samuel Bernsdorff, you have ruined thousands by your greed. The diamond will enable me to recoup some of them. If your greed has not choked all feeling out of your heart, perhaps some day you will be glad I have taken it.'

One appeal of the plot is undoubtedly the fact that two of the women friends of the four men were equal candidates for being the protagonist for interventionist justice in the style of a *James Bond* of the 1930s. Wilson's storytelling has such brilliance that the reader cannot exclude the possibility of more than one of the friends being in league together. Could it be the case that the newly promoted Inspector Cunningham has teamed up with Diana's best friend Myra to secretly deliver the justice he believes Bruce Coverdale was right to aspire to in his dreams? Or perhaps the richest among them, Templeton, is 'Mr Justice'. The luxury of an ample private income gives him nothing better to do but exercise his clandestine conscience and assuage the internal guilt of having been born with wealth and comfort while so many are committed to a struggle for day to day survival. Perhaps the real protagonist is the journalist

Willard, succumbing to the double temptation of generating an ongoing series of scoops and using the power of his own profession to iconise his secret and popular infamy? Wilson keeps the reader tantalised and intrigued to the very end, though some detective fiction aficionados have been given enough clues to harbour enough suspicion as to 'Mr Justice's' real identity.

Although written by a male author, the content of *Mr Justice* is a further example of Wilson's writing that is early proto-feminist in social and gender construction. Wilson had a refreshing inclination to construct thriller/crime novels where the central women characters not only had the upper hand but triumph morally and politically with characterisation that was counter-stereotypical in not straitjacketing them with *femme fatale* or hysterical breakdown tropes requiring the moral and medical deliverance of men. *Mr Justice* is an undiscovered classic of twentieth century popular crime fiction. Its plotting, characterisation, thematic structure, representation and ideology were pioneering and revolutionary in the 1930s and eighty years later the novel has a fresh and exciting criminology combined with adventuresome zeal that would crackle in any media dramatisation in its Art Deco and 1930s nostalgic context.

Mr Justice had and has the potential for serialisation in novel, radio and filmic/ television form. Since the novel poises key characters with unconsummated romantic love interests and unresolved cliff-hanger directions of narrative, it is astonishing Herbert Jenkins did not press for a follow-up. Alexander Wilson's agent, John Farquharson had a storytelling source for radio drama serialisation and screenplay with powerful global production potential in the UK, USA, British Empire, and European markets.

The death of the author

The author, Alexander Douglas Gordon Chesney Wilson, died in October 1942 at the Battle of El Alamein. He had been a Lieutenant Colonel in the British Indian Army serving in the First Punjabis regiment. That was the uniform the young Mike Shannon last saw his father wearing when waving goodbye to him on the platform of a railway station on the Yorkshire Dales in 1941. That was the uniform his father was wearing in the last photograph he had of his father. And that was how his uncle Reg and mother Dorothy told him his father had died around his ninth birthday in the autumn of the third year of the Second World War. If he had done any rudimentary checking later on in life, he would have discovered there was a Lieutenant Colonel Wilson who was killed in artillery fire at the first battle of El Alamein in July 1942 in command of a battalion of the First Punjabis.

In Mike's world it would not only have been his father who had been killed. The writing career of an author of 24 novels who had been so highly acclaimed across the English-speaking world also had to die. The significance of this subterfuge of being killed in action in heroic circumstances needed a cover story and real-life legend of action and consequence. Alexander Wilson, the writer, had to be mourned as well, perhaps by the writer himself. This may well be the significance of some of Wilson's unpublished manuscripts bearing a completely different 'Wilson' identity: 'Colonel Alan C Wilson.' The real Alexander Wilson knew he had to begin from scratch if he wanted to resurrect his writing career. His new manifestation of authorial identity could not present himself to a publisher with the line: 'By the way I'm the Alexander Wilson who wrote all those *Wallace of the Secret Service* novels.' Because that Alexander Wilson was dead to his second wife Dorothy and his son by that marriage, Michael Chesney Wilson.

And it was not just Alexander Douglas Gordon Chesney Wilson who had been killed in the desert sand of the El Alamein battles. There was the Michael Chesney pseudonym that had authored another promising series of espionage and military thriller novels between 1938 and 1939: *Callaghan of Intelligence*, *"Steel" Callaghan*, and *Callaghan Meets His Fate*. The Colonel Geoffrey Callaghan character of British military intelligence was gathering momentum and following throughout the English-speaking world. The Callaghan books were being reviewed strongly from Singapore to Nottingham where a regional paper would say of *"Steel" Callaghan* in February 1939: 'A tale of hair-raising adventures among the tribesmen of the North-West Frontier. An interesting character created by Mr. Chesney is a very Westernised Mohammedan girl who gives considerable assistance to the political police in frustrating a projected outbreak by the tribesmen.'

The author Michael Chesney had to be killed as well. In selecting this pseudonym Alexander Wilson was giving honour and an expression of love to the son he had christened 'Michael Chesney' in 1933, but for unaccountable and unexplained reasons he would have to abandon forever nine years later. When the last Callaghan novel was written and published in late 1939, both publisher and author gave every sign the series would continue.

In the final chapter of *Callaghan Meets His Fate* we learn *en passant* that the Colonel has reached the age of forty and married Leila whose romantic figure is lovingly created in the novel's opening paragraph: '"Her eyes are a soft, velvety shade of brown, veiled by long dark lashes, and there is something magnetic about them. Her nose is small and straight, and she has a little mouth with lips as red as […] not more than five feet, but somehow, in spite of her littleness, she doesn't give one the idea that she is the type of woman who requires protection. She simply radiates capability."' This is classic Wilsonian romanticism and so typical of his description of women characters. At the end of the final Callaghan novel we also learn that Colonel Geoffrey has also been appointed Director of Military Intelligence at the War Office. The novel's police detective characters Slater and Weaver 'were both expecting to be attached to Intelligence before very long' because '"Steel" Callaghan has ideas!'

But those ideas and the many others that the writer Alexander Wilson might have had would be snuffed out and liquidated in all the chaos and enigmas of his bizarre and still largely unfathomable professional and private life. We can also not rule out the possibility of the veil being pulled over his writing career because of the turn of fashion and interest in popular writing after the Second World War.

Chapter Ten

Scoundrel or Sentimental Crook?

It is tempting to judge Alexander Wilson only by his criminal behaviour. Once one strips away the chaff and decoy of possible intelligence fantasy and potential nonsense about the undercover operation which for reasons of national security he could never explain, what is left is unpleasant and disreputable. Wilson was a crook. He even confessed to being one with the title of his 1934 novel *The Sentimental Crook*. He may have been a villain with emotions, but also recognised perhaps that he was a dyed in the wool cad and scoundrel.

The Sentimental Crook had previously been sold to another publisher with the title *Confessions of a Scoundrel* - only the first and last chapters were changed. Everything else was largely word for word. A New Zealand critic spotted the con with an article titled 'Talk about "stolen thunder"'. He contacted the publishers. Had Alexander Wilson ripped off Geoffrey Spencer or Geoffrey Spencer ripped off Alexander Wilson? He never twigged they were one and the same man.

Wilson was busted for most probably card sharping returning Great War veterans of their hard-earned savings having risked life and limb in the trenches of the Western Front, and did six months hard labour in one of North America's toughest penitentiaries. But he got away with employment as an English professor in British India with a fake CV, a degree and masters from Oxford he never earned. He even went round Lahore as Sir Alexander Wilson.

He inveigled himself into MI6 with another fabricated CV- Repton School, Cambridge University, cousin to Winston Churchill? All lies. He faked a burglary at his home in war-time London. That got him chucked out of MI6. MI5 were convinced he even made up the bugged calls he was listening to. He was arrested for wearing a Colonel's uniform and medals he was never entitled to and did time in Brixton Prison in 1944. He left his hand in the till when cinema manager in Hampstead and did three months in 1948.

For the rest of his life he got away with fraud and pecuniary advantages by deception. He forged his third wife's signature to get educational grants their sons were not entitled to. She had to pay everything back after he 'dropped dead' in their kitchen. He had promised that the truth of his heroic life as a great spy would be revealed to her after his death if she cared to examine his wallet.

When she did so in front of the priest administering the last rites, it was empty.

Two very similar books

Confessions of a Scoundrel was published by T Werner Laurie in 1933 under the pseudonym Geoffrey Spencer and The Sentimental Crook by Alexander Wilson was published under the name of Alexander Wilson in 1934. Geoffrey Spencer was in fact Alexander Wilson. Publisher's correspondence survives and Alexander Wilson gives an address in the Piccadilly Circus area of Soho. It also reveals that 'Major Wilson' changes his agent from Curtis Brown to John Farquharson. Unfortunately, all documents and papers that Herbert Jenkins may have had on Alexander Wilson have not survived. Even more frustratingly all the papers of Wilson's agent John Farquharson were destroyed in a storage fire.

The New Zealand reviewer spotted the potential publishing fraud of both books being nearly identical when reviewing The Sentimental Crook. 'Now here's a case' said the writer. The reviewer continued: 'Certain incidents have been given a slight "twist in detail," but generally the settings and characters are the same.' Both publishers were contacted on the 'coincidence' and said they were 'going into the question.' Wilson never had a book published under the name of Geoffrey Spencer for T Werner Laurie again. But he continued to be published repeatedly and with great success by P.G Wodehouse's publisher Herbert Jenkins.

It is not the fact that he had apparently got away with selling what amounted to the same book twice that is significant. Both books are first person narratives and written in the style of a confession. Confessions of a Scoundrel was so realistic that the reviewer for the Times Literary Supplement talked about it as if it were non-fiction. Alexander Wilson never kept a diary and did not write any autobiography. As the novels explore the motivation of a criminal's character as well as representing real-life incidents in Wilson's life there may be clues in both texts that can explain his character and conduct.

Aggrandisement

Alexander Wilson consistently misrepresented and exaggerated his background, education and status throughout his life. During the Great War he only reached the rank and responsibility of an acting lieutenant. Yet on his second son's birth certificate he described himself as a former Captain. When taking on the role of commanding a university cadet force at Islamia College, University of the Punjab from around 1926, he appears to reward himself the rank of Major. A major is usually in charge of a company. His cadet force was no bigger than half a company. The rank would have been honorary, but there is no surviving documentation indicating that he had any official sanction for calling himself Major Wilson. The same self-promotion seemed to have happened in

London in 1940 when he was working for the Secret Intelligence Service. He suddenly presented himself as a Lieutenant Colonel in the British Indian Army. He was not entitled to do so, and this led to his criminal prosecution and conviction in October 1944.

Despite having served a jail sentence for misrepresenting himself as a Colonel by wearing a bogus uniform, he continued to present himself as a retired Colonel of the Indian Army in all kinds of documentation to all and sundry for the rest of his life.

He had a similar problem with medals and decorations. He was not content with the Silver War Badge that he was awarded for service during the Great War which was a special tribute from King George V to members of the armed forces wounded or invalided. When arriving in Lahore to take up his role as a Professor of English Literature, he began claiming a Distinguished Service Order, Military Cross, Mention in Despatches, and a Legion of Honour from France. He had never been awarded any of these medals and decorations. During the 1930s and once again in 1948 he wrote to the War Office asking for First World War medals, but they wrote back to him explaining that as he had never been posted to any overseas unit, he was not entitled to any.

He continued to pretend that he was an RAF pilot, and went around wearing RAF wings, and the ribbons for DSO, DSC, mentioned in despatches badge, and the Croix de Guerre during the Second World War. This also led to criminal prosecution and a jail sentence at Marylebone Police Court in 1944. *The Evening Standard* branded him *'The Bogus Colonel Who Wore Wings,'* a headline that haunted and profoundly upset his second son Dennis who was, himself, an honourable infantry officer nearly killed in action during the Battle of Normandy. Yet Alexander Wilson continued to claim some of these decorations in various forms of official documentation afterwards.

During the Second World War he used his father's First World War blue officer's book probably to corroborate his false Colonel's status. His father, also called Alexander Wilson, had been a Lieutenant Colonel in the RAMC and died of exhaustion in 1919 having been mentioned in dispatches for his invaluable work at the Western Front in organising medical supplies. The blue book should have been returned to the War Office. Instead somebody, and we assume it was his son, amended the date of birth from 1864 to 1894. This was done with scratching and ink. It was most probably used by his son as part of his bogus Colonel performance.

Wilson told the Stipendiary Magistrate in 1944, when he admitted the impersonation and false medal offences, that his motivation was stupidity and vanity: 'he hated being out of khaki at this time, and the masquerade was "sheer madness.'" This was a clear admission of his uncontrollable inferiority complex. He could never be content and easy in his own skin. He had to be as good or better than the people he admired or was jealous of. It is so sad and tragic that a man so talented, gifted, charming and popular should resort to such pathetic devices.

Fake education

Alexander Wilson had an excellent education. He went to the famous St Joseph's College in Hong Kong and when his father was stationed in Plymouth he had all the benefits of bilingual day teaching from the De La Salle brothers at St Boniface Roman Catholic cathedral school. His father's successful career as an RAMC quartermaster commissioned officer meant the Army subsidised Alexander's schooling. Yet, this was not good enough. In a highly class-structured society where the public school system determined elite and superior social status, Alexander decided to fake his enrolment at the Repton public school. He obtained the professorial teaching post at Islamia College by falsely claiming a degree from Oxford University which oscillated in publication and documentation from BA Oxon to MA Oxon. Even more bizarrely Wilson as a Professor and Principal at the College was being presented as 'Sir Alexander Wilson' with the Baronet nominal after his name.

The Times advertisement for the Islamia College Professorship required a first degree qualification. He may have needed to fake this aspect of his curriculum vitae, but Wilson's tremendous success as a lecturer, academic and University College principal clearly demonstrates he did not need to take on the multiple adornments of a Baronetcy, and all his other gongs.

There is no doubt that Wilson was hugely gifted as a linguist. He claimed facility in Cantonese Chinese, French, German, Arabic, Urdu, and Persian. His fluency has been witnessed and corroborated. He would have been very rigorously tested by specialist examiners before being recruited as a linguist/translator for the secret section at MI6 bugging the calls of London embassies. Yet, this was not good enough for him. He decided to falsely claim a BA and MA in modern languages from the University of Cambridge. Incredibly these qualifications matched another Alexander Wilson who had served as a Lieutenant during the Great War and also had a father called Alexander Wilson. The real Alexander Wilson entitled to the qualifications went on to teach languages at Manchester Grammar School.

The Marlborough fantasy

Alexander Wilson's parents had climbed the social stratosphere from very humble origins. His mother Annie had defied her Republican family in Ireland to travel thousands of miles to marry her British Army sergeant in Hong Kong in 1886. By the end of the Great War his father had served 40 years in the Army having joined as a boy soldier at the age of 15 in 1869. He had risen through the ranks to earn a commission and died a Lieutenant Colonel having provided distinguished service during the Boer War and receiving the Queen Victoria and King Edward the Seventh medals. But this was not enough for Alexander Wilson. He needed to be the son of somebody much more noble and exciting. Colonel Gordon Chesney Wilson and Lady Sarah Wilson's son had died from septicaemia after a burst appendix at the age of 9. His first initial was 'A' not for Alexander but Alan. Colonel Gordon Chesney Wilson had died an heroic death in the first year of the Great War. Alexander Wilson's real father had merely had a heart attack in the year after the conflict was over.

Alexander Wilson began claiming his connection with Colonel Gordon and Lady Sarah- a daughter of the Duke of Marlborough who was a swashbuckling war correspondent during the Boer War and whose glamour and wealth was so much more exciting and impressive than that of his Irish mother Annie, the daughter of a publican from Dublin. Yet again this dissembling is the manifestation of social inferiority. It is part of a general pattern that extended to all aspects of the legend that Alexander Wilson created for himself. He was a talented soccer and cricket player. It was not enough that he may have played amateur for Plymouth Argyle, a fact that the club was unable to corroborate. He had to claim two amateur caps for England; something that official records clearly demonstrate he had never achieved.

Alexander Wilson was always economically challenged. There is no evidence that he had ever owned any property. Yet this inadequacy would be countered by the fantasy that he owned a wonderful country home called Ringwood in the New Forest that had been requisitioned by the Army during the Second World War.

First criminal antecedent

The first evidence of an actual criminal conviction and sentence for Alexander Wilson arises from a record kept by British Columbia Board of Corrections from 1919. He had joined the Merchant Navy in the role of purser in May 1919, an occupation that his Royal Naval background and Army Commission in the Royal Army Service Corps clearly qualified him for. The merchant seafarer record reveals he was employed by the Glasgow based Scottish shipping line Shaw, Saville and Albion which ran passenger and freight routes to Australia, New Zealand, the Pacific, South and North America.

Wilson was accused of stealing the precise sum of £151 and two and a half old pence while on the high seas on 7th September in his role as the purser on the SS Prinzessin. This ship had been a German passenger liner surrendered to the allies at the end of the First World War.

The crew agreement for the ship shows that Wilson joined at Victoria Docks London at 1 a.m. on 13th May 1919 on a route from London to Vancouver via Yokohama, Shanghai, Hong Kong, Singapore, Penang and Colombo. It was described as his first ship, thereby excluding any indication of previous merchant navy service, unless he had signed on previously under a false name. This would not have been unknown. Going to sea like joining the Foreign Legion was a traditional refuge for men who had something to run away from or were seeking adventure in an escape from their desperately poor and dreary lives. The registration process seemed to invite them to create a new identity for themselves.

Traditionally the financial integrity of the purser in naval folklore has always been vulnerable. Tasked with quarter-mastering the ship's supplies and performing the role of ship's banker the perks of creaming a profit on the trading can easily lead to 'misunderstandings' in deck accounting.

On the day before his formal arrest in Vancouver, 19th September 1919, unknown to him, approximately 4,750 miles away his father had died of a heart attack in Minster, Isle of Sheppey while on leave from France- a country that was being devastated by the Spanish influenza pandemic and killing more soldiers in army camps than the recently ended war in the trenches.

No records of Wilson's trial before the Vancouver Stipendiary Magistrate H.C. Shaw on 7th October 1919 had survived. So it was not known if he pleaded guilty or not guilty. All that was known was the sentence: six months with hard labour at the Oakalla Prison Farm- the most notorious prison in Canadian criminal history. The SS Prinzessin embarked at London on 20th December 1919 with a passenger and crew list missing Alexander Wilson. The SS Prinzessin crew agreement is endorsed with a stamp from the Vancouver Police Court confirming that Alexander Joseph Wilson had been discharged into its custody on 20th September 1919 by the ship's master Arthur Neagle.

£151 in 1919 is worth just over £8,000 in 2018. It is also possible Wilson had been caught 'card-sharping'- cheating at card-games such as poker. At least two of his sons remembered that he shuffled cards with the dexterity and confidence of somebody who knew how to play and win games with stakes. His duplicated novels reveal expert knowledge of how to manipulate card gambling and gaming. *The Sentimental Crook* has an entire chapter 'A Manipulator of Cards' devoted to the art of card-sharping. The fiction in the first person provides a narrative of a young man travelling across the world having signed on under a false name; something the real Alexander Wilson might have been able to do between 1912 and 1914. An added element to this 'facility' is that his sons Gordon and Nigel remembered he was also something of a competent magician. He could do plenty of magical card tricks. And others too such as apparently melding together bits of string he had previously cut to pieces with scissors into one robust strand.

Fiction as truth?

The entry on the Provincial Gaol Record form under the title 'Marks on the body of the prisoner,' provided official documentary evidence of injuries that Wilson had to have experienced prior to October 1919 and most probably during the First World War. Three scars were recorded on the lower arm, four to the forearm, several on his left breast, two on his left collar bone, one on his right wrist and a large scar on the inside to his left knee. This was a precise and independently verifiable description of the shrapnel scars noted by Alison and his surviving children. The implication is that Alexander Wilson experienced two violent incidents during his service in the Great War. War office records only documented the accident that damaged his knee and necessitated an operation.

The large number of shrapnel scars distributed across the left side of his body had no official explanation, but Wilson had included a passage in *The Confessions of a Scoundrel* suggesting these wounds arose from shelling at the front. The character Geoffrey Spencer described in the first person how he was blown up by a bomb dropped by an aircraft during the Battle of the Somme. This battle took place after Wilson had been invalided out of the army: 'As I was giving my orders a German aeroplane, flying low, came over. A bomb burst nearby, and every man, prisoners and Tommies alike, made a rush for shelter. I was following, when came another shattering roar. I felt a terrific shock, the world seemed to be spinning round, jumbling in hopeless confusion khaki and grey figures, tank and trench. A silence surrounded me and a dreadful darkness.'

Wilson's RASC transport duties took him to within a few miles of the Western Front. It is not inconceivable that he could have been subject to either shellfire or aeroplane bombardment. His army records do not include any of the completed medical examination reports that fully determined his invalidity status. If his body scars did not represent shrapnel or blast wounds it is also possible they may have related to injuries sustained in the crashing of an early Royal Naval Air Service plane very briefly referred to during his interview for the emergency war commission reserve in 1940.

His Great War medical papers make euphemistic references to problems with sleeping indicating symptoms that would now be recognised as post-traumatic stress related issues. The clear evidence of receiving scarring injuries from a

173

violent incident apart from the knee accident provides some explanation for this. His son Dennis speaks with the authority of an army officer who has experienced battle when he affirms that his father's descriptions of front line fighting in *Confessions of a Scoundrel* were realistic.

There can be no doubt that the six months of hard labour at Oakalla deeply affected Wilson. The prison farm could not be described as some agricultural holiday camp on the Pacific coast. In *The Sentimental Crook* it would seem Wilson decided to depict the experience for his first person character Michael Granville as lasting three years: '...and a little later I was transferred to the penitentiary, there to lose my identity under a number, and suffer hell not for three years, but for three eternities. I cannot think of those years without a shudder. Years of acute torment suffered under the most humiliating conditions to which men can be subject. God! The surroundings alone were enough to break one's spirit for ever. The cell with its scanty few feet of space; the hard cot; the iron galleries; the barred doors, which clanged with metallic reverberations that seemed to sear my heart every time they shut. Then the odious striped uniform, the guards everywhere, their commands jerked out in harsh, grating tones that I would not have used to a dog. I was a beast among beasts, a thing of no account, toiling day by day through the wearisome abasement of a timetable that only paused to continue again its degradation on the morrow.'

There is no doubt that the passages in this novel about the day of release are invested in great authenticity and feeling. This is prose written by an author who has experienced what he is writing about: 'After the morning meal I sat in my cell, shaking like an aspen leaf, unable to believe that my term had really expired, dreading that there might be some mistake. It did not seem possible that I was to be at liberty again, free to go where I liked, do what I liked, hear the laughter of men and women, the happy voices of children. I could not keep control of my thoughts – they were racing through my brain in mad confusion, but all the time one rose paramount above the rest, and kept repeating, "I am free; I am free!" until I found my foot tapping in consonance with it.

A dead silence reigned round me, for all my associates in that block were at work somewhere, either in the shops, or outside the prison, and I was entirely alone, waiting for the summons that I had ached for, yearned for, yes, prayed for, for three years. Abruptly the stillness was disturbed. I heard a soft tread mount the iron steps, and come along the gallery. As it approached nearer an intense nervousness, almost a feeling of shyness, took possession of me, and I kept my eyes fixed on the ground. A shadow darkened the cell.

"Come along, six-twenty," ordered a voice, which strangely had no longer the rough accents to which I had grown accustomed.

I rose to my feet, trying to appear unconcerned, but was compelled to sit down again, because of the absurd trembling of my legs. I looked at the warder apologetically, and, to my surprise, saw a very human smile upon his face. It seemed all wrong somehow. He had always looked so harsh and stern before.

"Guess you're feeling a bit upset," he observed in kindly tones. "It's only the old hands who can walk in and out as though they owned the place."

Presently I was able to follow him along the gallery and down the stairs to a room where I discarded my uniform of shame, and put on the garb of respectability. Then he led me on once more towards freedom. As in a dream I heard doors clang to behind me, crossed a large open space, where two convicts, polishing the floor, glanced up at me and winked their farewells. The last obstacle of all, a ponderous, steel-barred affair, opened to let me through, and closed with a wonderful air of finality behind me. A few words with the warden in his office, and I stepped out into the sunshine a free man. That was the greatest moment of my life.'

The most detailed history of Oakalla Prison farm was written and published by one of its former correctional officers, Earl Andersen, in 1993. *Hard Place To Do Time* reveals that Oakalla was probably Canada's most notorious prison where between 1912 and 1991 'forty-four men were "hanged by the neck until dead" on Oakalla's gallows' and where 'for many years prisoners were forbidden to speak, except by special permission from the Warden.' Wilson served his time during those years under the power and control of the first warden William G. McMynn who ruled 'in strict military fashion.'

Alexander Wilson's description of Michael Granville's US penitentiary matches in great detail many aspects of the brutal *Shawshank Redemption* style external and internal architecture, and brutal and oppressive atmosphere.

When Wilson writes of horror and hell in *The Sentimental Crook* his writing is based on the truth of his personal experience. He was not exaggerating the reality of Oakalla in any way. He started his sentence within weeks of the prison's first capital execution. Prisoner 2883 Alec Ignace was hanged from temporary gallows erected in the very yard Alexander Wilson walked over when entering the prison on the 9th of October 1919 and when leaving it on 23rd February 1920. Alexander Wilson was inmate number 3096 and the physical and mental terror of his hard labour regime broke his health for his gaol record discloses that he was removed to the General Hospital between 5th January and 10th of February 1920.

Unlike Michael Granville, his crime had not been on the scale of lifting half a million dollars. In reality it would seem the young Alexander Wilson was utterly alone and nobody; not even any member of his family, let alone his wife Gladys, had the faintest idea of where he was and what was happening to him. He was in a foreign country unknown to anybody. There was no evidence from the British Columbia records that he had had any respite in terms of working in the prison library or doing special light duties.

Wilson's description of penitentiary life hits home with the multisensory depiction of internal and external squalor, the bullying and brutality of prison officers and the pathetic observations of human behaviour that could be cruel one moment and kind and humanitarian the next. His moving description of Granville's panic and fear of the loneliness and insecurity in being freed again represents an inner core psychological understanding of the experience of having lived in that reality. Wilson's description of his character's despair on learning that his fiancé had abandoned him, known as the 'Dear John' letter by soldiers serving in the frontline of war, would have been likely witnessed by Wilson as the experience of another inmate.

Earl Andersen's book contains a formidable photograph of the Oakalla prison officer staff circa 1920, the very people in charge of Wilson. Twenty five men and the one woman, presumably the prison matron, project hard hearts through their cold and unfeeling countenances.

Criminality in perspective

In truth, all of the evidence of Alexander Wilson's criminal wrongdoing does not reveal some major figure in organised crime. If he was a crook, his offending was minor. His crimes were misdemeanours and not felonies for he was never tried for any offence at the Crown Court. The longest sentence he ever received was six months in Canada. The imprisonment for being the bogus Colonel who wore wings was only in default for not being able to afford the fines. The penalty for the misunderstanding over the takings at the Playhouse Cinema in Pond Street, Hampstead amounted to only three months. The amount of money involved was £223 the equivalent of around £8,200 in 2018 values. It is curious that the value of the amount taken was the same as he was accused of stealing from the SS Prinzessin in 1919.

His explanation to the court was all rather sad. He told the investigating detective: 'I have been very foolish, you may not believe me; but I didn't have any of the money. I had £141 stolen from the office during last October, and again about a month later I lost, or had stolen from me at Edgware Road £94 after I had cashed one of the firm's cheques.'

When he was asked about the two bank paying in vouchers which appeared to have been altered, he replied: 'I did that to cover up the loss.' His plea to the magistrate was that he had not in fact stolen any money at all. Since he had lost

176

the money, or been robbed, he had been paying in money received two days after he got it to cover up the deficiency. He was expecting money in regard to some books he had published and hoped to make good the loss of his employer's money. These are the rather feeble words of somebody who has never really understood the principle of managing a business's takings. If it is fraud, it is pretty incompetent, minor and rather farcical.

Again, this is criminality on a rather pathetic level. The surviving court papers for the case in 1948 reveal Alexander Wilson was originally arrested at 6.05 p.m. on 21st April four months before his eventual sentence. It would appear that the stipendiary magistrate wished to give him as much time as he could to make restitution to his employers and thereby substantially mitigate the sentence. The long period between his first court appearance in April and his sentence in August is also explained by several instances when it was reported he was too ill to appear in court.

In the absence of any evidence that Alexander Wilson was thieving for personal extravagance and greed, it can be assumed that his criminal convictions represent a course of fraud and dishonesty in order to sustain the needs of his many families. The investigation by the police in 1942 into what they suspected as a fake burglary at his flat in West Hampstead did not proceed to prosecution. It is more than likely they realised he had staged the burglary in order to cover up the fact he was selling jewellery he had recently given to his wife in order to pay her medical bills. Was the card-sharping on SS Prinzessin or unlawful profiteering with the ship's stores a way of bringing back some funds to help set up home with Gladys and their 2-year-old son Adrian in Southampton?

The military uniform offence and fake decorations had nothing to do with trying to obtain a financial advantage. The cinema management embezzling may well have been a matter of dishonesty getting the better of him because of the desperate need to make things better for Alison and their two young sons, and to also send something to his first wife Gladys in Southampton.

He faked his applications for the Professorship in Lahore in 1925 and the intelligence officer's job at the Secret Intelligence Service in 1939 so he could do good for his country and make a living for his family, or we should say families.

He forged his wife Alison's signature in educational grant applications so that their sons could have the best schooling available. This was another fraud, and Alison had to pay back all £300 after his death. His actions were, of course, dishonest, but the motive again was doing wrong to do right for his children. The behaviour lacked moral judgement and was another example of his stupidity. All well and good if he got away with it. But after his death his grieving widow had to face the music and recompense the local authority.

Bankruptcy

Alexander Wilson does not appear to have been capable of doing bankruptcy properly. It was not a crime in January 1944. It was not relevant to his prosecutions in 1944 and 1948, yet it might have been useful in mitigation or to help the magistrates judge his social and financial circumstances. He was supposed to have undergone a public examination, but there is no evidence at all that this was reported anywhere.

It had been advertised on the front page of *The Times* on 1st January 1944 but not one member of his family had any knowledge of it, and no subsequent record existed that he was ever discharged, a process that has to be registered whether or not he had been able to pay his debts.

Wilson had the full attention of the Senior Official Receiver, Mr. L.A. West in Carey Street who would have investigated and evaluated in great detail every possible trail of income and assets that would have stretched from London to Southampton; even to Dorothy in Bridlington. His agent and all his publishers would have been contacted and a charge put on any royalty payments.

When he took up cinema management in Lincoln in late 1944 and early 1945, then moving to cinema jobs in Purley and Palmers Green, the Official Receiver would have had the power to place a charge on his salary. It seems inconceivable that he would have been able to obtain this employment if he had been a declared bankrupt with criminal convictions for deception. Cinema management placed him in a position of considerable trust as he was responsible for collecting and banking hundreds of pounds in cash every week.

Whatever he did or wherever he went, the burden of the bankruptcy would have followed him if it had been real. He would have been allowed no bank account, he would be blocked from obtaining loans, the Official Receiver as trustee in bankruptcy would have liquidated all his assets in order to pay back the ordinary debt he owed to the licensed money lenders E.L. Lear Ltd at 39 Broadway, Stratford. Wilson would only have been allowed 'necessary clothes, bedding and tools of his trade.' Yet it is as though the bankruptcy process had never happened.

Bigamy

There is no doubt that Alexander Wilson committed the crime of bigamy on at least two occasions. The marriage certificates for Alison in 1941 and Elizabeth in 1955 provide the proof. It is now apparent from Christopher McGill's research in Lahore in 2015 that Wilson most probably tricked Dorothy into thinking there was a marriage there in 1928. The Bishop of Lahore is convinced there was a ceremony without official certification.

Bigamy is a significant deception in human relationships. Again, there is no evidence at all that Wilson did bigamy for financial advancement. The dishonesty here was emotional. The motive was love in every case. If he wanted sexual relationships and all the indulgences of affairs with more than one woman, there was not necessarily a need to marry them. The decisions to engage bigamous marriages were not taken with enthusiasm. It could be argued he agreed to marriage as a mark of respect. It offered the women in his life the status of respectability and a feeling of stability.

And it is also clear that the victims, if and when they became aware of their husband's double, triple and quadruple families had no desire to bring in the authorities. There was the need to protect their children who adored a father who adored them. Gladys always suspected that Alec would find the love and comfort of a woman if he was away and alone. Dorothy's anger against her husband suggests she may have suspected or indeed known about her husband's bigamous tendency. But there is no evidence that there had been any complaint on her part to the police. After her move to Bridlington she began a respected career as a police civilian worker. Alison was fooled into believing that he had been convicted and punished for it in 1944. But her loyalty and love to him was such that there had never been any temptation on her part to seek redress and vengeance by reporting him either when he was alive or afterwards. She confessed to feeling dread whenever she saw a police vehicle in the street.

Why? Problems with his father?

Alexander Wilson's fantasizing about himself and materialising this as proposed reality in everyday life is what people in the military call 'Walting' - based on the character Walter Mitty. It has to stem from some deep-seated insecurity and inferiority. It may lie in inadequacies arising from his relationship with his father- the formidable Lieutenant Colonel Alexander Wilson. It may be the case that Alexander Wilson junior could never live up to his father's achievements and expectations. If he could not be as successful in the army as his father, perhaps a part of him decided he would simply make it up; particularly if it was easy to persuade people and make them believe in him. He had the same name. During the Second World War he had his father's Great War officer's book which was the same colour and largely the same design used for the 39-45 conflict.

Two of his published novels contained realistic descriptions of young male central characters being abroad when their beloved and estranged fathers had died. In *The Sentimental Crook* (Herbert Jenkins 1934) the character Michael Granville has a furious row with his father before leaving home to travel the world as an adventurer, card shark and jewellery thief:

'"Mother's darling!" he sneered. "You always were tied to her apron-strings, weren't you? What a pity it is you were not a girl. Love and devotion indeed! Pshaw! I have noticed for some time how happy you seem to be in the presence of women. You have gushed over them, and flirted with them until you have nauseated me. Do you think I haven't observed how you run after them during your holidays, holding their hands, kissing them, and giggling with them. You sentimental fool! That's the sort of thing you imbibed from your mother. If she had– "

"Stop!" I shouted. "If you say a word against her, I won't be responsible for my actions. At least, if I do show a fondness for female society, it is nothing to my discredit. I admit that girls do attract me, but is there anything to be ashamed of in that? There is no harm in it. I don't think I shall ever come a cropper on that account."

"For heaven's sake," he snapped, "try and be a man if you can. Women have nothing to do with your present circumstances. Let us leave them out of it. What do you think you're going to do now? As far as I am concerned I've finished with you. I want no gambler and thief as a son. You've disgraced your name – you can expect little more from me. The most I will do for you will be to find you a clerkship in some office. Apart from that I wash my hands of you."

"I have told you," I replied quietly, "that I intend to make my own way for the future. I want none of your clerkships."

"Your way will probably end in a jail," he sneered.

"Wherever it ends it will be my business – not yours."

His eyes narrowed, his lips met in a thin hard line as he sat contemplating me for a few seconds. Then he made up his mind.

"Very well, you shall go your own way," he remarked. "And, remember this, I do not want to have anything to do with you again. Here" – he unlocked a drawer, and withdrew a bundle of banknotes, which he threw on the desk – "take those, and go. Don't come back for any more, for henceforth the doors of this house will be closed to you. It will be no use writing. Letters from you will be destroyed unopened."

I picked up the notes, and pocketed them.

"Is that all you have to say?" I asked.

"That is all I have to say."

He rose from his chair and walked to one of the windows, where he stood with his back to me. I hesitated a moment; then slowly left the room, and the house.'

After years of philandering Granville decides to call on his father while in

London sorting out the fencing of the goods from a high-class jewellery heist only to discover that he is too late:

"'He is dead, sir."

The blow caught me totally unprepared. Not once during my years of absence from home, when my thoughts had dwelt on my father, had the possibility of death occurred to me. I staggered back before the shock, unable for some moments to do more than repeat the awful fact that the father, with whom I had had little in common but whom I had so deeply grieved, was no more. Presently, like a blind man, I groped my way into the morning-room, and sank into a chair, Birks following me in and regarding me curiously.

"When did he die, Birks?" I asked.

"Six months ago, Sir. Desperate efforts were made to find you when it was known that he was dying, but without success."

"Just leave me alone for a little while, Birks, will you?"

He quietly left the room, and I was alone.

Six months ago, and I had only just found out! While my father was dying I had been on the Riviera robbing people by trickery at cards. Just for a little while a feeling of the most utter shame came over me, and I bowed my head before the consciousness of my own abasement. But that state of mind did not last long. It would be hypocritical to pretend that I was cast down with grief. I was sorry of course, but there had been an absence of understanding between us and so little sympathy, that he had, after all, been but a father in name. My greatest regret lay in the fact that coming home in the hope of making my peace with him, I had found I was too late. Gradually the rawness of the shock wore off, and I regained full control of my emotions. I called Birks back, and learned from him that my father had suffered from heart disease for two years before his death. Apparently he had made great efforts to find me, but all in vain.'

In *Confessions of a Scoundrel*, Wilson's first person central character Geoffrey Spencer has a similar estrangement with his father, sparked by an expulsion from school involving some hanky panky with a female followed by working his passage in the Merchant Navy around the world, working in stage management 'down under', and then various criminal card-sharping, and jewellery robbery adventures throughout the world. While Granville's mother had died before the blow up with his father, Spencer's mother is still on the scene and unlike Granville he returns home in uniform as a soldier.

Is it possible that the tragedy of an estrangement from his father and the enduring insecurity that he could never measure up to the person he thought his father hoped him to be was a contributing factor in Wilson's almost pathological desire to pretend to be somebody much more successful and important than himself? The father's raging words about his son wasting his life and ending up with a dead-end 'clerkship in some office' did indeed prove to be ironically prophetic for Alexander Wilson. The character of the father in Wilson's first person novels also predicts that his son's flawed personality would eventually lead to jail. Again a prescient and sadly accurate prediction of the fate of the author of these prose narratives.

Why? The trauma of Clarice?

Alexander Wilson's habit of falling in love with women, marrying them bigamously and having their children was and is not normal behaviour. Individuals do have consecutive relationships and marriages, but they normally progress with divorce and custody arrangements before moving onto the next experience and process of remarrying. As already indicated the happenstance of falling in love again during marriage was usually managed by people through clandestine extra-marital affairs. The new woman on the scene was accorded the status of mistress. But Alexander Wilson clearly wanted the new women in his life to be more than that. As a Roman Catholic, divorce in the 1920s, 30s, 40s and 50s was a very difficult process. It required religious permission as well as a difficult and usually humiliating legal process. It was the tradition for men to fabricate evidence of adultery in hotel rooms with the help of private detectives hired by solicitors.

There was no evidence that Wilson stopped loving the women in his life even when the relationships were multiple and simultaneous. He did not want to divorce them and he certainly did not want to lose contact with his children. The situation with his second wife Dorothy was clearly different. Their separation had been hostile. We do not know why.

His behaviour was irresponsible, unethical, deceiving and while it might be possible to explain his conduct by way of mitigation, he will always be judged to have failed in his moral and legal duty according to the values of his time and also the present.

Confessions of a Scoundrel and *The Sentimental Crook* offer a shocking prose narrative of their central characters falling in love with a woman called Clarice while working in professional theatre in Australia. It is heavily implied that she is married to a bisexual or homosexual man. The relationship is presented as the first real love for Geoffrey Spencer and Michael Granville. Were Spencer and Granville the embodiment and representation of Alexander Wilson between the ages of 18 and 21 when he may have been travelling the world in the merchant navy?

Both novels are undoubtedly invested with the truth of the author's life. The intensity of the passion between Wilson, aka Spencer and Granville, and Clarice can be gleaned from this exchange:

' "Oh, Why didn't I meet you before I married him?"

"Do you love me?'

She looked up at me, and her eyes were full of tears.

"Oh, I do, I do" she cried. "It may be wrong, but I can't help it. You have become all that matters to me in life, Michael."

The love affair is represented as the happiest and most blissful period in the life of the first person character. Granville and Spencer though are so much in love with Clarice that jealousy overtakes them. When she apparently responds to an excess of attention and affection from a leading actor in one of their productions, he knocks the man down and is chided by Clarice: "'Oh Michael," she rebuked me between tears and laughter, "How silly you are! Mr Furness was doing no harm here. You had no right to behave as you did and knock the poor man down."' In the ensuing row Michael insults her cruelly. She leaves him a note saying their affair is over because it is clear he cannot love her: "'Oh, Michael how could you? How could you?"' They both break each other's hearts. In *The Sentimental Crook* Michael is denied any reconciliation when Clarice drowns in a tragic collision at sea outside Hobart.

But in *Confessions of a Scoundrel* the twist of fate is much more cruel. In the row that follows the punching of Mr Furness, Clarice is unsteady on her feet, sinks into a chair sobbing and reveals that she is pregnant. Spencer immediately assumes that Furness is the father: 'I sprang to my feet so suddenly that she fell over sideways. I can visualize her now lying there, the strained look in her white face, the fear in her eyes. Instead of taking her into my arms and fondling her, instead of pleading with her for forgiveness, I, the thing calling myself a man, glared down at her malevolently.

"Is it mine—or his?" I snapped. "Well, I don't want your brat— I'd never be sure whether I was the father or not."'

In despair Clarice decides to have a back street abortion to get rid of the child. The procedure leaves her dying from septicaemia. He returned to beg for her forgiveness too late. A doctor is called but her condition is fatal: '"You have been living with that girl, haven't you?" he asked in a more kindly tone. I nodded numbly. "Well," he went on, "She has had an abortion, and it has been deliberately brought on by somebody. Blood-poisoning has set in, and—" He shrugged his shoulders. In one stride I reached him and caught hold of his arm. "Doctor," I faltered, "you don't mean to say that Clarice is—is going to die." For a moment he looked at me; then very slowly he nodded, and patted me on the shoulder.'

If it were the case that this modern and realistic account had been a personal experience of Alexander Wilson, this may be some clue as to Wilson's near pathological tendency to take on new love and commitment through parallel marriage and parenting. Had his first true love ended with a devastating quarrel so that the woman bearing his child thought it best to obtain an abortion? And had his attempted reconciliation and apology been too late? Had he actually experienced her death as a result of the illegal operation? Of course, we will never know for sure. His fiction is inevitably a mixture of fact, fantasy and reality, but without calibration with his diary or many more contemporary accounts, it is very difficult to fix issues of truth in the fictional prose of an author. We can, however, recognise 'dramatic truth.' And in that respect the Geoffrey Spencer, Clarice, abortion, and death sequence resonates very strongly with emotional and humanitarian understanding of such matters.

Was Alexander Wilson always subconsciously trying to revisit and repair the trauma of his love for the real Clarice that ended so tragically? It is certainly the case that his chaotic and disastrous private life repeatedly led to losing love and children. It is clear he had to die from the world of his son Michael. As his 9-year-old boy was left to grieve for a father he would never see again, so Alexander Wilson had to come to terms with the fact he could never see his son again. Elizabeth Wilson left him for Scotland after two years and took their two-year-old boy Douglas with her. Wilson was never to see them again. This was another example of love and parenthood being taken away from him. Of course, he was the author of his own misfortune, but to what extent did he really have any emotional control over his predilection to love so unwisely?

Chapter Eleven

Discovery, forgiveness and reparation

Alexander Wilson's life is a truth-defying narrative of mystery, paradox, charm and alarm and enduring humanity and in the end heroic forgiveness, love and understanding. All his children remember him as a wonderful father who gave them love and confidence and hopes and dreams. He was a quintessential story-teller dancing and spinning on the edge of fantasy and reality, fact and fiction. Perhaps we should remember Spike Milligan's recollection of being woken up at 3 o'clock in the morning by his father Leo to confess: 'The tiger...I never shot him. I'm sorry. But honestly. What would you have preferred? The entertaining lie, or the boring truth?' If Wilson had elected more 'boring truth' in his life, the women and children in his life would have been spared much hurt and consternation.

All of Alexander Wilson's children decided that the dramatic truth of their father's chaos, adventure, and indeed patriotism was the thing to take from the extraordinary heritage he left for them. His third wife Alison investigated, interrogated, tried and condemned the man who gave her so much love, grief, sorrow and fun. She articulated the forgiveness that his surviving children would agree on when they consecrated a gravestone in 2008 at Milton cemetery Portsmouth bearing the words from Shakespeare's Othello 'He loved not wisely, but too well.'

In the end there is a balancing of scales, where the good in a complex, perplexing and enigmatic man is recognised over the troubling chaos of a charm and patriotism that became for him unavoidably misanthropic. And the real triumph rests with the women he loved and who loved him, and children who went on to have successful and fulfilling lives.

Wilson derived nothing materialistic or financial from his marriages. There was no evidence of profligacy, extravagance or financial incontinence. If he lived beyond his means, it was simply because he had to borrow or spend in surplus on the bare necessities. In fact, his third wife Alison was always impressed with how little he spent on himself: a few ounces of tobacco, a pint of beer and taking his children to see cricket and soccer matches. She admired his qualities as a father, his spiritual and moral guidance to their children, his mentoring and the faith, confidence and ambition he gave to them.

In the same way he never boasted or blabbed about his intelligence work, Wilson achieved a discretion and separation between his multiple families that one assumes could only be achieved by an experienced and effective operator in the world of espionage. When Wilson was living a near hand to mouth existence of temporary lodgings with Alison and their two young sons in the later years of the war and through the grim post war years of rationing, he would meet his first wife Gladys and their adult children in London town looking prosperous and dapper.

The narrative has the ritual of a secret service operation. When he took young Michael to have tea with the Captain of the Queen Mary in Southampton, his older son Dennis was working in the same port and at the same time with a firm of photographers, which took portraits of the famous liner's passengers.

All four of Alexander Wilson's wives stayed true to him in the sense that whatever their suspicions, sense of disappointment and betrayal, not one of them made any complaint to any authority. The loyalty they gave him was equal to the loyalty and patriotism he expressed and demonstrated in his service to his country. In this respect and many others it should be remembered that each of them made a powerful and easily understated contribution in terms of their service to their country too.

Wilson married his first wife Gladys in 1916 and she was on the home front in two World Wars bringing up and educating three children and for most of her married life she was a single parent. Nobody could deny that she had the patience, forbearance and forgiveness as well as the discretion and loyalty of a saint. She had to fill the vacuum of authority, love, and discipline of the absent father. She had to make all the key decisions about the education of their children and perform the financial miracles of dividing loaves and fishes when her husband no longer sent any cheques in the post.

She had to deal with all the insecurities and loneliness of a marriage without a husband who after 1925 and but for the brief period between 1933 and 1935 was constantly 'abroad'. Even in the early years of their marriage, Gladys had to deal with the responsibilities of raising a baby son on her own while it is presumed an invalided Lieutenant Wilson sought employment anywhere in the later years of the Great War and signed up for the Merchant Marine in 1919. She was on her own at the military funeral of her husband's father Colonel Wilson RAMC in East Minster, Isle of Sheppey in 1919. There came a time when she realised that Alec, as he was known by his wives and children, would never be coming back and she dealt with the situation with a quiet dignity and rational presence of mind that avoided self-pity and outrage.

The deeply held roots of his love for Gladys could be discerned in his literature. Throughout his life he had articulated in different forms the dream of living together with any one of his families in a country house in the village of Ringwood in the New Forest area of Hampshire and the opening pages of his 1933 short story 'Bound In Morocco' that formed chapter 2 of *Wallace Of The Secret Service* hints at the unattainable romantic aspiration that Alexander and Gladys may well have shared in the early years of their marriage: 'Although his duties kept Sir Leonard Wallace in London most of the year, he spent every available moment at his estate close to Lyndhurst in the New Forest. In fact, during certain summer months he lived there, travelling daily to the metropolis by car, and returning in the evening.

His country residence is a small but beautiful Tudor house set in an old world garden, with a farm attached, and encircled by the majestic trees of England's most noble forest. Both Sir Leonard and Lady Wallace loved the place, and if it had been possible would have resided permanently there. London held little attraction for them and, though they were to be seen at most functions during the season, and entertained liberally themselves, their hearts were in the New Forest.

Lady Wallace loves flowers, and is never happier than when pottering about the garden herself, while her little son Adrian has inherited her love for beautiful things and, if possible, will always escape from his governess whenever he catches sight of his mother wearing her old gardening gloves, and preparing to assist the gardener in his daily warfare against slugs, green flies, and all the other pests sent to try the horticulturalist. Sir Leonard is also very fond of flowers but, as he admits himself, cultivating them does not appeal to him. He prefers to see other people doing the work, and admire the result.

"You see, Molly," he observed one day a few weeks after his return from Egypt, as they lounged on the terrace, "gardening is all very well for the young and innocent. What do you think your precious flowers would feel like if a hoary old sinner like myself messed them about? Besides, the real art of gardening is to sit and watch things grow."

She laughed.

"How would you expect them to grow," she asked, "if they were not cultivated?"

"Of course someone must do the cultivating," he admitted, "but the real artist is he who sits and appreciates."

"Thank you," she murmured sarcastically, her eyes twinkling with merriment. "You're a fraud, Leonard," she went on; "a lazy old fraud."

"I confess it, but it's humiliating to be unmasked by one's wife."

She laughed again in that attractive way of hers, and lay back in her chair, her hands behind her head, in an attitude he loved. Never tired of admiring her, he watched her now. Lady Wallace is as clever as she is sweet, as accomplished as she is charming. Her beauty is not only physical, it is mental as well, and that is perhaps why she is as popular with her own sex as with the other. It would be impossible to dislike her, impossible to think lightly of her. Her glorious deep blue eyes, *retroussé* nose, perfectly shaped scarlet lips, and clear complexion are too well known to require description. She and her husband adore each other and jointly worship Adrian. In this twentieth century of broken marriages, divorce, unrequited love, Sir Leonard and Lady Wallace have proved that the perfect state of connubial happiness is still possible.

Wallace had given himself a well-earned holiday and, for a week, had been engaged in proving, at least so he said, that it is possible to reach an ideal state of indolence. For the time being a deep, blissful peace had entered Molly's heart, a glad relief from that feeling of anxiety which always pervaded her when he was actively engaged on those dangerous duties which so often took him away from her. Though often she felt that he undertook ventures which might have been left to others, nevertheless she would not have thought of attempting to dissuade him from them. But she dreaded the necessity which so often compelled him to risk his life. Proud of him, as she was, and of his position as the head of a department upon which the well-being and welfare of the British Empire so greatly depended, she yet prayed for the time to come, when she would have him entirely to herself, and no longer be subject to the heartache and trepidation she felt when he was away from her.

It was a glorious day in September, and the sun was sinking gradually behind the great trees that stood like sentinels to the west of their domain, as they sat on the terrace of their beautiful home. They had been playing tennis together, and were resting after their exertions. Everything was peaceful and quiet with that languid stillness which is the country's greatest charm. A feeling of contentment was in Molly's heart; she had entirely forgotten for the time being the existence of a Secret Service; was, in fact, living in the present and treasuring up every moment of the delight she felt at having her husband with her.

"Visitors," grunted Sir Leonard suddenly.

In the distance could be seen a motor car coming rapidly along the winding drive towards the house, and they watched it casually as it approached.

"It's old Humphrey's car from the station," decided Sir Leonard presently. "Now who can have come by train to visit us?"

As he spoke a premonition that her happiness was about to be interrupted came over Molly, and she sighed. Somehow the beauty seemed to have gone out of the day, she even felt a little chilly, and involuntarily shivered. Sir Leonard glanced at her, but asked no questions. He understood quite well what she was thinking.'

In this passage it is possible to imagine Alexander Wilson expressing the great tenderness that could exist in any of his marriages and all the hopes and dreams of future happiness and security that we now know would be thwarted either by his own folly or a combination of circumstances utterly beyond his control. He would never be able to realise his dream of living in the Tudor style country house in Ringwood. His son Gordon recalled the legend as it developed in his childhood: 'I have a feeling that he actually claimed that it was built in the inter-war years and he certainly claimed that it had been requisitioned in the war. As I grew up it seemed to be a sort of nirvana that was never handed back and there were certainly many cases of requisitioned properties not being returned after the end of the war.' The writing in 'Bound in Morocco' perhaps hints at the chilling effect that the spying game cast on the author's life. He may have been representing the disruptive and destructive shadows of two World Wars that seemed to cast him into financial, professional and personal chaos and misfortune, perhaps exacerbated by the weaknesses and vulnerabilities of his own personality.

But for all those flaws of character, there was certainly a consistency of attitude that for him all of the women in his life, Gladys, Dorothy, Alison and Elizabeth were in a way Lady Wallace to his Sir Leonard. They had to be left so that he could struggle to fulfil his duties as a husband to the others and be a parent to their children. It was an impossible formula. It is extraordinary that he was able to generate and maintain so much respect, happiness and love in all this chaos.

It is presumed Wilson married his second wife, the professional actress Dorothy Wick, in British India. It has been impossible to trace any marriage certificate and the recent research by Wilson's great grandson Christopher McGill in Lahore suggests he may have organised the ceremonial ritual of the marriage in the City's Roman Catholic cathedral, but avoided the official licensing and concealed this from Dorothy. The wickedness in such deception is breath-taking. Their relationship began on the high seas when finding each other on the same ship to India in 1925.

She began appearing as Mrs Dorothy Wilson in Lahore newspapers in 1928. Two photographs in the Indian album inherited by Mike from his mother show his parents garlanded with flowers. No annotation indicates whether these are wedding images. Mike's understanding of his mother's character is that he thinks it would have been inconceivable that they had not married: 'She had an adherence to moral values and social respectability.' It was also the case that she identified Alexander Wilson as her living husband in her will signed and witnessed in 1951.

It is possible that Dorothy had some intelligence connections. After leaving Wilson in 1941 she upped sticks and moved to Yorkshire. She brought up their son Michael on her own, and worked hard and tenaciously throughout her life, latterly as a civilian administrator in the East Riding of Yorkshire Constabulary. Mike Shannon recalled an incident during the Second World War when it would appear that Dorothy agreed to perform the role of a mysterious alien gypsy woman in a village adjacent to an army base to test the security, alertness and vigilance of the soldiers guarding it. He remembered seeing her using theatrical make-up, a wig and costume to perform the role and how when she removed her disguise, the threat to the realm and national security evaporated in a flash of theatrical illusion.

This event, combined with the apparent discipline and ruthlessness in the way she maintained the legend of her husband's death and erased any trace of his existence in her life, suggests she was a woman trained and practiced in the arts of intelligence tradecraft. At the very least there was evidence of enormous strength of character, independence of spirit and a robust mentality. Dorothy might have been physically petite, but emotionally her mind was immense. She was already a successful professional actress making her own way in the British Empire on tour in India when she met Wilson. Surviving documentation demonstrates she managed and organised his writing career. She made the decision that she had had enough of her marriage and organised and constructed her own way of metaphorically killing her husband through dramaturgy that was pure tradecraft. Alec would die in the desert sands of Egypt and there she buried him with a determination that brooked no sentimentality. In the dour post war years of rationing Dorothy knuckled down.

So impressive was her service as a civilian administrator of intelligence records with the East Riding Police, the chief constable and senior officers celebrated her retirement with a reception more fitting for a Detective Chief Superintendent. Throughout her life she was a stalwart producer of charity revues and these continued to utilise her musical, performance and directing skills. She pledged and provided security, protection and education for her son Michael and liquidated and erased all traces of her husband's existence. To this day Mike believes that had she not accidentally left one of his published novels in her flat in Bridlington he would have had no key at all for the unlocking of the secrets of his father.

Wilson married his third wife Alison in 1941. They had worked and met while on the front-line of Britain's intelligence war between 1940 and 1942. Alison had got into intelligence as a young woman on her own merit. These were the darkest years of the Second World War, punctuated by defeat after defeat. They worked the double shifts at MI6 headquarters in Broadway, St. James's, Westminster, at the height of the London Blitz and would dodge bombs and shrapnel on the walk back to their lodgings. Each of their respective lodgings, on different occasions in 1940 and 1944, would be blown to smithereens by high explosive and doodlebug. Alison extricated herself out of the wreckage of her digs in Harrington Gardens in November 1940 having cheated death by being in the right room on the right floor at the right time. It was a mark of her humanity and selflessness that she found it difficult to forgive herself for not responding to the cries of an injured housemate even when she knew that had she done so she would have died falling through an obliterated staircase.

Alison endured poverty, humiliation, exasperation, and confusion throughout her 22-year marriage to Alexander, but she loyally sustained his activities and accepted his explanations, however fantastic and incredible. She worked conscientiously, mothered and protected their 2 sons, and fought ferociously to give them a decent and secure upbringing. Alison was in a way as good a writer as her husband as evidenced by the narrative brightness and moral precision of her memoir. At the core of her personality was a sense of ethical certainty and honest dignity that would cut no corners. After Alexander died in 1963 instead of relying on a solicitor's sophistry to wriggle out of the implications of her late husband's fraudulent forging of her signature on educational grant applications, she paid back every pound, shilling and pence.

Her sons recalled and respected the power of her spiritual integrity and following her conversion to Roman Catholicism she devoted the rest of her life to a study of religion and philosophy. As a mature student she successfully studied for a divinity degree and her postgraduate research and knowledge of world religions secured her lecturing at the prestigious Heythrop College. She wrote a complex and impressive treatise on religious philosophy. There is no doubt that intellectually and morally she had the full measure of her late husband's enigmatic, equivocal and duplicitous character. She had fully triumphed and soared above all of the disappointments of her marriage and in her exploration and investigation of her faith asserted a dignity and confidence in her intellectual and ethical identity. It can be argued that whereas Alexander Wilson had surrendered to the moral ambiguities of the Great Game, Alison Wilson had resoundingly defeated them.

Wilson married his fourth wife Elizabeth, a senior state registered nurse, in

1955. Elizabeth was an independent, professional young woman who would never have a harsh or critical word to say about her husband even though he had clearly lied about his age and background. She took their young son Douglas to Scotland and remarried after Alexander Wilson's death in 1963. She was another intelligent young woman who met and fell in love with this secret agent and author, found her own way of dealing with the consequences of that fate, and ensured that her child would have everything a parent could give and provide. It would appear they lived a parallel existence with Wilson's third family in Ealing for a period of about two years between 1955 and 1957. The reason for her decision to move to Scotland with Douglas two years into their marriage can only remain a matter of speculation. She must have had great reserves of self-resourcefulness to set up and run a one-parent family home in Scotland for six years until her husband's death in Ealing in 1963. This is also another episode in the curious sanitizing of letters and documents by one of Wilson's wives and the compression and construction of distorted history for one of his children.

First gathering of all four families 2007

Gordon Wilson hosted the first gathering of relatives from all four families at his home in Liphook, Hampshire in 2007. Dennis Wilson, as the oldest surviving relative of his father and affectionately crowned the patriarch of his newly extended family, offered a moving and sensitively worded speech to this unique and special gathering. He emphasized the importance, courage, forbearance and honour of his father's wives and their enormous achievement as mothers in the most difficult years of the twentieth century while married to such a complex, talented and challenging husband.

But he said the truest and most valued legacy of the events of the past was the brilliance and talent of the people before him and the joy of discovering and meeting individuals he was so privileged and proud to recognise and cherish as family.

This was history with an impact on present day lives. Those individuals affected responded with good heart, an excellent human spirit and all of the enthusiasm captured in Nigel's words 'that all of us will have a more complete Christmas. The presence of Daphne and some of her family put the proverbial icing on the cake.'

Dennis wrote 'the discovery of my 28 new blood relations plus spouses (if I have added up correctly) has made 2007 one of the best years of my life, and 9th December one of the happiest days.' Dennis had painstakingly and comprehensively constructed a genealogical family tree of his new family reaching as far back as his grandparents and extending to his father's great grandchildren many of whom were playing happily together in Gordon's garden on that mild Sunday in December. They were the heroes and heroines of the saga now in taking on board all the implications with consummate dignity and understanding. The family research project had delivered Mike Shannon into a wider family clearly enjoying each other's company with such ease. Alexander Wilson's gregarious and charming nature, and the multiplicity of his talents seemed to be represented in the generations of his children and grandchildren; many of whom have pursued successful careers in professional drama, teaching, journalism and the media, and public service.

Wilson's youngest surviving son Douglas travelled from Edinburgh to Hampshire with his three daughters Tamsin, Bryony and Rowan to join the gathering and intelligently engage in the discovery and celebration of family history. After obtaining his MA in history from Edinburgh University, Douglas had worked for a charity in Pakistan and often travelled to and from Lahore, the very city that had been so critical and influential in his father's intelligence and literary career. He had read widely in the literature and history of the Great Game in this region of Imperial India, was familiar with the myths, realities, and legends of espionage and above all the romance of story-telling and human adventures associated with this region, little knowing how much his father had been involved.

Alexander Wilson's multiple and parallel marriages do not fit into any pattern of criminological frame apart from being a breach of statutory law. There is no evidence he married for money. The marriages did not advance his social and financial status. Wilson was recruited to the post of Professor of English at Islamia College, Lahore by its then Principal, Abdullah Yusuf Ali, and Wilson's second novel *The Devil's Cocktail* indicates Yusuf Ali became in all probability a friend and mentor. Wilson may have learned from Yusuf Ali that the divorce process was so utterly catastrophic in the damage to father and child relations as well as the emotional hurt between the married parties that any avoidance would be the lesser of two evils. As Zafar Ishaq Ansari observed in his foreword to Dr. M.A. Sherif's impressive biography of Yusuf Ali: 'For Yusuf Ali suffered the shock of two successive broken marriages and the ensuing agony was further exacerbated by the disrespect shown to him by his children.'

A major contributory factor in the breakdown of Yusuf Ali's marriages to two English women was the problem that his service to Empire in India meant that they could not follow him. It was a custom in the early 20th century that the wives of Englishmen with young children serving the Raj would stay behind in England. Such long term separation must have placed a considerable strain on husbands and wives. The tragedy in Yusuf Ali's case is that the inherent racism of the Raj would not tolerate the performance of a mixed-race marriage in Lahore or any other part of Imperial India. Wilson represents a dimension of this racism in *The Devil's Cocktail* through the characterisation of the Eurasian Olive Gregson who is pejoratively depicted as a predatory gold-digger:

'[Oscar J. Miles] "Say," he said; "I guess you had a narrow escape with that girl. You have to be mighty circumspect with Eurasians, or they'll raise Cain!"

Hugh looked at him in astonishment.

"Eurasian!" he exclaimed. "Why she's as pure-blooded as I am."

"Not on your life! She looks the goods all right, but if you get the chance take a peek at her finger nails; and didn't you notice that peculiar rising inflection in her voice? When you hear that, Shannon, you can bet your bottom dollar the tar brush has been about."'

Of course, these sentiments in 2018 are deeply insulting and offensive, but Wilson was accurately representing contextual attitudes and prejudices in 1928. Yusuf Ali's divorce in relation to his first marriage on the grounds of his wife's infidelity in 1912, and separation from his second wife through estrangement in 1941 may have been known to Wilson. Yusuf Ali drew up his will in 1940 and ruled out any legacy or benefits to the 4 children of his first marriage: 'These children by their continued ill-will towards me have alienated my affection for them, so much so that I confer no benefit on them by this my will.' Dr. Sherif discovered in his biographical research that the bulk of this great man's estate went to the University of London with limited legacies to his second wife and their son who had become a commissioned officer in the Indian Army.

This was a truly tragic vista of human despair that would have horrified Alexander Wilson. Racism and separation by travel and work had done their worst. It may be surmised that Dorothy could have discovered the extent of his duplicity in human relations and if this were the reason for the charade of his death at the Battle of El Alamein and losing any contact with his son Michael for the rest of his life, Alexander Wilson's determination to keep the existence of multiple parallel marriages and children part of his secret world can be readily understood. His Roman Catholic faith and the social stigma of divorce in England in the first half of the 20th century are of course other factors that would have weighed heavily on his mind. Certainly, his ability to live and perform two different identities between 1925 and 1963, to take on and sustain at any one time two and three marriages demonstrates espionage dramaturgy at the highest level. But this was spying not for his country, but for the very core of his human identity and existence.

Even when investigated by the police and the subject of criminal prosecution for other matters in 1944 and 1948 he was able to avoid discovery and prosecution for bigamy. One explanation is that his extraordinary private life was known to the authorities. If there had been any truth in the prosecution claim in 1944 that he had been under surveillance for some time because 'he had been living beyond his means' it seemed inconceivable that the Metropolitan Police detectives would have failed to discover that the reason was that he was married polygamously to three different women and responsible for five going on six children. It seemed incongruous that there was no mention in court that he had been declared bankrupt and subject to public examination in 1944.

Dedication of the headstone and monument to Alexander Wilson

Dennis Wilson believed that involving all of his brothers and sister in the commissioning of a proper monument to their father at Milton Cemetery would provide an opportunity to bring an element of spiritual closure to all the hurt and trouble created by the tragedies, paradoxes and follies of Alexander Wilson's life. All agreed with Dennis's suggestion on the wording that it would have the names Alexander Joseph Patrick Wilson at the top, followed by 'also known as Alexander Douglas Gordon Chesney Wilson, author and patriot', followed by the appropriate dates, and then the quotation 'He loved not wisely, but too well,' and after that the names of the other incumbents.

And so over 45 years after his passing away at 13 Lancaster Gardens, Ealing, in the late summer of 2008, his surviving children gathered together on a fine sunny day to expiate and forgive the misunderstandings and mystifications of the past. Douglas had previously given his brothers and sister ties and a scarf bearing the tartan pattern of the Scottish clan Wilson and on this day each and every one wore the tartan proudly and as a symbol of their family solidarity. Within feet of the monument to another MI6 agent, Commander Lionel 'Buster' Crabb, Alexander Wilson, the intelligence officer and author was immortalised with an inscription bearing the full names of both his identities and an appropriate quotation from Shakespeare's *Othello*:

'In loving Memory of Alexander Joseph Patrick Wilson also known as Alexander Douglas Gordon Chesney Wilson, author and patriot, 1893 –1963.'
He loved not wisely but too well

Dennis had prepared a simple though profoundly considered religious ceremony by which each living child of Alexander Wilson would be able to address the memory and spirit of their father. Dennis declared: 'Almighty God, we ask you to look down in mercy on our father Alexander. He grievously offended You and broke Your commandment, but he loved You all his life, and served You in his own inadequate fashion; and he encouraged all his children to love You and to serve You also. We ask you to forgive him his sins, and to give him eternal rest with You in Your Heavenly Kingdom. [...]

We say together:

We his children, on behalf of ourselves and on behalf of our respective mothers Gladys, Dorothy, Alison and Elizabeth, and on behalf of our brother Adrian, dedicate this headstone to the memory of Alexander Joseph Patrick Wilson; to his mother and our grandmother Annie Marie; to his sister and our aunt Isabella; and to Annie Elizabeth Allnutt; and we ask Almighty God to give them eternal rest in His Heavenly Kingdom. May their souls, and the souls of all the faithful departed, through the mercy of God, rest in peace. Amen.'

Each of Alexander Wilson's children then lay their roses on the plinth of the headstone, one by one in order of seniority, saying a silent prayer or message as each of them wished. Those messages remain private to each and every individual. Dennis hugged his sister Daphne as they both placed a red rose on behalf of their brother Adrian. Gordon's personal message quoted from the writings of the anti-Nazi and dissident Lutheran Pastor Dietrich Bonhoeffer who was executed by the Gestapo in 1945, Douglas recited a Scottish Gaelic poem, and Mike recited a new poem he had written in January of that year:

For A.J.P.W.

I will light a candle for you, Dad,
Although your guiding light I never had.
I'll think upon a friend I was denied
And fatherless: so many times I cried.
Did you forget when Mum took me away
The son who with such joy you used to play?
The bedtime stories ending with your kiss
That soothed me to my sleep in perfect bliss?
The dreams I used to dream that we would meet
By chance one day on any London Street;
I know at last that this will never be,
The father that I lost I'll never see,
But now, with new relations celebrate;
To reaffirm my love is not too late.

I will light a candle for you Dad
Although your guiding light I was denied,
I'll think upon the friend I never had
And fatherless became, the day you died.

Mike Shannon and his newly found half brothers and sister had had a father

196

with substantial and significant writing ability, a powerful output of best-selling and highly acclaimed thrillers and spy novels, which explicitly and implicitly indicated that the author was an experienced and very well-informed British intelligence agent or officer. Alexander Wilson was a great adventurer of the twentieth century spanning and scaling the social, political, military and cultural vicissitudes of the reigns of Queen Victoria, King Edward VII, George V, Edward VIII, George VI and Queen Elizabeth II, two World Wars, the decline and fall of the British Empire, independence and partition in India, the Cold War, the development of the Information age of mass media culture, and the sexual and moral revolutions in developing gender equality, distribution of wealth and no fault divorce.

In his living and in his writing he seemed to fundamentally touch and engage in these tectonic movements of human society on a micro and macro dimension. There was also something inherently truthful about his complex story. There was a dangerous excess of daring, wit, risk, and ambition in his life that he pursued not only for himself, but for the women he loved and the children he fathered. Despite the recklessness of many of his adventures in human relationships perhaps it could be said there was more truth in the adventures of his flawed genius than the security and predictability of those who conceal and control their supposed weaknesses and foibles.

It is impressive how his surviving children could remember relating to him as a father and cherished their memory of his *joie de vivre* and outgoing personality. He radiated charm, imagination and a sense of fun. He was the father who would play football with his boys in the park when well into his sixties, or pick up his Ukulele and raise the spirits with an anarchic singsong. But the complexities and ambiguities of his life meant that his sons Michael and Douglas both 'lost' their father at very tender ages and in their mature years have had to understand and reconcile themselves to this fact. Michael had direct memories of a father and son relationship. Douglas had indirect memories negotiated by his mother.

Every one of Alexander Wilson's first generation children has had to engage the totality of their father's life with immense emotional courage and they have shown so much grace and equanimity in the midst of devastating and challenging revelations about their family history and the continuing frustration of being denied important official information that might explain the painful paradoxes and ambiguities of Alexander Wilson's life and times.

The shades of light are inevitably cast with shadows of darkness. The counterpoint of truth is of course deception. Wilson led many secret lives in terms of the ultimate human relationship of husband and wife, a bond regarded as sacred in his Roman Catholic faith. The price of that betrayal resonates in a sentence from Wilson's novella 'That Bloody Afghan' in the early part of the characterisation of Aziz Ullah: 'Nobody knew actually whence he came, who he was or, in fact, anything about him.' The novella depended on the intelligence twist that Aziz Ullah was in fact Captain Hugh Shannon of the British Secret Service.

In the first chapter of John le Carré's novel *The Secret Pilgrim*, George Smiley warned trainee spies of the death of their own natures that could result from 'the manipulation of their fellow men, and the truncation of their natural feeling.' Alexander Wilson's spy writing colleague had a profound understanding of the ethics of the Great Game: '"By being all things to all spies, one does rather run the risk of becoming nothing to oneself," he confessed sadly. "Please don't ever imagine you'll be unscathed by the methods you use. The end may justify the means- if it wasn't supposed to, I dare say you wouldn't be here. But there's a price to pay, and the price does tend to be oneself. Easy to sell one's soul at your age. Harder later."'

The tragedy for Alexander Wilson is that he sold his soul not for espionage, but in human love. Alexander Joseph Patrick Wilson was in fact Alexander Douglas Gordon Chesney Wilson. As a result, so many of the people he loved discovered that when he was alive they really had not known whence he came and as a result he may well have become nothing to himself.

Appendix I Alexander Wilson Biographical Timeline

(1886 14th January) Alexander Wilson's father, also called Alexander and his mother Annie O'Toole married in Hong Kong. He was the son of Hugh Wilson, a private in the Army Hospital Corps, who died at the age of 31 in 1870 and was buried in the grounds of Netley Hospital outside Southampton. Annie's father was a publican in Dublin.

(1887 13th August) Alexander's older sister Isabella Marie, who became known as 'Auntie May' was born in Hong Kong.

(1893 24th October) Born Dover, Kent as Alexander Joseph Patrick Wilson-daughter of Annie O'Toole who fled a Republican family in Carlow, Ireland to marry a sergeant in the British Army Hospital Corps also called Alexander Wilson.

(1899-1900)   Mauritius. Father serving in Army Hospital Corps. Alexander's younger brother Harold born.

(1900-1903)   England while father, now lieutenant in Boer War, South Africa serving as a quartermaster supplying hospital trains in the Royal Army Medical Corps.

(1905 12th October) Alexander Wilson's younger brother Leonard Arthur born in Hong Kong.

(1903-1908)   Hong Kong. Educated at St Joseph's College, a famous Catholic school in the colony while father posted there. In Singapore for 6 months in 1907. Colombo, Ceylon 3 months in 1908. Fluent in Cantonese Chinese.

(1908-1912)   Educated St Boniface College, Plymouth where teaching by De La Salle Brothers was bilingual in French and English. Father promoted to Captain RAMC in 1910.

(1912-1914)   Midshipman in Royal Navy and reservist, Devonmouth, serving in the cruiser HMS Andromeda. Soccer player- amateur for Plymouth Argyle. Active amateur cricket player. It is possible that between 1912 to 1914 he may have been travelling the world having signed on with merchant ships under a false name. His time and work for the period between the ages of 18 and 21 (1911-14) are largely unaccounted for.

(1914-1915)   RNAS- Royal Naval Air Service. Crashes his plane. Father promoted to Major in RAMC in 1914.

(1915) Leaves Royal Navy to take up commission as Lieutenant in Royal Army Service Corps. Motor transport officer- escorting convoys of supplies from Avonmouth to Le Havre and Rouen, France.

(1915 May)   Crippling injury to knee in incident in France. At the same time or in a separate incident he may have received massive shrapnel wounds with severe scarring across the left side of his body. Sister Isabella serving as nursing sister in Malta at the same time as Vera Brittain (author of 'Testament of Youth')

(1916) In March Marries Gladys Kellaway in Lyndhurst, New Forest, England. In June invalided out of the Army. Awarded Silver War Badge for wounds/ injuries while on active service.

(1916-1919) Army pension. Tries to resume his army commission in July 1917, but his return blocked by his invalidity status. First son Adrian born 1917. Father promoted to Lieutenant Colonel 1918 and commander of all medical supplies to the Western Front, and is Mentioned in Despatches. From 1918 regular visitor to Naples, Milan, Genoa Italy, Paris, Marseilles, Amiens, France.

(1919) Merchant Navy- Purser on SS Prinzessin, London, Colombo, Penang, Singapore, Hong Kong, Shanghai, Yokohama, Vancouver.

(1919-1920) Unexplained accusation of theft on board ship (£151), 6 months hard labour in Canada's most notorious penitentiary, Oakalla Prison Farm, British Columbia. Father dies while on leave in Minster, Isle of Sheppey 18th September 1919. Therefore, misses his father's military funeral with gun carriage and guard of honour provided by 300 soldiers of the Cheshire Regiment.

(1920-1925) Runs touring repertory drama and theatrical revue company with Gladys and travels throughout England performing in provincial theatres. Second son Dennis born 1921, daughter, Daphne in 1922. Brother Harold dies in 1922 from pneumonia after a bone lodged in his throat. He was 23 years old.

(1925) Alexander Wilson applies for and appointed Professor of English Literature, all Muslim Islamia College, University of Punjab, Lahore. Interviewed by college Principal Yusuf Ali in London (a pro-British Empire Indian with intelligence connections and later translator and interpreter of the Koran.)

Wilson travels to British India on the steamship City of Nagpur from Liverpool to Karachi on 25th October. The actress Dorothy Wick, who describes herself as a 'theatrical', is on the same passenger list.

Wilson is active in Lahore, Rawalpindi and Peshawar, travelling North West Frontier region. Honorary Major Indian Army Reserve, officer commanding University Training Corps at Islamia College until 1932- connected to Punjabis Regiment. First evidence of the use of his identity 'Alexander Douglas Gordon Chesney Wilson'. Becomes fluent in Urdu while in India and acquires fair knowledge of Persian.

(1926) First academic book- co-editor *Selected English Prose Stories for Indian Students*, published in Lahore.

(1927-8)   Manuscripts of first 2 novels *The Mystery of Tunnel 51* and *The Devil's Cocktail* accepted and published by Longmans, Green & Co. First publications featuring the fictional Sir Leonard Wallace and his British Secret Service who appear to be based on the first 'C' Mansfield Smith-Cumming and MI6.

(1928) Second academic book. Editor of *Four Periods of Essays*. Appointed Principal of Islamia College. First appearance of second wife Mrs Dorothy Wilson (neé Wick) in Lahore newspapers. She is a professional actress. Acts of terrorism by revolutionary independence movement in Lahore. Murder of assistant commissioner of police J.P. Saunders and Sikh police inspector, by pro-independence group led by Bhagat Singh.

(1929) *Murder Mansion*- crime and murder thriller published by Longmans, Green and Co. Represented by literary agents Curtis Brown. Lahore Conspiracy trials in relation to terrorism incidents.

(1930) *The Death of Dr. Whitelaw* crime thriller published by Longmans, Green and Co. 3rd academic book *Selected English Essays: From Steele to Benson*, published Lahore. Wilson and Dorothy likely witnesses to assassination attempt on Governor of Punjab at degree ceremony in Lahore, Sikh police inspector killed. In Colombo, Ceylon for 6 months.

(1931) Leaves Islamia College in the wake of global Great Depression to relieve the College of the burden of paying a European academic salary. Awarded honorary fellowship of Punjab University. Appointed editor of a newspaper in Lahore.

(1932) In Arabia and Palestine for 8 months. Possible intelligence activities. Becomes fluent in Arabic.

(1933) *The Crimson Dacoit* by Herbert Jenkins (P.G. Wodehouse's publisher) A political and intelligence thriller depicting the impact of terrorism in the fight for Indian independence, and the infiltration of a mole, Kim Philby- style into India's police intelligence establishment. *Confessions of a Scoundrel* written in pseudonym of Geoffrey Spencer, published by T Werner Laurie. A modernist crime thriller addressing child abuse by a priest, abortion, homosexuality, sexual violence against women and the idea of crime being determined by environment. Second wife Dorothy returns to England pregnant. Their son Michael Chesney Wilson (later changes name to Mike Shannon) born Paddington October 23rd 1933. *Wallace of the Secret Service* published by Herbert Jenkins. Strong sales lead to reprints.

(1934) Poached by literary agency run by John Farquharson who would later represent John le Carré. *Get Wallace!* and *The Sentimental Crook* published by Herbert Jenkins. Returns to England. Double-life staying with Dorothy and

Michael in London, and Gladys and three children in Southampton.

(1935) *The Magnificent Hobo*, a popular romantic comedy, later optioned by Hollywood, published by Herbert Jenkins. Has row with first wife's aunt in Southampton and moves to London to live with Dorothy and Michael. Though remains in contact and on good terms with Gladys and their children until his death.

(1936) *His Excellency Governor Wallace* published by Herbert Jenkins. Evidence he may have travelled to Spain during the civil war. Alexander Wilson's mother Annie died in Southsea in December aged 71.

(1937) 3 novels published by Herbert Jenkins: *Double Events, Mr Justice*, and *Microbes of Power*. Assumed he might be working as an intelligence agent for Security Service, SIS (Z-Section) and/or Sir Robert Vansittart's private intelligence gathering network linked to Winston Churchill.

(1938) *Wallace At Bay* published by Herbert Jenkins. 2 pulp fiction novels published under name of Gregory Wilson (*The Factory Mystery* and *The Boxing Mystery*.) Witnessed by the young Mike Shannon meeting and speaking fluent German to Hitler's Foreign Minister Joachim Ribbentrop at the German Embassy in London's Carlton House Gardens. Possible this was part of a message courier intelligence operation just before the Nazi takeover of Austria. Leonard Wallace short story published in Faber and Faber anthology, *My Best Spy Story* and reprinted until 1956. Begins a new series of three intelligence thriller novels based on the central character Colonel Geoffrey Callaghan which are published by Herbert Jenkins. The first volume *Callaghan of Intelligence* is published in this year. He uses the pseudonym 'Michael Chesney' the forenames of his son from his second marriage with Dorothy.

(1939) *Wallace Intervenes* and *Scapegoats for Murder* published by Herbert Jenkins. Accepted in Emergency Army Officer Reserve. Evidence he has repeatedly offered his services to intelligence organisations since 1935. Emergency war police constable for the London Metropolitan Police September 1939 to March 1940 serving in Fulham and Hammersmith. Joins Section X of the Secret Intelligence service in September 1939. He was recruited as an intelligence officer translating and analysing embassy and diplomatic communications in London. This covert unit may have been based at Broadway, St James's. Two more Callaghan novels by Wilson's pseudonym 'Michael Chesney' are published: *"Steel" Callaghan* and *Callaghan Meets His Fate*.

(1940) Dorothy and Michael leave London for Yorkshire. Apparent separation. Wilson meets and develops romance at MI6 with secretary Alison McKelvie who learns that he is known as 'Buddha'. Last novels published by Herbert Jenkins: *Double Masquerade* and *Chronicles of the Secret Service*.

(1941) Waves goodbye to Michael for the last time at Leyburn railway station in North Yorkshire. Marries Alison McKelvie in her 21st year in a temporary church in Kensington High Street. Their first son Gordon is born early 1942.

(1942) Met Police investigation into suspected fake burglary at Wilson's London flat. The embarrassment caused to SIS is such that they persuade the Met Police not to investigate to full charge and trial, but at the same time decide to dismiss him from the Service. Investigation begun by the Security Service MI5 into Wilson's intercepts of telephone communications to and from the Egyptian Ambassador in London and his Embassy staff. Wilson tells Alison that MI6 have decided to send him into the field as an agent. Informs sons Adrian and Dennis that if anything happens to him Sir Alexander Cadogan or Sir Robert Vansittart would provide an explanation. He explains to Alison that his apparent sacking and any 'fall from grace' are aspects of an intelligence operation. Alison experiences near poverty as they continually move lodgings. 9-year-old Michael (Mike Shannon) told that his father was killed at the Battle of El Alamein and never sees or hears of him again. He does not discover the truth until revealed by an academic researcher with the University of London in 2006.

(1943) Alex Kellar's MI5 report on Wilson's Egyptian Embassy intercepts alleges he fabricated a false pro-Nazi plot by the ambassador to collect intelligence in London against Great Britain and Allied interests. The Chief of MI6 accepts the findings. The Director-General of MI5 Brigadier Sir David Petrie says that the fact he was no longer in the service was: '...perhaps some small compensation for the amount of trouble to which his inventive mind has put us all. A fabricator, such as this man was, is a great public danger.' The then 'C' of SIS Sir Stewart Menzies wrote: 'I do not think it at all likely that we shall again have the bad luck to strike a man who combines a blameless record, first rate linguistic abilities, remarkable gifts as a writer of fiction, and no sense of responsibility in using them!' The head of MI5 Petrie vows to ensure that Wilson is never allowed to have any post of public responsibility and it is implied he will be watched from now because of the danger he can bring.

(1944) Apparent bankruptcy in London, but never discharged. (All bankruptcies are discharged even if the debts are not paid off) Second son Dennis seriously wounded at the Battle of Normandy 1st July 1944 with disabling injuries. Alexander Wilson's apparent prosecution for wearing colonel's uniform and fake medals, and serves 2 month jail sentence October 1944 instead of paying fine of £10. Wilson tells Alison this is an intelligence stunt and operation. This claim is supported by the fact that the police case is in part based on a false premise. Second son with Alison, Nigel, born in November 1944.

(1944-1948) Develops career in cinema management, but jailed for 3 months in '48 for embezzling takings at a cinema in Hampstead.

(1948-1961)   Continues to write fiction under his real identity or 'Colonel Alan Wilson'. 4 unpublished manuscripts have survived. One is a post war spy novel with a new 'C' of the Secret Intelligence Service based on the second real chief of MI6, Admiral Hugh 'Quex' Sinclair. Unpublished writings indicate continued connections with intelligence in terms of research and themes.

(1949-1963)   Hospital porter Central Middlesex Hospital Ealing, then clerk at Sandersons wallpaper factory Perivale. He references continuing intelligence work though Alison increasingly sceptical and disbelieving. But his son Gordon remembers his father being physically affected when learning of the death of Lord Vansittart in 1957.

(1955) Marries 4th wife Elizabeth Hill in Ealing in January and carries on a double-life in the area for two years before Elizabeth moves to Scotland with their son Douglas who is born much later in the year.

(1959) Alexander Wilson's sister Isabella Marie Wilson dies in Maidenhead aged 71 in March. She was unmarried and ran a hospital and nursing home in Southsea which moved to Devon during the Second World War.

(4th April 1963) Alexander Wilson dies from heart attack at Lancaster Gardens Ealing in his 70th year. Buried with mother and sister at Milton cemetery Portsmouth feet away from the grave of MI6 agent Commander Lionel 'Buster' Crabb. Extraordinary funeral attended by two widows: Alison and Gladys. All four wives are informed of his death though apart from Alison and Gladys they are not aware of each other's existence and locations. Gladys had no idea that Alison was another of her husband's wives until after his death. Alison thought the marriage to Gladys had been annulled by the Catholic Church.

(1983) Alexander Wilson's younger brother Leonard, who was born in Hong Kong in October 1905, dies in September. He was a retired army officer and had lived in Farnham, Surrey.

(1986) Alison Wilson, now a graduate of theology with the University of London, writes a two part memoir describing and reflecting on her life with Alexander Wilson, the lies and deception, the sorry story of him struggling to find work after 1942, the family of four passing through seventeen different dwellings in seventeen years, the pressure she had from her brother and mother to persuade her to give up her second son for adoption.

(1991) Alexander Wilson's first wife, Gladys, passes away at the Royal Hampshire Hospital in Winchester in June 1991 at the age of 95.

(1992) After the tragically unexpected death of Gordon's second wife, Alison decides to share the first part of her memoir 'Before' with her two sons. She also confides the contents and story to her granddaughter Ruth Wilson destined to become the award-winning actor and producer.

(1998) Alexander Wilson's first son Adrian, by his marriage to Gladys in 1916, passes away at his home in Chandler's Ford near Southampton. He had been a school-teacher after a career in the regular British Army where he had represented the Hampshire regiment in sports and served in signals and ciphers during the Second World War.

(2005 July) Mike Shannon, now a 71 year-old veteran Shakespearean actor and performance poet, asks Tim Crook, an academic researcher with the University of London, to investigate the mysteries of his father's past. Alison Wilson dies on 3rd August 2005 only a matter of days after Mike commissions his family history search. Her sons are able to read part 2 of her Memoir 'After' in which she sets out her discovery of faith in God and Catholicism and was able to find forgiveness for all the wrongs, hurt and pain that her late husband's lying and dishonesty had caused her.

(2007 May to August) Tim Crook makes contact with Dennis Wilson, the second son of Alexander Wilson's first family and then establishes contact with Gordon and Nigel Wilson of the third family and finally Douglas Ansdell of the fourth family.

(2007 December 7th) Gordon Wilson hosts first gathering of all the families with the majority of relatives meeting each other for the first time.

(2008 August) 45 years after his death, Alexander Wilson's six surviving children dedicate a monument at his grave giving his real and second identity, describing him as an 'author and patriot' and quoting Shakespeare's *Othello* 'He loved not wisely but too well.'

(2010 May) Second gathering of the four families hosted by Nigel and Mary Wilson at their home in Shepperton to celebrate the completion of Tim Crook's writing of the biography. Mike Shannon diagnosed with non-Hodgkin's lymphoma. Ruth Wilson wins the first of two Olivier theatre awards beginning with Best Supporting Actress for her portrayal of Stella Kowalski in *A Streetcar named Desire* and followed by Best Actress for the titular role in *Anna Christie* also at the Donmar Warehouse in 2011. These would be among multiple future awards received for performances in television, film and theatre.

(2010 October) Alexander Wilson's fourth wife, Elizabeth, died after having been in care with Alzheimer's disease since 2001. Her funeral takes place in Scotland in October. At the same time there is the publication of Alexander Wilson's biography *The Secret Lives Of A Secret Agent: The Mysterious Life and Times of Alexander Wilson* by Tim Crook with feature newspaper coverage in *Independent*, *The Times*, and *Evening Standard*, and considerable coverage online. Book launch lecture by Tim Crook at Goldsmiths, University of London.

(2010 21st December) Mike Shannon, who initiated the extraordinary project to discover the mysteries about his father, passes away peacefully at his home in Bromley.

(2011 February) Tim Crook presents an academic paper on Alexander Wilson's representation of the first 'C' of MI6 in his Sir Leonard Wallace Novels at a conference at Cambridge University.

(2012 to present) The wider extended family continues to be close and regularly meeting, including a memorial celebration of Mike Shannon's life in the Spring of 2012 and the scattering of his ashes off the Hampshire coast later that year. Alexander Wilson's oldest surviving son, Dennis (now in his 92nd year) receives national media coverage for the publication of his poetry, including a significant poem of the Second World War based on his personal experiences of combat in Normandy.

(2013) Dennis Wilson invited to be guest of honour by Her Majesty the Queen and the Duke of Edinburgh at the Buckingham Palace reception for Contemporary Poetry. He is described as the Wilfred Owen of the Second World War and is interviewed by John Humphrys on the BBC Radio 4 *Today* programme. The Foreign and Commonwealth Office release to the National Archives a file on 'The Egyptian Ambassador' revealing the disgrace of an MI6 surveillance officer suspected of fabricating 'special material' transcripts on communications to and from the Egyptian Embassy. Although the file redacts the name, there is no doubt it refers to Alexander Wilson. Tim Crook appointed visiting professor at Birmingham City University and in his inaugural lecture presents new analysis and evidence that the MI5 report claiming Wilson fabricated the Egyptian Embassy intercepts could be wrong.

(2015) As a result of representation by the Blair Partnership, Allison & Busby begins republishing the nine Wallace of the Secret Service Novels by Alexander Wilson to strong sales and new critical acclaim. Tony Parsons says 'Without Alexander Wilson, there is no James Bond, there is no Bourne, there is no George Smiley. Unmissable'. The *Daily Mail* declares 'James Bond may find he has a worthy rival.' Dennis Wilson appointed honorary fellowship by Southampton University for services to poetry and literature.

(2016) UK Information Tribunal (first tier) rejects application by Professor Tim Crook under the Freedom of Information Act for the release of the Alex Kellar's MI5 report and other SIS files about Alexander Wilson.

(2018) Ruth Wilson is executive producer and performing the role of her grandmother Alison in a three part television film drama called 'Mrs Wilson' to be broadcast by the BBC and also in America. The scripts have been written by Anna Symon. The production company films a new family gathering in

Southampton on June 23rd. Dennis Wilson is now 97 years old and his sister Daphne 96. The Foreign and Commonwealth Office carries out another security sensitivity review into the withholding from the Public Record Office of the MI5 Alex Kellar report accusing Wilson of fabricating his telephone interception reports. Even after 75 years MI6 still believes the information cannot be released for national security reasons. Tim Crook completes the second edition of *The Secret Lives of a Secret Agent: The Mysterious Life and Times of Alexander Wilson*.

November 27th to December 11th 'Mrs Wilson' series broadcast by BBC 1 at 9 p.m. on Tuesday evenings to wide critical acclaim. More than seven million viewers watch each episode- the highest audience for BBC midweek drama in this year.

The publication of the second edition of *Secret Lives* on 30th November is attended by best seller status and reaches number 3 in the Amazon.co.uk Espionage Biography chart.

Tim Crook makes an application through his MP that the Home Secretary and Foreign Secretary ask the Security Service (MI5) and Secret Intelligence Service (MI6) to exercise compassion in releasing as much information as they can on Alexander Wilson's intelligence activities.

(2019) January. The e-book/Kindle and US editions of the second revised edition of *The Secret Lives of a Secret Agent* are published.

'Mrs. Wilson' premieres on US television in the prestigious Masterpiece series broadcast by PBS from Sunday, March 31st 2019.

Appendix II

Literary works of Alexander Wilson

The Mystery of Tunnel 51* - 1928 - Longmans, Green & Co

The Devil's Cocktail* - 1928 - Longmans, Green & Co.

Murder Mansion - 1929 - Longmans, Green & Co.

The Death of Dr. Whitelaw - 1930 - Longmans, Green & Co.

Confessions of a Scoundrel [Written as Geoffrey Spencer] - 1933 - T Werner Laurie

The Crimson Dacoit - 1933 - Herbert Jenkins

Wallace of the Secret Service* - 1933 - Herbert Jenkins

Get Wallace!* - 1934 - Herbert Jenkins

The Sentimental Crook - 1934 - Herbert Jenkins

The Magnificent Hobo - 1935 - Herbert Jenkins

His Excellency, Governor Wallace* - 1936 - Herbert Jenkins

Double Events - 1937 - Herbert Jenkins

Mr. Justice - 1937 - Herbert Jenkins

Microbes of Power* - 1937 - Herbert Jenkins

Wallace at Bay* - 1938 - Herbert Jenkins

The Factory Mystery [Written as Gregory Wilson] - 1938 - Modern Publishing Company

The Boxing Mystery [Written as Gregory Wilson] - 1938 - Modern Publishing Company

Callaghan of Intelligence [Written as Michael Chesney] - 1938 - Herbert Jenkins

Wallace Intervenes* - 1939 - Herbert Jenkins

Scapegoats for Murder - 1939 - Herbert Jenkins

"Steel" Callaghan [Written as Michael Chesney] - 1939 - Herbert Jenkins

Callaghan Meets His Fate [Written as Michael Chesney] - 1939 - Herbert Jenkins

Double Masquerade - 1940 - Herbert Jenkins

Chronicles of the Secret Service* - 1940 - Herbert Jenkins

Academic Publications - India

Selected English Prose Stories for Indian Students [Co-edited and written with Mohammad Din. - Lahore - Editor - 1926 - Shamsher Singh & Co.
Four Periods of Essays - Lahore - Editor - 1928 - Rai Sahib M. Gulab Singh and Sons.
Selected English Essays (From Steele to Benson) - Lahore - Editor - 1930 - Uttar Chand Kapur & Sons

Unpublished Manuscripts - UK

Murder In Duplicate - UK - Written as A.J.P. Wilson at 88 Sheen Park, Richmond, Surrey.
The Englishman From Texas - UK - No identification in terms of author's identity or location of writing.
Out of the Land of Egypt - From 1958 - Written as Col. Alan C. Wilson at 13 Lancaster Gardens, Ealing, London W.13.
Combined Operations [Title assigned by his son Dennis B. Wilson] - UK -1961 - Did not disclose his writing name on his script, but written at 13 Lancaster Gardens, Ealing, London W.13.

Anthologies - UK
*My Best Spy Stories: A Collection of Stories by their own Authors** - 1938 to 1956 - Faber & Faber Limited. Page 355 to 384 'Brien Averts A War'

* Books featuring the character of Sir Leonard Wallace, his fictional British Secret Service and his officers and agents.

Bibliography

Books

Andersen, Earl (1993) *Hard Place To Do Time: The Story of Oakalla Prison 1912-1991*, New Westminster, British Columbia: Hillpointe Publishing.

Andrew, Christopher, (1987) *Her Majesty's Secret Service: The Making of the British Intelligence Community*, Harmondsworth, England: Penguin.

Andrew, Christopher (2009) *The Defence Of The Realm: The Authorized History of MI5*, London: Allen Lane.

Crook, Tim, (2010) *The Secret Lives of a Secret Agent: The Mysterious Life and Times of Alexander Wilson, First Edition*, Essex: Kultura Press

Curry, John (1999) Andrew, Christopher introd., *The Security Service 1908-1945: The Official History*, Kew, London: The Public Record Office.

Drabble, Margaret ed., (1987) *The Oxford Companion To English Literature: New Edition*, London: Guild Publishing.

Greene, Graham & Hugh (1957, 2006) *The Spy's Bedside Book*, London: The Folio Society.

Head, Dominic ed., (2006) *The Cambridge Guide to Literature in English: Third Edition*, Cambridge: Cambridge University Press.

Hennessey, Thomas & Thomas, Claire (2009) *Spooks: The Unofficial History of MI5*, Gloucestershire: Amberley Publishing.

Hinsley F. H., Thomas, E. E., Ransom C. F. G., Knight, R. C., (1979) *British Intelligence in the Second World War: Its Influence on Strategy and Operations, Volume One*, London: Her Majesty's Stationery Office.

Hitz, Frederick P. (2004) *The Great Game: The Myths and Reality of Espionage*, New York: Vintage Books.

Homberger, Eric (1991) 'English Spy Thrillers in the Age of Appeasement' in *Spy Fiction, Spy Films, and Real Intelligence*, edited by Wesley K. Wark, London: Frank Cass & Co.

Howard, Michael (1990) *British Intelligence in the Second World War: Volume Five Strategic Deception*, London: HMSO.

Hubin, Allen J., (1979) *The Bibliography of Crime Fiction 1749-1975*, Del Mar, California: University Extension University of California, San Diego.

Hussain, Syed, Sultan, Mahmood (2009) *56 Years of Islamia College Lahore 1892-1947,* Lahore: Izharsons

Jefferey, Keith (2010) *MI6: The History of the Secret Intelligence Service 1909-1949* London: Bloomsbury.

Judd, Alan, (1999) *The Quest for C: Mansfield Cumming and the Founding of the Secret Service*, London: Harper Collins.

Knightley, Phillip (1987) *The Second Oldest Profession: The Spy as Patriot, Bureaucrat, Fantasist and Whore*, London Pan Books.

Le Carré, John (1963, 1992) *The Spy Who Came In From The Cold*, New York: Ballantine Books.

Le Carré, John (1990) *The Secret Pilgrim*, London, New York, Sydney, Toronto: Guild Publishing.

Levi, Primo, first edition 1958 (2000), *If This Is A Man* (title in the USA *Survival in Auschwitz*), London: Collier Books.

Liddell, Guy, (2005) West, Nigel ed., *The Guy Liddell Diaries Vol.II: 1942-1945: MI5's Director of Counter-Espionage in World War II*, London & New York: Routledge.

Mackenzie, Compton, (1932) *Greek Memories*, London: Cassel & Co. Ltd.

Mackenzie, Compton (1933) *Water On The Brain*, New York: Doubleday, Doran and Company Inc.

Mackenzie, Compton (1968) *My Life And Times, Octave Seven, 1931-1938*, London: Chatto & Windus.

Masters, Anthony (1984) *The Man Who Was M: The Life of Maxwell Knight*, London: Basil Blackwell.

Masters, Anthony (1987) *Literary Agents: The Novelist as Spy*, Oxford: Blackwell.

Maugham, Somerset W., (1928) *Ashenden: or The British Agent*, London, New York: Doubleday, Doran & Company, Inc.

McCormick, Donald (1977) *Who's Who in Spy Fiction*, London: Elm Tree Books.

McCormick, Donald & Fletcher, Katy (1990) *Spy Fiction: A Connoisseur's Guide*, New York: Facts on File.

Miller, Joan (1986) *One Girl's War: personal exploits in MI5's most secret station*, Dingle, Co. Kerry, Ireland: Brandon.

Mukhopadhyay, Ashoke Kumar (1997) *India and Communism: Secret British Documents*, Calcutta: National Book Agency PVT. Ltd.

Muggeridge, Malcolm (1981) *The Infernal Grove: Chronicles of Wasted Time Vol. II*, London Fontana.

Panek, L. LeRoy (1981) *The Special Branch: The British Spy Novel, 1890-1980*, Bowling Green, Ohio: Bowling Green University Popular Press.

Philby, Kim (1969 1st edition, 1989 with new introduction by Phillip Knightley) *My Silent War*, London: Grafton Books.

Polmar, Norman & Allen, Thomas B., (1997) *Spy Book- The Encyclopedia of Espionage*, London: Greenhill Books.

Punjab University Enquiry Committee, 1932-33 Report, (1933), Lahore: Superintendent, Government Printing, Punjab, India.

Qureshi, Major Mohammed Ibrahim (1958) *The First Punjabis- The History of the First Punjab Regiment 1759-1956*, Aldershot: Gale & Polden Ltd.

Read, Anthony & Fisher David, 1984, *Colonel Z: The Life and Times of A Master of Spies*, London: Hodder and Stoughton.

Rimington, Stella (2006) Introduction to Greene, Hugh & Graham (originally 1957) *The Spy's Bedside Book*, London: 2006 The Folio Society.

Rockwell, Joan, 'Normative Attitudes of Spies in Fiction, in *Mass Culture Revisited* (1973) edited by Bernard Rosenberg and David Manning White, New York: Van Nostrand Reinhald.

Sansom, Major AW (1965) *I Spied Spies*. London: George G. Harrap & Co

Shannon, Mike (2008) *Upside Down*, Colchester Essex, England: Kultura Press.

Sherif, M.A. (2004) *Searching for Solace: Biography of Yusuf Ali*, New Delhi, India: Adam Publishers & Distributors.

Singh, Navtej (1998), *Challenge to Imperial Hegemony: The Life Story of a Great Indian Patriot Udham Singh*, Lahore: University of Punjab/Publication Bureau.

Smith, Michael, (2004) *The Spying Games: The Secret History of British Espionage*, London: Politicos.

Smith, Michael (2010) *Six: A History of Britain's Secret Intelligence Service, Part 1: Murder and Mayhem 1909-1939*, London: Dialogue, Biteback Publishing.

Smith, Myron J., (1982, 2nd Edition) *Cloak and Dagger Fiction: An Annotated Guide to Spy Thrillers*, Santa Barbara, California: ABC-CLIO INC.

Stafford, David (1989) *The Silent Game: The Real World of Imaginary Spies*, London: Viking.

Stafford, David (1997) *Churchill & Secret Service*, London: Abacus.

Nation Associates (1948) *The Record of Collaboration of King Farouk of Egypt with the Nazis and Their Ally, The Mufti: Memorandum Submitted to the United States*. New York: The Nation Associates.

Thomas, Gordon (2009) *Secret Wars: One Hundred Years of British Intelligence Inside MI5 and MI6*, New York: Thomas Dunne Books, St Martin's Press.

Tomlinson, Richard (2001) *The Big Breach*, Edinburgh: Cutting Edge Press.

Tsarev, Oleg and West, Nigel (2009) *TRIPLEX: Secrets from the Cambridge Spies*, New Haven & London: Yale University Press

Usborne, Richard (1953) *Clubland Heroes*, London: Constable.

Wark, Wesley K. (1998) 'The Spy Thriller' in *Mystery & Suspense Writers: The Literature of Crime, Detection, and Espionage, Volume II*, edited by Robin W. Winks, New York: Charles Scribner's Sons.

West, Nigel (1985) *MI5*, London: Panther Books.

West, Nigel (1985) *MI6: British Secret Intelligence Service Operations 1909-1945*, London: Granada Panther Books.

West, Nigel ed., (1993) *The Faber Book of Espionage*, London: Faber & Faber.

West, Nigel (2005) *Mask: MI5's Penetration of the Communist Party of Great Britain*, London, New York: Routledge.

West, Nigel ed., (2005) *The Guy Liddell Diaries, Volume 1: 1939-1942, MI5's Director of Counter-Espionage in World War II*, London and New York: Routledge.

West, Nigel (2006) *At Her Majesty's Secret Service: The Chiefs of Britain's Intelligence Agency, MI6*, London Greenhill Books.

White, Rosie (2007) *Violent Femmes: Women as spies in popular culture*, London & New York: Routledge.

Whitwell, John, a.k.a. Leslie Nicholson (1966) *British Agent*, London William Kimber.

Wilson, Alexander & Din, Mohammad eds., (1926) 'Preface' in *Selected English Prose Stories For Indian Students*, Lahore, Pakistan: Shamsher Singh & Co.

Wilson, Alexander (1928) *The Mystery of Tunnel 51*, London, New York, New Delhi: Longmans, Green & Co.

Wilson, Alexander, (1928) *The Devil's Cocktail*, London: Longmans, Green & Co.

Wilson, Alexander (1929) *Murder Mansion*, London: Longmans, Green & Co.

Wilson, Alexander (1930) *The Death of Dr. Whitelaw*, London: Longmans, Green & Co.

Wilson, Alexander (1933) *The Crimson Dacoit*, London: Herbert Jenkins

Wilson, Alexander (1933) *Wallace of the Secret Service*, London: Herbert Jenkins.

Wilson, Alexander pseud. Spencer, Geoffrey (1933) *Confessions Of A Scoundrel*, London: T Werner Laurie Ltd.

Wilson, Alexander (1934) *Get Wallace*, London: Herbert Jenkins.

Wilson, Alexander (1934) *The Sentimental Crook*, London: Herbert Jenkins.

Wilson, Alexander (1935) *The Magnificent Hobo*, London: Herbert Jenkins.

Wilson, Alexander (1937) *Microbes of Power*, London: Herbert Jenkins.

Wilson, Alexander (1937) *Mr Justice*, London: Herbert Jenkins.

Wilson, Alexander (1939) *Wallace Intervenes*, London: Herbert Jenkins.

Wilson, Alexander (1940) *The Chronicles of the Secret Service*, London: Herbert Jenkins.

Wilson, Alexander (1956) 'Brien Averts War' in *My Best Spy Story*, London: Faber & Faber.

Wilson, Dennis (2008) *The Poetry Of A Marriage*, Essex: Kultura Press.

Wilson, Dennis (2012) *Elegy of a Common Soldier* and other poems, Essex: Kultura Press.

Wright Peter (1987) *Spycatcher: The Candid Autobiography of a Senior Intelligence Officer*, Toronto, Canada: Stoddart.

Archives

The UK National Archives

FO 371/23372/4242, Complaint made by Egyptian Ambassador, 1939

FO 371/27488, Activities of Egyptian Ambassador at Tehran, 1941

FO1093/263, 'C', Chief of the Secret Intelligence Service (SIS): report on the Egyptian ambassador, 25 May – 2 July 1943

FO 371/41392, Activities of Hassan Nashat, Egyptian Ambassador in London, 1944

HW 1/1376, Egyptian ambassador, London: discussion with Soviet ambassador on Feb 11 on attempts to pressurise Egypt into aligning herself with Soviet Union and China, 17 February, 1943

HW 1/1341, Egyptian ambassador, London: rumours of German peace proposals discussed at Casablanca, 29 January, 1942

WO 372/21

B11/65. High Court in Bankruptcy: Registers of Petitions 1940-1944

KV 4/227. 'M.S. Report' by Maxwell Knight.

KV/2/2699 Secret CX/12650/1988, Captain Miller, Scotland Yard, 8.2.29.

KV/2/2699. I.P.I W. Ogilvie 4/2/42.

KV 2/827. Sidney Reilly's MI5 file.

GCHQ/ HW 1/2565 & 1/2573

City of London Metropolitan Archives

Ms 1631/28 from London Guildhall Library has been preserved in the transfer of the Hodder and Stoughton accounting and sales figure ledgers to the London Metropolitan Archives.

PS/MAR Marylebone Magistrates Court Registers 1884-1988. Quarterly registers for Marylebone Police Court: 1944 and 1948.

India Office Archives, British Library

IOR: L/P&J/12/377. Lahore Conspiracy Case P&J (S) 79, 1929.

IOR: L/P&J/12/20, 21/3 and 20/5. Fortnightly report on the internal situation of the North-West Frontier Province for the second half of April 1930 & the first half of May 1930.

IOR: L/P&J/12/20, 17/6: Fortnightly report on the internal situation of the North West Frontier Province for the first half of June 1930.

IOR: L/P&J/12/403; File 938D/1929, Terrorism in India 1917-1936. Intelligence Bureau, Home Dept, Govt of India. Simla, 1937.

IOR: L/P&J/12/377, P&J (S) 79, 1929, Lahore Conspiracy Case document 5. Copy of Telegram, New Delhi 10th January 1929.

IOR: P&J (S) 79/29 333, 1931, Lahore Conspiracy Case document 23., The Secretariat of the Communist Party of Great Britain, 'Lahore Conspiracy Case, 5th March 1931.

IOR: L/P&J/12/377. P&J (S) 79, 1929, Lahore Conspiracy Case document 6. Copy of Telegram, Simla 6th July 1929,

IOR: P&J (S) 79/29 111 3, 1929. Lahore Conspiracy Case document 11. Secret.

IOR: P&J (S) 79/29 4th July 1929, Lahore Conspiracy Case document 13 & 14. Secret.

IOR: P&J (S) 79/29 189, 1930. File No P&J (S) 466/36. Lahore Conspiracy Case document 19.

Ministry of Defence

Alexander Joseph Wilson Ministry of Defence Army Personnel File, P/92962/3 (Records)

19A Letter from Records Department, The War Office, 71 Eaton Square to A.J Wilson, Esq., 39 Norfolk Avenue, Bowes Park, London N.13, 21st July 1948.

War Office Army Form E564A, E/13675 1A 25/5/39, Alexander Joseph Wilson 1A.

3B 31st May 1939 100/Reserve/1634 (A.G.5.(E)) 13675 John Farquharson to The Under Secretary of State, The War Office,

3A May 29th 1939 Father Aydon, St. Mary of the Angels, Moorhouse Road, Bayswater W.2. to the Under Secretary of State, The War Office.

10A Army Form B2164, File no: 48045/4, Examination of Member of the A.O.E.R. at No. 22 Reception Unit.

16A P/92962/3 (A.G.12.e.) 13th May 1940 to A.J. Wilson, Esq., 56, Woodlands, Golders Green, N.W.11.

1Af, 48045, Letter from Alexander Wilson to The Secretary, The War Office, S.W.1 7th October 1935.

Letter from Alexander Wilson to the Secretary of State for War, 29th October 1937.

Letter from Alexander Wilson to the Under Secretary of State, The War Office,

27th September 1938.

6A Letter from Alexander Wilson to the Under Secretary of State, The War Office, 20th June 1939.

7A Letter from Alexander Wilson to the Under Secretary of State, The War Office, 23rd July 1939.

Medical Certificate from Lieutenant Randel MacCarthy RAMC, Military Hospital, Avonmouth, 21st September 1915.

48045/4 (M.S.1.) Letter from Major General Robb, Military Secretary to The General Officer, Commanding-in-Chief, Aldershot Command, 24th May 1915.

48045, Letter from Alexander J. Wilson, 'Gaulter', Kimmeridge, Corfe Castle, Dorset to The Secretary To The War Office, 9th June 1916.

Letter from A.J. Wilson late A.S.C. Foxbury, Lyndhurst, Hants to The Secretary, War Office, 5th November 1916.

Letter from A.J Wilson to The Secretary, War Office, London S.W. 23rd November 1916.

48045, Letter from Alexander J. Wilson, late A.S.C., Marguerite Lodge, Checkendon, Reading, 7th February 1917.

Letter from Major I H. Grant, Recruiting Officer, Brockenhurst to The Secretary D.R.L., War Office, London, S.W. 25th July 1917, A 444, 18117.

48045/9 (D.R.1) Letter from Captain H. Hanks, Director of Recruiting, War Office to The Recruiting Officer, Brockenhurst, 24th August 1917.

Army Form E564A, E/13675 Part IIA. – Previous Service (If Any) in H.M. Forces, 'Application for Registration in the Officers' Emergency Reserve For Appointment To A Temporary Commission in His Majesty's Land Forces on Mobilization, Recd 25 May 1939.

General Register Office

Application 575952-1, marriage solemnized between Hugh Wilson, 25 years old and Elizabeth Bracken, 22 years old, 12th November 1863 at the Congregational Church in the District of Winchester. Copy retrieved 30th September 2008

Wilson Family papers

Before & *After* Alison Wilson memoir, (1986) strict copyright estate of Alison Wilson.

Wilson, Alexander (date unknown c 1950s) Out of The Land of Egypt, unpublished.

Letter from Alexander Wilson to Adrian Wilson 17th March 1940.

Letter from Alexander Wilson to Adrian Wilson 19th May 1940.

Letter from Alexander Wilson to Adrian Wilson 26th March 1944

Letter from Alexander Wilson to Adrian Wilson 5th July 1944.

Letter from Alexander Wilson to Alison Wilson written in J.C. Ward, King Edward VII Hospital Ealing W13, 9th March 1962.

Letter from Alexander Wilson to Alison Wilson from 13 Lancaster Gardens, Ealing W13, 1st February 1963.

Letter from Alexander Wilson at 99 Ebury Street, London S.W.1 to Adrian Wilson, Hampshire Regt. Depot, Winchester, 26th September 1935.

Letter from Alexander Wilson at 'Bruerne' 2 Merton Road, Southsea to Private Adrian Wilson, The Hampshire Regiment. 4th January 1937.

Letter from Alexander Wilson at 2 Whitehall Court, The Authors' Club, London SW1 to Adrian Wilson, 5th July 1944.

Letter from Alexander Wilson to Private Adrian Wilson, 31st March 1937.

Wilson, Alexander (28th August 1937) Letter to Adrian Wilson.

'Great Public School Teams, Repton, 26' a document loaned to the author by Douglas Ansdell and probably written and produced by his father sometime in the 1950s.

Letter from Lieut. Colonel P.J. Emerson to Douglas Ansdell, 4th July 2002.

'A Souvenir of Colonel Gordon Wilson' provided to Douglas Ansdell by Major (Retd) A.W. Kersting, curator Household Cavalry Museum, September 1998.

Wilson, Dennis (2007) extracts from a letter sent to Gordon and Nigel Wilson and copied to the author 24th August 2007.

Letter from Kevin Baverstock to Dennis Wilson 16th April 2009.

Interviews and correspondence

Mike Shannon

Dennis Wilson

Nigel Wilson

Gordon Wilson

Douglas Ansdell

Tamsin Ansdell

Richard Shannon

Christopher McGill

Jean Rose, Random House

Captain (Retd) P H Starling, Curator The Army Medical Services Museum

Dr M A Sherif

Confidential sources

Newspapers and Periodicals

The Bookseller, Leventhal, Lionel (August 13, 2004) 'Bookselling can kill you', pg 21(1) No. 5141 ISSN: 0006-7539.

Civil & Military Gazette, pg. 5 col 3, 'Lahore Students arrested', February 20th 1930, Lahore, British India.

Civil & Military Gazette, pg 11, April 17th 1931, Lahore, British India.

Civil & Military Gazette, pg. 10 December 10th 1931, 'International Music: Punjab Literary League's Success', Lahore, British India.

Civil & Military Gazette, pg 7 December 18th 1931, 'Our Dumb Friends', Lahore, British India.

Civil & Military Gazette, pg 1, September 11th 1931, col 1, 'Punjab Murder Plotters To Die' Lahore: British India.

Civil & Military Gazette, December 16th, 17th, 18th, 19th, 23rd, 24th, 1931, 'Lahore Cricket Controversy', 'Government College Offer Accepted, Sports Committee to Make Decision', 'Decision Still Not Made', 'Final Match To Be Replayed', 'University Final Re-played: 20 Wickets Fall in One Day', 'The Re-Played Final', Lahore: British India.

Civil & Military Gazette, December 30th 1931, 'Lahore Hindu-Muslim Riot Deaths', Lahore: British India.

The Daily Mail, Mackenzie, Compton, 'Two men recapture the magic of travel', 11th April 1935, London.

The Daily Mail, Porter, Monica, 'Betrayal and a masterspy's son', 3rd January 1998, London.

The Daily Mirror, 'Villain With Chivalry Streak' Wednesday, October 9, 1929, London.

The Daily Mirror, '** Very Good. *Good' June 24, 1937, London.

The Daily Telegraph, 14th June 2008, 'James Bond author Ian Fleming urged appeasing Adolf Hitler' by Andy Bloxham, London.

The Daily Telegraph, Chris Hastings, Public Affairs Editor, 'Lord Halifax tried to negotiate peace with the Nazis', 31st August 2008.

The Evening Star, Monday October 2nd 1944. Page 4. 'Vanity and Stupidity.'

The Evening News, Monday October 2nd 1944, Page 3, '7 Medal Man- He Had Won Only Three.'

The Evening Standard, Monday October 2nd 1944, Page 4, 'The Fake Colonel, D.S.O, D.S.C. and Wings- He Hated Being in Mufti.'

The Evening Standard, Monday 9th October 1944, Page 5, 'Bogus Colonel Wore Wings.'

St Marylebone, Paddington and City of Westminster Record and West London Times, Saturday October 14th 1944, page 3, 'Author Posed as Colonel.'

The New York Times Book Review May 6th 1928 page 23 Page title: 'New Mystery Stories' The Mystery of Tunnel 51, by Alexander Wilson, 345pp. New York: Longmans, Green and Co. $2

The New York Times Book Review December 30th 1928 page 15 Page title: 'New Works of Fiction' (continued from page 13) Sub-title: A Gang of Schemes The Devil's Cocktail by Alexander Wilson, Longmans, Green and Co. $2

New York Times Book Review Sunday December 1st 1929, page 48 Page title: 'New Mystery Stories' Murder Mansion: by Alexander Wilson, 343 pp, New York: Longmans, Green and Co $2

The Observer, Advertisement for Longmans 'New Novels 7 s. 6d. net each', 27th May 1928, London.

The Observer, p. 6 'Hush-Hush. Secret Service And Other Heroes' by Torquemada, Get Wallace by Alexander Wilson (Herbert Jenkins 7s. 6d.), 16th December 1934, London.

The Observer, p.7 'New Novels. Criminal Miscellany.' By Torquemada, His Excellency Governor Wallace, By Alexander Wilson, (Herbert Jenkins 7s 6d) 2nd February 1936, London.

The Observer, p. 6 'The Crime Ration' By Maurice Richardson, Wallace Intervenes, By Alexander Wilson, (Herbert Jenkins 7s 6d) 7th January 1940, London.

The Scotsman (1860-1950), Sep 28, 1933 'New Fiction'; ProQuest Historical Newspapers *The Scotsman* (1817-1950) electronic source same below; pg 2.

The Scotsman (1860-1950), May 28, 1934, Article 10 – No title; pg 15.

The Scotsman (1860-1950), Nov 19, 1934; Review 8 – No title; pg 15.

The Scotsman (1860-1950), Apr 15, 1935 'New Novels,'; pg 15.

The Scotsman (1860-1950), Sep 28, 1933 'New Fiction,'; pg 2.

The Scotsman (1860-1950), May 28, 1934, Article 10 – No title; pg 15.

The Scotsman (1860-1950), Nov 19, 1934, Review 8 – No title; pg 15.

The Scotsman (1860-1950), Nov 29, 1937, 'New Fiction,'; pg. 15.

The Scotsman (1860-1950), Dec 18, 1939, 'Four Mystery Tales,'; pg. 7.

The Sheerness Guardian and East Kent Advertiser, back page. Saturday September 27th 1919, The British Newspaper Library.

Stubbs Weekly Gazette and Supplementary List of Creditors, February 2nd 1944, London, England.

The Times, Tuesday, Dec 15, 1953; pg. 8; Issue 52805; col D ' Mr. A. Yusuf Ali Indian And Islamic Publicist.'

The Sunday Times, 'Only The Brave' by David Stafford, News Review Section, 30th July 2000.

The Times Literary Supplement, 'The Mystery of Tunnel 51', 24th May 1928

The Times Literary Supplement, 'The Devil's Cocktail' 29th November 1928.

The Times Literary Supplement, 'The Death of Dr. Whitelaw', 12th February 1931.

The Times Literary Supplement, 'Crimson Dacoit', 20th April 1933.

The Times Literary Supplement, 'Wallace of the Secret Service', 21st September 1933.

The Times Literary Supplement, 'Get Wallace! By Alexander Wilson', 20th December 1934.

Wood Green, Southgate and Palmers Green Weekly Herald, Friday August 20th 1948, page 4, 'Cinema Manager Charged with Falsifying and Stealing.'

Ruling of the First Tier Tribunal, Appeal Reference: EA/2015/0224, Determined without a hearing at Field House On 19 April 2016, Professor Tim Crook and the Information Commissioner and The Foreign and Commonwealth Office.

Illustrations

The dust jacket for *Wallace Intervenes* published by Herbert Jenkins in 1939 (By permission Dennis Wilson)

Alexander Wilson in Second World War uniform as he looked when saying goodbye to his son Michael at Leyburn railway station, Wensleydale in 1941 and wearing the cap-badge and officer's jacket of the Punjabis Regiment of the Indian Army (By permission Mike Shannon)

Dorothy Wilson (née Wick) as a young actress on tour in India in the middle to late 1920s. She was an accomplished singer and piano player. She also had considerable skills as a producer of revues and charity concerts. (By permission Mike Shannon.)

Alexander Wilson in India between 1925 and 1932. The reflective author with pipe. (By permission Mike Shannon)

Alexander Wilson's wife Dorothy outside their house at number 11 Masson Road, Lahore. (By permission Mike Shannon)

Dorothy Wilson (left) and friend with Alexander Wilson on board the liner to or from India. In the right picture Dorothy is on the left relaxing with her friend on the ship's deck and taking the sea breeze. (By permission Mike Shannon)

Dust jacket for one of the last of Alexander Wilson's published novels in 1940 *Chronicles of the Secret Service*

Alexander Wilson with pipe (on right) returning from India with Dorothy Wilson (centre) in 1933. They are posing with the Italian captain of the liner. (By permission Mike Shannon)

Dorothy Wilson with devoted dog in Lahore, India in the late 1920s. Dorothy Phyllis Wick met Alexander Wilson while going out to British India in 1925. She toured the country with Grand Guignol productions and had replaced Dame Sybil Thorndike who had pulled out of the tour. She also acted in the first radio drama productions ever transmitted in India at a radio station established in Calcutta. (By permission Mike Shannon)

Left: Alexander Wilson spent much of his childhood in the colony of Hong Kong. (By permission Dennis Wilson) Right: Alexander Wilson as a young teenager. He was educated at the Roman Catholic St Joseph's College in Hong Kong and later at St Boniface Roman Catholic College in Plymouth. (By permission Dennis Wilson)

Alexander Wilson as a naval Midshipman (probably far left standing) in HMS Andromeda, Devonmouth 1911/12 (By permission Dennis Wilson. Image enhanced by Timothy Caldbeck)

Alexander Wilson as a young man in the Edwardian Age, lounging with pet dog probably in the Colony of Hong Kong where he learned to speak fluent Cantonese.

Left: Wedding photograph of Alexander Wilson's first marriage in March 1916 to Gladys Kellaway. He was wearing the army uniform of the Royal Army Service Corps with the rank of Lieutenant. (By permission Dennis Wilson) It is noticeable that he is standing with his left leg straight and right leg bent, a likely sign of disability to his left knee caused by an accident while on transport duties to the Western Front.

Bottom: Wedding Day March 1916 in Lyndhurst, the New Forest with snow on the ground. The Kellaways to the left and the Wilsons mainly to the right. Alexander's brother in law Stanley standing behind him in private's uniform. Alexander's younger brother Leonard sitting. (He would reach the rank of Lieutenant Colonel in the Royal Army Service Corps). Alexander's sister 'Auntie May' far right, mother Annie sitting far right with father Major Alexander Wilson RAMC standing second from the right. (By permission Dennis Wilson)

Alexander Wilson, aged 25, posing for his merchant seaman's photograph after signing on as the purser for SS Prinzessin 12th May 1919. According to the crew agreement documents it was his first merchant sea service. He joined at Victoria Docks, London 1 a.m. the following day. He gave as his address Alnwick Cottage, East Minster, Isle of Sheppey, where his mother, wife and young son Adrian (aged 2) were staying at the time of his father's death in September of that year. (Strict copyright and by permission Southampton Archives)

Alexander Wilson's family life in Southampton in the late 1920s. His first son Adrian (standing) His sister Auntie May, first wife Gladys and mother Annie (right to left sitting) Daughter Daphne and second son Dennis (sitting on ground cross-legged) (By permission Dennis Wilson. Image enhanced by Timothy Caldbeck)

The bungalow at 11 Masson Road, Lahore, India where Wilson was living with his second wife Dorothy. (By permission Mike Shannon)

Alexander Wilson (right) and his mother Annie (left) during the middle to late 1920s. (By permission Dennis Wilson)

Dust jacket covers:

The Crimson Dacoit (1933)

and

His Excellency Governor Wallace (1936)

Alexander Wilson as the celebrated author of the 1930s with pipe in the style of Edgar Wallace. (By permission Dennis Wilson)

In order to supplement his earnings as a writer Alexander Wilson was prepared to 'ghost write' under pseudonym more sensationalist thriller fiction for the Modern Publishing Company. In 1938 he would complete *The Factory Mystery* and *The Boxing Mystery* using the nom de plume 'Gregory Wilson'.

Above Left: Dorothy Wick in 1915. The photograph was kept in her brother Reginald's album (By permission Richard Shannon)
Above Right: A portrait of Alison McKelvie in her riding costume when aged 15 or 16. (By permission Gordon Wilson)

Right: Alison Wilson (née McKelvie) at the time she met Alexander Wilson when working for a top secret MI6 surveillance unit in London in 1940. (By permission Gordon Wilson)

Alexander Wilson featured left on page 20 of the *Lahore Military and Civil Gazette*, Wednesday, Feb 20th, 1929 at the Punjab Olympic Athletic Trials. He is seen talking to Mr. H. L. O. Garrett right, Principal of Government College, and President of the Punjab Olympic Association, who acted as chief judge.

Islamia College on the Railway Road in Lahore has not changed in appearance much since the time of Alexander Wilson's Principalship between 1928 and 1931.
These buildings would have been familiar landmarks in his daily life at the College. (Images by Ajmal Jami)

Bottom: Ladies' Dining Room at the Authors' Club, 2 Whitehall Court, where Alexander Wilson courted Alison McKelvie when they both worked at SIS Broadway in 1940 and 1941. MI5 spymaster Maxwell Knight also used the dining room to recruit and brief his key women agents including Joan Miller. (By permission Authors' Club)

Alexander and Alison Wilson on their wedding day in Kensington in 1941. He was wearing the uniform of a Lieutenant Colonel of the Punjabis Regiment, the Indian Army, for which he would be subject to a prosecution at Marylebone Police Court in September 1944. (By permission Nigel and Gordon Wilson)

Below: Alexander Wilson left his third family in Ealing to attend the weddings of both his sons from his first family on the same day in 1951, while he remained fully separated from his second family, then living in Bridlington. (By permission Dennis Wilson)

Left: A dapper Alexander Wilson in the 1950s, an image that belies the humble job he held as a porter in the casualty unit of the Central Middlesex Hospital.

Right: An elderly Alexander Wilson dressed smartly for the passing out of his son Gordon at Dartmouth Royal Naval Training College. He never disclosed to Gordon that he had had any connection with the Royal Navy because his service had been in his real identity as Alexander Joseph Wilson.

A relaxed family picture of Alison and Alexander Wilson demonstrating that they were a loving couple wholly respected for the quality of their parenthood by their sons Gordon and Nigel. (By permission Gordon and Nigel Wilson)

Alexander Wilson on holiday with Alison and his sons at Deal, only a cinque port away from Dover where he had been born in 1893. (By permission Gordon and Nigel Wilson)

Alexander Wilson's fourth wife Elizabeth Hill. Left (when qualifying as a nurse) and right, at the time of their marriage in 1955. (By permission Douglas Ansdell)

Elizabeth Wilson feeding pigeons in Trafalgar Square with a friend. Elizabeth moved from Ealing to relocate in Scotland with their son Douglas. (By permission Douglas Ansdell)

The first gathering of the surviving sons of Alexander Wilson in 2007. Standing left to right Nigel and Gordon Wilson, sitting left to right Mike Shannon, Dennis Wilson (nicknamed 'The Patriarch') and Douglas Ansdell. (By permission Gordon Wilson.)

The discovery of the thespian tradition: Alexander Wilson's daughter Daphne, a professional actress and dancer who formed and ran her own dancing school in Hampshire, and Alexander Wilson's granddaughter Ruth (daughter of Nigel and Mary Wilson) the highly-acclaimed professional actress and Golden Globe nominee for her BBC film performance in Jane Eyre. This photograph was taken in December 2007. In 2010 she received an Olivier award for Best Supporting Actress for her performance in the role of Stella in *A Streetcar Named Desire* at the Donmar Warehouse the previous year. (By permission Deborah Wilson)

The six surviving children of Alexander Wilson from four separate and parallel marriages at the successful gathering of all the families in Hampshire in December 2007. Standing left to right, Douglas Ansdell, Gordon and Nigel Wilson. Seated left to right, Dennis, Daphne, and Mike Shannon (*né* Michael Chesney Wilson)

Alexander Wilson's children, grandchildren and great grandchildren. The event was hosted by Captain Gordon Wilson, RN. And the only non-relative is the author standing far right. (By permission Deborah Wilson)

Mike Shannon returns to 53 Blomfield Road, Little Venice. The top floor and two small windows were where he remembered his happiest days with his mother Dorothy and father Alexander during the late 1930s.

The homage to Blomfield Road was accompanied by Mike's award winning dramatist and director son Richard (right) and award-winning niece actress and film producer, Ruth Wilson, highlighting the strong Thespian tradition in a family that had been divided by espionage and mystery in the 20th century. (Copyright Tim Crook)

Dedication ceremony for the new headstone of Alexander Wilson's grave at Milton cemetery in Portsmouth. Left to right, his surviving children: Mike, Gordon, Dennis, Daphne, Nigel and Douglas.

His youngest son Douglas (born 1955) reads a poem in Gaelic to commemorate his father at the dedication ceremony in August 2008. The brothers and sister had agreed the following wording: 'In loving Memory of Alexander Joseph Patrick Wilson also known as Alexander Douglas Gordon Chesney Wilson, author and patriot, 1893 -1963', and the quotation from William Shakespeare's Othello 'He loved not wisely but too well.' Wilson's monument is feet away from the gravestone of fellow SIS agent, Commander Buster Crabb, who was killed in a diving operation to spy on a Soviet flagship moored at Portsmouth Harbour in 1956. (Copyright Tim Crook)

Alison on the left next to her solicitor father seated in the deckchair centre. He died in early 1941 just as he was trying to check on the background of Alexander Wilson. (By permission Gordon and Nigel Wilson)

The trace of Alison Wilson's (née McKelvie) career in MI6. On the back of a family photograph in the garden of her family home in Whitehaven are the scribbled notes of Colonels and telephone numbers for interviews in the vortex of secret service buildings triangulating the Westminster embankment, St James and Mayfair in 1940.

Dorothy Wilson was a stalwart raiser of funds through charity revues and concerts and this programme was for a show produced and devised by her for the ARP in Paddington after the outbreak of war in the autumn of 1939. (By permission Mike Shannon.)

Dorothy never ceased producing fundraising events throughout her life and even in the 1950s she was organising gang shows for the sea scouts in Bridlington. Money raised enabled the scouts to acquire two racing dinghies. (By permission Mike Shannon.)

Rare dustcover of first Herbert Jenkins *Wallace of the Secret Service* novel (1933)

Rare dustcover of a romantic comedy novel based on a family holiday destination. The graphical illustration of the cover design is somewhat misleading.

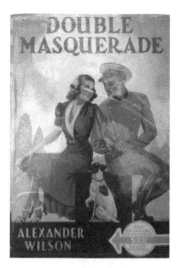

The front cover of one of Alexander Wilson's last published novels - the romantic thriller *Double Masquerade* published in 1940 when he was working for the Secret Intelligence Service. The title ironically hints at the masquerades deployed by the author in the relationships of his own life.

Extended Wilson family gathering of several generations in Southampton in 2013 celebrating the success and recognition of Dennis Wilson as a published poet. He is standing centre with his sister Daphne holding onto his arm on the left. Alexander Wilson's second son from his marriage to Alison, Nigel is standing third from the right at the front.
(Photograph copyright Marja Giejgo)

CPSIA information can be obtained
at www.ICGtesting.com
Printed in the USA
LVHW042308010419
612626LV00001B/98/P